NORMAN NICHOLSON'S
LAKELAND

*For Gwyn
and Christian
and Maisie*

NORMAN NICHOLSON'S

LAKELAND

A Prose Anthology

Chosen and edited by
Irvine Hunt

Drawings by
Bill Wilkinson

ROBERT HALE · LONDON

First published in Great Britain in 1991
© *Copyright Irvine Hunt, 1991*

ISBN 0 7090 4306 6

Robert Hale Limited
Clerkenwell House
Clerkenwell Green
London EC1R 0HT

Photoset in North Wales by
Derek Doyle & Associates, Mold, Clwyd.
Printed and bound in Great Britain by
Butler & Tanner Ltd., Frome, Somerset.

Contents

A View From a Window

The Shape of the Land

The Coming of Man

Along the Coast

Lakes and Dales

Shoot and Stem

Creatures Great and Small

The Weather in View

Way to the Dales

Man's Mark on the Land

8   CONTENTS

Stone Circles and Crosses

Nobbut God

Villages and Towns

Sports and Pastimes

The Names on the Land

A Local Habitation

The Explorers

Down the Tourist Trail

Poets and Writers

Tomorrow

Illustrations

At bottom the Lake District is a piece of rock. It is the rock which makes the land and the land has made the people. And even when industry came to the North-west, it came out of the rock, for it is iron and coal which made modern Cumberland and North Lancashire. The variety of the landscape, the texture of the fells, the form of the buildings and even the colour of a town street are all to be accounted to the rock. To look at the scenery without trying to understand the rock is like listening to poetry in an unknown language. You hear the beauty but you miss the meaning.

Portrait of the Lakes

Introduction

Norman Nicholson was a Cumbrian born and bred. All his life he wrote about the English Lake District as it really is, without the romanticism or the glibness of the commercial guides. He realized that the man who goes there goes for more than the scenery: he goes for the feel and the smell of the place; to enter, if he is lucky, another world where dale life and traditions differ from his own – a world where remoteness has bred a distinctive outlook and a way of life which had a large part of its origins in Viking times, and which has not entirely been wiped out. This realization underpins the writings of Norman's Lakeland.

In a way, he had the edge on those of us who have discovered and grown to love the Lakes, for he was born with the dazzle of the Irish Sea on the one hand and the whole of Lakeland stretching away on the other. From his vantage he looked into a world of mountains, lakes and dales and during the course of some forty years wrote about them and their people in poetry and prose with the insight and warmth of a man accurately in touch with his own beloved patch, his local habitation.

That Lakeland's mountains are the highest in all England, and the dales strikingly beautiful, was not lost on him, yet he sought to penetrate that aura, for his eye was that of a trained writer, his perception that of a fine poet. His deeper interest lay in the living company of Lakeland, the total scene, or as much of it as one man might hope to encompass.

He was practical in his approach. 'It's no good me writing just a guide-book,' he said. 'It must be a real portrait to be of any value.'

The books from which these writings are taken include many diverse portraits, backgrounds, landscapes, figures in a landscape, impressions and form. He began basically enough with what he termed the living rock – 30,000 feet of solid Cumberland, and from there he embraced the rest, the flora and the fauna, the people, their churches, villages and towns, their history and industry and, quite brilliantly, the arrival of the Lakers – those first adventurers and tourists – as well as that extraordinary and

13

fascinating group, the Lake Poets.

He wrote in engaging, often candid language. He saw the dale churches as having a gruff bareness 'that knocked at the heart like poverty'; or Furness Abbey, 'as functional in design as a blast-furnace'. Windermere, once the queen of the Lakes, had become a period piece – more of an ambitious municipal park than part of the Lakes, with everything from drives, walks and seats, to long-distance swims and tame ducks. Keswick he regarded as 'the least Cumbrian town' in the county, an observation that upset some but one which he felt qualified to make, for was he not Cumbrian to the core? Yet he was also fair, pointing out that the town 'is not without beauty' and plays an important part in the economy of the North.

People occupy a good part of the scene, particularly those from the outside world, the journalists and diarists, who from about the middle of the eighteenth century began to stumble into Lakeland as if they were exploring the wildest corner of earth. Indeed, that is how many of them thought of it. There was Daniel Defoe, a good journalist, 'an accomplished liar'; William Gilpin, 'travelling salesman of the Picturesque', and Thomas Gray who, in his memorable *Journal*, stepped cautiously, well muffled, and found mountains of inexplicable malice.

Bold Joseph Budworth, on the other hand, strode into Lakeland literature 'like Long John Silver' and by the time he had written about the discoveries he had made in the remote valley of Buttermere, the outside world was to relish a scandal of the grandest kind, the story of Mary Robinson, a sensation in its day.

Norman's knowledge of the Lake Poets was extensive and, as one might expect, poet to poet, Wordsworth occupied his attention to a profound degree. He regarded him as one of the supreme original minds of all English poetry, yet he was not overawed. He could be relied on to find the unexpected, for example, Wordsworth and Harriet Martineau conversing, always difficult, 'she with her ear trumpet and he without his teeth.'

As a literary critic, Norman was never dismissive. He approached an author's work with an open mind and, without minimizing any shortcomings, sought out the positive. The journal of Dorothy Wordsworth was as much celebrated as her brother's genius. Indeed a balanced view was one of the pleasing things about his work and that quality and his good prose won him many admirers.

While his knowledge about the Lake District was considerable, he did not pretend that he had been up every mountain, because he hadn't. Yet no one would persuade him, he wrote, that he had never seen the Lake District either, just because he had never climbed Napes Needle. Physically he could not have managed that, and I suspect that apart from Coniston Old Man, and Black Combe at his door, he never got all the way up any other mountain.

Judged against some writers' works his output was not large. He began writing poetry seriously in his twenties and first came to public notice in 1942 as the editor of the *Penguin Anthology of Modern Religious Verse*. Poetry and verse plays followed and in 1949 his first book of Lakeland prose, *Cumberland and Westmorland*, was published. It became a standard work.

Norman found his images not in his subconscious mind but in the external world. The sources of his inspiration ranged from the massed fells down to the silts of the coast; he turned, too, to the industrial towns of Greater Lakeland's fringes, Millom, his home town, among them.

Like Wordsworth, he had a feeling for the rock, and Wordsworth's own interests encouraged Norman to a deeper questing into the nature of his native countryside. He certainly saw the drama in it.

> Look at the side of Scafell that drops down to Wasdale. Here is volcanic rock at its hardest, a sheer wall of rock which could take bombing and blasting and dynamiting as if they were flea-bites. The ice and the weather have made their marks, it is true, and there are long vertical grooves as if the rock had been combed with an iron comb. In the gills, too, there are trickles and slidings of scree, but still the rock is harder and more lasting than history.

This was the Lake District that my father told *me* about as a child. This was the district that drew me in as a young blood to discover the mountains for myself, as it does now for thousands of newcomers every year.

Norman was equally at home in surroundings less dramatic than Scafell, whether describing the flowers of mountain pastures, the marks made on the land by farming and mining, or the sports and pastimes of his fellow Cumbrians, particularly Cumberland and Westmorland wrestling:

> It needs a calm concentration and watchfulness which leaves no place for malice or anger. If you lose your temper you will probably lose the fall. Often you will see men smiling quietly to themselves as they waltz round one another, waiting for a chance to attack, and when they fall they get up with the look of surprise that you see on the face of a very young child who knows that he cannot

walk without falling, but is never quite ready for the fall when it comes.

It is entertaining writing: the wrestlers smiling quietly as they waltz round ... you can see them most Augusts at the Grasmere sports. Here is the human side of the Lakes, part of the living company he is so good at describing.

Norman regarded the landscape as a living thing, changing as he watched, and adjusting itself in the slow world of wind and water. He thought, too, that many people have lost the art of seeing what the landscape really looks like. Many no longer enjoy the knack of recognizing differences of rock, soil and vegetation, methods of agriculture, even ways of building a wall.

He would probably have made a good geologist. But he might also have become an historian, or a botanist – indeed, to walk in the dales with him was to enjoy a botanical education. The fact that he did not pursue these followings was decided when he was still in his teens and diagnosed as having tuberculosis.

*

Norman Cornthwaite Nicholson was born in Millom in 1914 at 14 St George's Terrace, a Victorian house where he lived all his life. In 1867 his paternal grandparents, Richard and Maria Nicholson, had moved from the farming community of Cartmel to Millom where Richard took charge of the horse-drawn haulage at the newly opened Millom Ironworks. Richard came from Viking stock, and Maria, whose maiden name was Brennan, from Irish. She joined Richard a few months after he started his new job, crossing the mile-and-a-half-wide Duddon estuary at low tide in a carrier's cart. But when close to the Cumberland shore, she became upset by the sight of the miserable encampment of huts and sheds which was all there was then of Millom town, and ordered the driver to turn back. In this she was too late, for the tide had turned already and had cut off their retreat to the Lancashire side. Ten years later, Norman's father, Joseph, was born, one of fourteen sons, and thirty-seven years later, Norman himself.

As a child, Norman saw himself as 'chatty, natty, nervous, thin.' In 1925 he won a scholarship to Millom Secondary (Grammar) School and an academic career seemed likely, perhaps university, then teaching.

His father kept a men's outfitter's shop, and the family lived in the house above and behind. In 1919 when Norman was five his mother, Edith, died during an influenza epidemic and his father remarried, to Rosetta Sobey, 'a local-born young lady'[1] who managed a piano shop close to his home.

At the age of sixteen, racked by a perpetual cough, Norman was found to have tuberculosis of the lungs. As he recalled, there seemed only one way then to try to cure TB and that was with plenty of good food, plenty of fresh air, and lots of hope – hope being the chief ingredient and at that time not too plentiful. Despite the heavy expense, which his father met with unstinting love, nearly bankrupting his little shop, the young scholar was sent to a private sanatorium in Linford on the edge of the New Forest, where the further discovery was made that he had TB of the larynx. For the following two years the doctors strove to cure him.

This illness was to have a great influence on the future writer. At school he had already been composing his own poetry, he had already experienced the enjoyment of reciting aloud to audiences at the annual town festivals – and winning prizes – and now he was to undergo an experience which one day would find its outlet in the printed pages of his own life.

In the bedroom of his sanatorium chalet, open to all the winds of Hampshire, he suffered the worst of all frustrations for a loquacious, pert young fellow – he was forbidden to speak. He was told that he must rest the larynx and the only way to do that was to stop talking. It seems an impossible demand now, yet apart from saying ninety-nine for the doctors, never a word did he utter for the next twenty months, save in a whisper. It worked well. Because the chalet had a low wooden roof, the sound was enclosed and his whispers reverberated. All outside noise was blanked out and he found that he could talk to people effectively.

At the end of fifteen months he was allowed to get up from bed and go outside, where he found that whispering was hopeless. Upset because he could not converse easily any more, and fearing this was how it would be for the rest of his life, he bought a policeman's whistle to attract attention and command a listener, but once anyone fell silent he was often too embarrassed to continue.

There is a poignancy here. Yet this time of silence, from sixteen years old to his eighteenth birthday, became a kind of analogy for the type of writer he was to be. He was not destined to become a loud declaimer, filled with stridency, but something more subtle, a writer, a reader, a quiet reciter, able to persuade his public to

---

[1] *Wednesday Early Closing* (Faber and Faber, 1975).

listen by skill and personality and, most of all, because he had something to tell.

As to Norman the man, my family were lucky enough to know him as a friend, mentor, best man and much else. With his mane of grey hair, his flying sidewhiskers, he resembled an Edwardian; though there the resemblance ended, for he was sharply attuned to the twentieth century, well informed, and an astute critic of the foibles of our time. His outlook was large and compassionate, he was generous and enjoyed lively conversation, burning out our midnight oil on numerous occasions. His shrewd eyes were deep with humour, belying his claim that he had only four jokes, which was patently untrue. At a poetry-reading in a Cumbrian theatre on a cold winter's night, we stood backstage waiting to begin, he characteristically wheezing from his lifelong struggle with the after-effects of TB, and I panting from a like experience of asthma. 'Nay,' he said at last with a certain grim smile, 'there's not one man here between us tonight, I'll swear!' We made a good job of it, even so.

In 1956 a further happiness was added to his life when he married Yvonne Gardner, whose love, enthusiasm and help proved a great strength. They travelled far together in the twenty-six years that followed. Yvonne died in 1982 and Norman five years later, in 1987. They are buried in St George's churchyard, Millom.

*

Five of Norman's books were the main hunting ground for this anthology. Three were of a like nature – *Cumberland and Westmorland, Portrait of the Lakes* and *Greater Lakeland*; and two, *Provincial Pleasures* and *The Lakers*, afforded a considerable and effective contrast. One extract came also from *The Lake District: An Anthology* which Norman compiled in 1977. It is one of the most satisfying books of its kind, presenting a wide range of the writings and poetry of Lakeland from the early seventeenth century to the present day.

The first, *Cumberland and Westmorland*, was published in 1949 in Robert Hale's County Books series. It was Norman's first extended exercise in writing about the Lake counties and despite its title, it also embraced much of that part of Lakeland that included North Lancashire. For long before the Lake counties were renamed Cumbria, in April, 1974, he had recognized the area for what it is – one country where the people are one people. The book was a success and was soon regarded as a standard work.

The second book, *The Lakers*, 1955, was not so much about the Lakes, but more about the way in which people look at the Lakes. Though not strictly topographical, it is certainly relevant here and in its way is a classic, raising the whole question of man's view of the area, from the visits by the first tourists to the present day. It also sets the Lake Poets in a proper relation to the district in which they lived.

As to *Provincial Pleasures*, there are people whose faces instantly light up with delight when it is mentioned. Published in 1959, it is a description of life in a small Cumbrian town, in fact Norman's Millom, though the names in the book are lightly disguised. There is a touch of the *Under Milk Wood* about *Provincial Pleasures*, which is a poetic book laced with humour and marvellous undertones. The pseudonyms allowed him to get under the skin of the town he knew so well. In the present anthology the extracts afford an entertaining understanding of the Cumbrian way of life as well as glimpses of Norman's own milieu.

In 1963, *Portrait of the Lakes* was published and it superseded *Cumberland and Westmorland* as the standard work. It grew out of the latter and while a good part of the text was the same, it is possible to see how he had rewritten and improved on his original work. First ideas were sharper, the text had been tightened up, some sections were cut back, others enlarged, and of course he had revised where necessary.

The fifth of the topographical books is *Greater Lakeland*. Published in 1969, it stretched to include most of the county we now call Cumbria, taking in the outer suburbs of the Eden valley, the Solway, Morecambe Bay and so on. The Lakes is at the core of the book, as in *Portrait* (and there is some duplication), yet it offers a wider perspective of the Cumbrian people, reaffirming Norman's view of the one-ness of the new county and its local loyalty.

The bonus of compressing five of Norman's volumes into one work was that it gave me a chance to re-read many enjoyable passages. Selection was not always easy and whenever I was undecided between one or another I sat back and imagined how they would have sounded had Norman been reading them. It was an uncanny feeling but I could conjure up his voice, and the choice was made.

In the editing, wherever the new name of Cumbria could substitute successfully, it has been used, but when only the old names of Cumberland, Westmorland or North Lancashire were relevant – as in the Cumberland plain, for example – the older form remains.

Cuts in passages have been made mainly to avoid duplication, but also to keep within my brief. Where original text has been omitted, the use of ellipses has been minimized, to avoid spoiling the flow, and because too many would have proved unsightly. Opening lines of some passages have been modified where the original contained references to preceding material not included, and in places the text has been brought up to date. Thus it is now the former Coniston railway station, because the original no longer exists; the Roman fort half-way up Hardknott Pass is now in the care of English Heritage and not H.M. Ministry of Public Buildings and Works; and the old ruined farm of Hinning House in Dunnerdale has become an outdoor study centre.

Each text is identified by the initials of its book of origin – *Cumberland and Westmorland: C.W.; The Lakers; L.; Portrait of the Lakes: P.L.; Greater Lakeland: G.L.;* and *Provincial Pleasures: P.P.* In the last named, for Odborough read Millom; Black Fell – Black Combe; Dunner estuary – Duddon estuary. All five volumes are out of print, though libraries often have copies.

*

There is a characteristic irony in Norman's view that the last catastrophe in the Lakes was the coming of man. That is as true today as ever it was. But what of Cumbria now? Is the Lake District of Norman Nicholson intact? In many a Cumbrian farm kitchen – and the county has some seven thousand farm holdings – there is no doubt that many of the old ways still exist, but in numerous Lakeland villages and some of the towns, alas, they do not. The wave of tourism that has swept into Lakeland since Norman wrote *Cumberland and Westmorland* has grown immensely, particularly in the last decade. Everyone, it seems, has been trying to sell Lakeland to the tourists, and succeeding; perhaps *oversell* might be appropriate. The basic shops, the butcher, the baker, the grocer, have been disappearing. It is harder now to find a loaf of bread on sale in villages such as Grasmere than it is to buy a woolly sweater. The gift shops have taken over. Indeed, the central Lakes villages and hamlets are adjusting to a new kind of existence: a mixture of retirement–visitor–farming communities, with younger people moving in to run businesses. A major change is that there are more people in the whole district all the year round now, and of course more cars. Better to avoid the mountain passes on holiday weekends than suffer the frustration of traffic jams among the peaks. Years ago it would have seemed inconceivable that people would suggest closing whole valleys to cars; yet that possibility is brought out from time to time, particularly if you live in Langdale. Norman did not want to see the area being turned into a museum, yet that is what many of us who live in Lakeland fear is happening; he did not want to see it smothered in good taste, either, though that too seems nearer. Nor are all the changes at dale level. Mountain paths have been worn away, so that teams of path-builders have appeared. The mountains are patrolled, and conserving Lakeland has become a useful school project. The Lakes, in short, are under pressure. The sheer numbers of people and their cars are at the heart of it.

Norman anticipated many of the changes that were to afflict the Lakes. He realized that even writing books about his home ground might be part of the destruction process. It is perhaps remarkable that he himself ever managed to write any books at all, for throughout the whole of his life he was never strong, though he had a certain 'home-bred gumption' and somehow he managed. To see him the day after a poetry reading, exhausted, often totally drained, was to appreciate how great a toll his illness had exacted.

From his TB days he retained a distinctive sound or catch in his voice, something very pleasing that grew, as his audiences grew, into a husky cosmic whisper; and there lay part of his strength, for so often his appeal was, at heart, of a quiet nature. 'My life still drifts in whispers,' he wrote. 'I shout out loud to no crowd.'

The whisper, I like to think, is still being heard.

Irvine Hunt
Bishop Pot, 1991

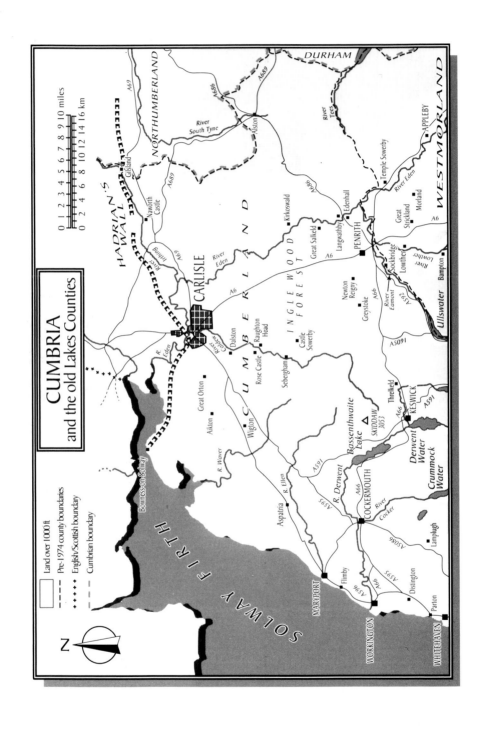

CUMBRIA
and the old Lakes Counties

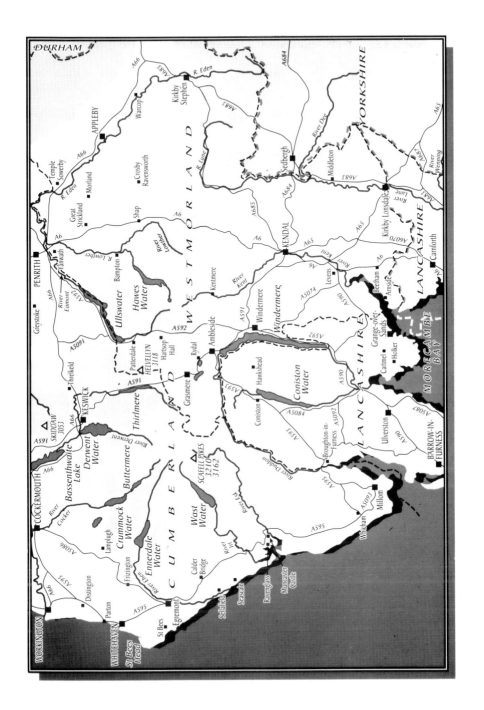

A View from a Window

Rock Country

*Norman worked in an attic room two storeys up in his house in St
George's Terrace, Millom. On cold winter mornings he often wrote while
sitting in bed, wearing fingerless gloves, working slowly with pen and
paper. Later, perhaps as an act of mercy, he typed it out on his old green
Imperial portable for those of us – the majority – who could not fathom his
handwriting. The view from his window of the mountains is unchanged,
but the old ironworks has gone, and most of the slag-banks have been
lowered and are now green slopes.*

When I look from my bedroom window across a huddle of roofs and
aerials, I can see rock country only about a mile and a half away. In
autumn the larches burn through green-yellow to brown-purple behind
the haze of the town smoke. In spring the first unpacking of the bracken
is as obvious from two thousand yards as it would be at a distance of
two feet. In summer, when the cows climb to the crest of the hill during
the hot nights, each single beast can be seen, neat as a ladybird, in the
morning light. Behind the hill, only two miles further away, is the hulk
of a fell visible in clear weather from both south Scotland and Wales.
And further round, if I lean out of my window, I can see the skyline of
the central fells – Scafell, Scafell Pike, Great End, Harter Fell, Bowfell,
Crinkle Crags, Coniston Old Man – an horizon unsurpassed in England.
No one, surely, could doubt that this is the true district of the Lakes.

Yet, if I go round to the back of my house, I get another view. For now,
closer than the rocks at the front, are the cliffs of a slag-bank, and bigger
than the trunks of the larches are the chimney-stacks of old furnaces.
And only a little further away are the pit-shafts and spoil-heaps of an
iron mine and a cargo-pier jutting out into the estuary. This, many
people would say, is not the Lake District at all.

But they would be wrong. For the furnaces used to smelt Lake District
ore with Lake District limestone, and the town itself, are built of Lake
District slate and Lake District flags. The men of the town, to a large

Hanging Knotts, Bowfell

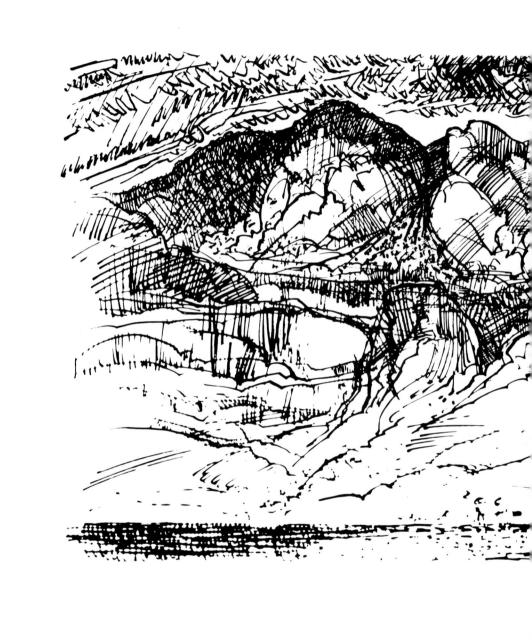

extent, come from the same stock as the men of the dales, and they speak the same kind of language. As with the hill-farmer, the shepherd or the quarryman, their life has grown out of the rock. Their work once came from the rock, and they live roofed, walled and pavemented by rock like dwellers in caves. Every bit as much as the water-ousel and the Herdwick sheep they can claim to belong to the Lake region of Cumbria.

P.L.

Silurian Hill

As I write, I can look out to a small knot of Silurian rock. It is built over now, being the oldest part of a market village which, when industry came to South Cumberland, became the suburbs of the new town. The slates pile up each behind the other, in sharp angles of roof, dormer window and gable end. From hidden plots of garden the tops of elders and apple trees puff out a green smoke among the smokeless chimneys of summer. At the very peak of the hill is a former noncomformist chapel, in buff sandstone, now turned into a bakery. The drab nineteenth-century houses are heaped and jumbled by the heave of the hill to make a mining-town St Michael's Mount. Its name is Holborn Hill, and it was by this name that Millom was known when first it began to grow into a town. The name, of course, looks like a reference to London, and there are many such references, and references to places as far apart as California, Gibraltar, and Jericho to be found among the farms of the district. But though Holborn Hill cannot be traced back beyond the eighteenth century, and hence survives in no early form, it seems at least possible that it may preserve the memory of Hallbjörn, an old Viking.

P.L.

A Deeper Tide

Here, high above the backwash of the streets, I feel a deeper tide flow over me – a 500-million-year tide, at the bottom of which the town and its people lie like grains of sand, like dregs in a teapot. Here, among chimney-pots and aerials, I feel the weight of the tides of the Ordovician Age – slow estuarine tides in which the mud sank and settled to form the rock which is now heaped in a hill above the town. In the night ebb Black Fell becomes once again a dark underwater rock scoured by the tides.

Then in a jiffy of millennia the sea begins to simmer. Volcanoes break out like carbuncles. A red-hot pus of lava bursts through the under-skin of the ocean, and the vapour stinks and fumes, boiling in tidal waves against the coasts. Under-sea deluges of ash stain the water black as a sewer where the cooled lava creates a new, slag-like landscape. Slowly under the scrubbing and bludgeoning of the tide, lava and ash, in their turn, consolidate to rock, and in the fishless seas there begins to take shape what one day will be known as Scafell or Langdale Pikes.

Once more the seas decline to sluggish shallows and the mud dreams itself into hills as gentle as the swash of its own tides. For 300 million years ago almost all that goes to make the outer landscape of Odborough was already formed if not yet shaped – Black Fell, the volcanic mountains of the Lakes, and the low Silurian hills across the Dunner estuary. Even the town itself was beginning to form, like bones within an embryo.

In the rocks which would make up the hill of Old Odborough waited the stones which would make up the houses and inns and chapels of new Odborough. And in the hills of Furness, across the estuary, the strata were still uncleaved which one day, as I lie in bed, will slate the roof above my head.

Yet this is not all that remains in the memory of the town's bones. Down beneath the sea it all went once again, and the tide flowed over it, warm and white as milk. Coral bloomed on the sea-floor in rhododendrons of stone, and a slow snow-storm of calcium descended through the water. The limestone which emerged when the seas had ebbed and steamed away is scarcely visible around the town – only a few clawings of rock at Odborough Point, where the River Dunner meets the sea. Yet it was in this stone that the town quickened into life. For the iron ore in the veins of the rock infused blood into the bones so that here, out of the belly of the mines, the town was brought forth. Every Odborough child is joined by an umbilical cord, stretching back through the ooze to the shelled, creeping creatures of the warm lagoons.

P.P.

The Shape of the Land

The Coming of the Ice

It has been said that when God made England his finger touched but did not press, but that is not true of Cumbria. He pressed there all right. What is more, he used his nails. And the nails were ice.

If the ice had not come the general shape of the country, the cartwheel of dales and ridges, might be much the same as it is now, but the features would have been very different. There would have been few cliffs or crags, no waterfalls, no gills, and perhaps no lakes. The ice invaded the north of England from two main directions. From Scandinavia it came to the north-east coast, covering much of Durham and Yorkshire, but rarely crossing beyond the Pennines; from Scotland it came down the west coast, covering the Carlisle plain and filling the sea-basin between there and the Isle of Man. This Scottish ice carved deeply into the spurs of the western fells, which once sloped gently to the sea, but now drop steeply to the two-or-three-mile-wide coastal plain. It pushed arms of ice up the estuaries. It broke chunks off the Eskdale granite and left them deposited on Walney Island and further south. It blocked the mouths of some of the western valleys, forming lakes such as the 'Whicham Lake' beneath Black Combe, which must have been rather like the Bassenthwaite of today.

The main glaciation, however, was home produced. As the mean temperature fell and more and more snow accumulated every year a glacier began to form in each dale, until eventually the lower hills were submerged and only the higher central peaks stood like an archipelago above the slow tides of ice. Perhaps even these went under in the end. The reverse must have been the case when the ice retreated. First it ebbed from the central dome, then left bare the radiating ridges, and finally oozed out of each separate dale. As the coastal glaciers, the Scottish ice shrank back, step by step, from the south, the waters burst out of the valleys.

P.L.

Dale Glaciers

The two Langdales demonstrate very clearly the effects of the ice on the scenery of the inner Lakes. The district had, in fact, taken its present ground-plan long before the Ice Age, for when rain falls on a dome-shaped object it is bound to flow downwards and outwards, so that the rivers will carve out valleys radiating roughly from the centre. There may have been no lakes in pre-glacial times, but you could probably have found your way rather blunderingly from dale to dale with the aid of a modern Ordnance Survey map.

Yet the Ice Age brought an immense change. Up to then, the landscape had been shaped mainly by the erosive power of running water; now it was to be chiselled by ice. Greater Lakeland underwent glaciation both from the outside, from the great Scottish glaciers which slid down the coast, and from the inside, from the home-bred glaciers, which formed on the tops of the fells and descended along the lines of the valleys till they met the Scottish ice of the coast.

It was these dale glaciers which were the real sculptors of Lakeland. Towards the foot of the valleys they flowed over the lower ridges, leaving them smooth, rounded and upholstered by thick cushions of boulder clay. In the upper valleys, where the ridges were higher, they dug deeply into the groove of the dale, flattening the bottom and chopping off the sides, turning it from the more normal V-shape to the characteristic U-shape. Great Langdale is a splendid example of this, with beckside meadows, flat as a tennis court, running the whole length of the upper dale from Chapel Stile to Mickleden. Often, too, the ice would scoop down into the floor of a dale and then plane up again, leaving a hollow, which, when the ice melted, became a lake or a tarn. That is what happened in Little Langdale, and the result is Little Langdale Tarn. At other times it would pluck at the rocks of the floor-bed until they snapped away in one solid piece. And that is what happened at Skelwith Force, below the meeting-place of the two Langdales, where the River Brathay drops clean away, the whole width of it in one break, giving the Lakes one of their most spectacular waterfalls, as well as one of the most accessible. The other kind of Lake District waterfall, of which Dungeon Gill in Great Langdale is one of the finest examples, is yet again a product of ice engineering, but in a different way. For when the glaciers carved off the sides of a dale, the little tributaries were left hanging in the air, and the becks, which before then had trundled evenly down to the main stream, either dropped sheer, in one long streak, as at Dungeon Gill, or cut back into the rock in a series of minor falls and chasms as at Tilberthwaite. What the ice did, in fact, was to exaggerate all the native characteristics of the Lake rocks, making the steep hills steeper, the round hills rounder, the crags

Langdale Pikes

craggier and the dales more cleft-like and secluded. And nowhere was its over-emphasis carried out with more exuberance and effect than in the greater and lesser valleys of Langdale.

G.L.

Two Cartwheels

It was Wordsworth who first compared the pattern of ridges and dales of Lakeland to a cartwheel. He noticed, also, that the system really falls into the shape of two cartwheels, separated by the north to south geological fault in which lie Thirlmere, Grasmere, Rydal Water and Windermere. The hub of the western wheels is on Esk Hause; that of the eastern, on Helvellyn. Perhaps the most satisfactory image for the western system, however, is that of a lemon-squeezer, with the dales gouged out of the dome and sloping radially to the rim.

If, now, you imagine that the right side of the squeezer, as you hold it in your hand, has been broken off, then you will get something of the effect of the Thirlmere–Windermere fault. For on that side of the dome the dales are all cut short. Easedale and the two Langdales break off into Windermere, while the little valleys on the south-eastern slope of Wetherlam and Coniston Old Man turn into Yewdale and Coniston Water. But through the whole of the western semicircle, from Keswick in the north to Millom in the south, the dales radiate in regular order: Borrowdale, the Buttermere–Crummock–Lorton valley, Ennerdale, Wasdale, Eskdale and Dunnerdale, with smaller dales like Newlands, Miterdale, and the valleys of the Calder and the Bleng, to fill up the cracks, or, rather, to make minor grooves between the major ones. The eastern cartwheel, which lies largely in the old county of Westmorland, is much less complete. It has two major dales, Patterdale and Mardale, both of which lie north-east. Westward there are only the gills which run to the Thirlmere fault. To the south, the Troutbeck valley flows into Windermere, while to the south-east a number of smaller valleys (Kentmere, Longsleddale and Bannisdale) find their way eventually to the course of the River Kent.

The main lines of communication, by road and railway, enclose both these cartwheels in a rough, bulging circle, of which the four corners, if one may call them so, are Whitehaven, Barrow, Kendal and Penrith. Across the diameter of the circle there is no railway, but a road runs from Keswick to Ambleside, by the Thirlmere–Windermere trough, over Dunmail Raise. For two centuries this has been the main trans-Lakes thoroughfare for the tourist.

The eastern cartwheel is bisected by the main road from Patterdale over Kirkstone Pass into Troutbeck and Windermere. But the western one at one time could not be crossed except by foot, though the passes of

Honister and Newlands and roads over Cold Fell and Birker Moor all cut off considerable corners. Today, of course, the route from Ambleside to the west coast is open to cars – by Little Langdale, Wrynose Pass, Hardknott Pass and Eskdale. Hardknott is the most severe test that faces any motorist in the district, but the surface is good, and the road takes you through country hardly seen, at one time, by any but the most adventurous tourist. The tarmac is new, and that is not conspicuous. But what a difference it makes, for even when no car is in sight – which, in the holiday months is not often – the former loneliness, the remoteness, is gone.

Yet perhaps on an October evening, with the dusk gathering above the river gravel and the mist clotting in the V of the pass, the bracken sodden and brown and the bitter-orange fruits of bog asphodel rotting into the mosses – perhaps, then, you can sense something of the almost Icelandic isolation in which the people of these dales once lived.

P.L.

Greater Lakeland

Perhaps Greater Lakeland could be defined as the country where the Lake fells are in sight. But the unity is greater than that. It comes from the rock, from the shape of the land, from its history, and from the stock and breeding of its people. It embraces places which the visitor to the Lakes may not want to see and aspects of life and society which he comes here to forget. But it is no good trying to forget them. Greater Lakeland does not just mean Derwentwater, Blea Tarn and the Wasdale Screes: it also means Sellafield nuclear power station, the Marchon chemical factory at Whitehaven, Workington steelworks, Barrow docks; wharves, warehouses, bus-stops and parking-places; schools, adult-education centres, the county libraries; churches, chapels, Sunday schools, cinemas and dance-halls; sports fields, allotments and cemeteries; the new housing estates and the old, shabby Victorian terraces; hardware stores, chemists, fish-and-chip shops, pubs and coffee-bars; the dairy herds, the turnip fields and a thousand lowland farms; one cathedral, one teachers' training college, one submarine-building yard – in fact, all that goes to the life and death of the people of Cumbria. Forget all this, and what all the rest of the country calls Lakeland will turn moribund, dying slowly from the edges inwards, to become in the end little more than a beautiful, embalmed corpse in a rotting coffin.

G.L.

A True Whole

How greatly the mountains divide the people who live among them can be seen from the case of the two Seathwaites. Both are dale villages. From one to the other is less than ten miles as the raven flies and even to men the route by Esk Hause and Moasdale, though rough, is not much further. But one Seathwaite is in Borrowdale, which runs due north, and the other is in Dunnerdale, which runs south. The farmer's wife in Borrowdale does her shopping in Keswick; her next-dale neighbour beside the Duddon goes down to Broughton, and beyond to Ulverston or Barrow. Barrow and Keswick are not widely separated to anyone with a car, but at one time, the dalesman did not usually own a car, and if he tried to make the journey by rail, he would have been lucky to manage it in four hours.

Yet in spite of all these barriers and divisions, the lake areas of Cumbria form a true whole. At one time they formed almost a small, separate, self-contained kingdom, locked off from both England and Scotland. This was partly due to the common Norse ancestry of the people, and partly to the character of the land, which imposed upon them a peculiar and uniform way of life. From about the tenth century onward there grew up in the dales a group of small communities, poor, austere, largely self-subsistent and always self-reliant. Even when the Industrial Revolution opened up the mining districts of West Cumberland and Furness, the same tradition persisted, for mining had been known there for 2,000 years.

P.L.

Seven Rocks: Skiddaw Slate

Skiddaw slate is the foundation stone of the Lakes and is essentially the Cumbrian rock, for it scarcely appears outside the old county.

The old rocks – and they are among the oldest in Europe – are harder and tougher than the newer rocks, and form the central hub of the Lake District with its spokes of ridges and dales.

The oldest of the lot is the Skiddaw slate: a mud-rock, laid down at the delta of a river on the shores of a shallow sea. It is softer than much of the Borrowdale rocks, and although it is called a slate, it is not very slaty – that is, it does not easily split into thin slivers like roofing slate. Here and there it breaks up into small fragments and forms screes, mostly scabby and small, but on the whole the surface disintegrates into soil, so that grass can grow and heather. It wears smoothly into rounded outlines with even slopes. These rocks occupy most of the northern part of the district. Bassenthwaite, Crummock and Loweswater lie entirely in

Skiddaw slate; Derwentwater and Buttermere, almost so. Ennerdale Water and Ullswater have their lower reaches among it – though the Ullswater patch is detached from the main block. This main block includes Skiddaw itself and Saddleback; all the fells around the Newlands valley; Grasmoor and the fells around Whinlatter and westwards to the edge of the iron-ore district. There are also a few outlying patches: one in the Eden valley on Crossfell, and one in the south which includes Black Combe.

Skiddaw and Saddleback are among the most mathematically ordered of all the fells, and might have been planned by a cubist painter. Yet, at the same time, they are alive and animal. The volcanic rocks, too, are alive, but with a fantastic life, as if they were grotesque, contorted creatures of folklore, but the Skiddaw fells are like prehistoric monsters.

The smoothness of the rock emphasizes its animal look, for instead of the patch and jigsaw texture of the craggier hills, we find an even-coloured hide of grass or bracken bulging round flanks and haunches. Saddleback does not suggest any specific animal shape, and Skiddaw is more of a pyramid – though an animal, too, as if a pyramid could turn sphinx. But Black Combe, in the south, is the Sphinx itself. Look at it from Silecroft Shore or Layriggs – the head has gone, but the chest muscles are there, the paws with a gulley between them, and the back stretching to White Combe with the ribs and the loins swelling above Whicham Valley.

Each of the Skiddaw fells has its own individuality, yet they are all of the same family. They are epic or just narrative verse rather than the dramatic poetry of the volcanic rock. Perhaps their finest and boldest effect comes from size and solidity, from sheer cubic content. Hollow out Saddleback and you would have a dish-cover that would fit over London.

Moreover, many of these fells are rather isolated, so that, unlike those of the central dales, you can see them whole and separate: Skiddaw, for instance, seen from Ashness Bridge, slanting straight from top to lakeside. Most isolated of all is Black Combe, with only a bleak sprawl of moorland to join it to the Eskdale fells ten miles away. Black Combe, indeed, is well known to many who have never visited the Lakes, for it dominates a large area, even as Criffell dominates the Scottish banks of the Solway. On a summer evening, from the north pier at Blackpool, you can see a blunt-headed mountain bullocking into the green of the twilight and leaping, apparently, straight into the tide. That is Black Combe, and that is Skiddaw slate.

P.L.

The Borrowdale Volcanic Series

After the Skiddaw slates had been deposited, a number of volcanoes burst out, probably under the sea, and ejected great masses of lava,

The screes, Wastwater

ashes and volcanic dust. None of the volcanoes remain, though it is thought that the largest crater may have been near where Bassenthwaite is today, but the material which they poured out formed the rocks known as the Borrowdale volcanic series, which make up the central dome of the Lake District. They run side by side with the Skiddaw slate, roughly parallel with the former Penrith-Keswick railway. They then skirt Derwentwater and cross over Honister, missing Buttermere and Crummock and leaving Ennerdale to the granophyre. Next down to Wasdale and along the edge of the Eskdale granite to the Duddon estuary. Their south-eastern boundary runs from Broughton-in-Furness, through Coniston and Ambleside and across the Shap fells to the limestone of the Eden valley. This volcanic area includes nearly all the fells of the centre – the Scafell group, the Coniston–Wetherlam group, the Langdales, Helvellyn and the High Street range. Of the dales it includes Borrowdale, Wasdale, Upper Eskdale, Dunnerdale, Mardale and most of Patterdale. Of the larger lakes only Thirlmere and Haweswater lie entirely in volcanic rock, though Wastwater nearly does.

P.L.

The Screes

Look at the side of the Scafell that drops down to Wasdale. Here is volcanic rock at its hardest, a sheer wall of rock which could take bombing and blasting and dynamiting as if they were flea-bites. The ice and the weather have made their marks, it is true, and there are long vertical grooves as if the rock had been combed with an iron comb. In the gills, too, there are trickles and slidings of scree, but still the rock is harder and more lasting than history. Where cleavage is greater, however, we find larger screes or a wreckage of broken-off boulders. The rain dribbles into wrinkles of the rock and there freezes, and, as it freezes, swells. This is a sort of geological rheumatism. The needles of ice swell in the joints of the rock, and split it, till deep cracks are formed, and the surface chips and flakes away. The screes which result are very characteristic of the dale scenery. A scree, academically, is a slope of loose stones in a state of unstable equilibrium – in other words, if you step on one it slides. Sometimes the stones are quite large, sometimes, if they are left undisturbed, soil accumulates and grass grows over them. Sometimes torrents form among them in times of heavy rain, and wash them into lakes or rivers, making little stony deltas.

The screes which the climber recognizes, however, are the long cindery slopes of small stones which slither under the feet. The most magnificent examples in the district are those of Wasdale. Here, at the lower end of the lake, there is a huge curtain of scree, falling stones held in suspension, dropping 1,500 feet into the water. The screes, as they slide, grow and gather like streams, widening and curving, till at the foot they fan out into a series of scallops on the shore of the lake. The whole slope stands in fluted tapering columns, shaped like the fan-vaulting of a cathedral turned upside down.

G.L.

The Silurian Rocks

The Silurian rocks are not very assertive. They make up, in the main, the easy-going country south of Coniston and Windermere and between Kendal and Kirkby Lonsdale.

The hills here are not very high, and shape themselves often into flattish, rather desolate moorland, dinted with broad, shallow valleys. This is not a picture-postcard country, though Coniston, admittedly, has the volcanic range of Dow Crag, Old Man and Wetherlam on one side of the lake, so that John Ruskin, who lived on the other side, said that he looked out on the first great up-thrust of mountain Britain.

The contrast is even more memorable when seen from the terminus of the closed-down Foxfield–Coniston branch line. Yewdale Crags looked so near that you felt you must be staring through binoculars. They are vicious crags, not very high, but fanged like a tiger, with slaverings of scree and bright green whiskers of larch and birch. Beyond is Raven Crag and the road winding beneath Tom Heights to Ambleside. All this is volcanic. But below you you can see Coniston village, with a road leading to the lake, beyond which, and behind Ruskin's Brantwood, are the wavy, unemphatic moors of the Silurian slate.

P.L.

Eskdale Granite

Long after the central rocks had been formed a number of igneous rocks were thrust up among them, probably in the period known as Old Red Sandstone. The main masses are the granite of Shap, Skiddaw and Eskdale, the granophyre of Ennerdale, the micro-granite of Threlkeld and the general mix-up of rocks on Carrock Fell. There are also many dykes and minor intrusions including a patch of the rare minette on Sale Fell near Bassenthwaite.

The best known commercially of the granites is that of Shap which is quarried for road material and for making kerbs and setts for pavements. Shap granite will take a high polish, when it looks like frozen potted meat and is used as an ornamental stone. But the Eskdale granite is much more extensive than either of these and has a far greater effect on the landscape. It varies a good deal in colour, being sometimes a mercury-like grey with only a hint of pink, and sometimes the dark red of iron ore which has, in fact, been mined in the dale.

P.L.

The Newer Rocks: Mountain Limestone

The mountain limestone is one of the loveliest rocks to be found in the whole district, and forms a soft, white ruff round the head of the slates. Not that it is always soft. The Pennines are not soft and descend westward in magnificent escarpments into the Eden valley from Brough to Appleby. Nor is the fell country round Askham and Bampton in any way soft, though it is not magnificent either. It is bare, but not with the clean-cut bareness of Skiddaw slate. Instead, it seems a landscape of utter poverty – as if a flock of monstrous, prehistoric fowls had scratched and scratched till the rock were scored and scurfy.

The best-known part of the limestone country, however, is that around the shores of Morecambe Bay where the rock is much gentler and more agreeable. Most visitors to the Lakes pass through this limestone area, entering it round about Carnforth. And, immediately, they must notice a difference in the *feel* of the land. It is still quite an ordinary type of landscape, quiet, grassy and green, though beautifully clean and washed after the grime of central Lancashire. The little chips which break through the soil here and there are as white as daisies. The stone walls, the cottages, the farms look as if they had been scrubbed.

P.L.

Coniston Limestone

Coniston limestone is a very different rock from mountain (or carboniferous) limestone. They are of vastly different ages, their only common link being their chemical composition – lime. Coniston is much older, dark grey, and has little impact on the scenery. Mountain limestone, quite the opposite.

A geologist, looking at the view from the site of the former Coniston railway station, would have been aware of the Coniston limestone, lying between the volcanic and the Silurian rocks. It lies between them both in space and time, having been laid down after the volcanic and before the Silurian rocks. It appears first at Beck Farm, near Millom, and then runs as a narrow strip along the division between the two slate rocks from the Duddon estuary to Shap. In the north it changes from limestone to what is known as the Stockdale shales. The limestone is hard and bluish, and where it crops up through the surface we get a little island of blue-white rock. A patch of it can be seen in Church Beck, where it flows through Coniston village. As this rock makes little difference to the scenery I will not say much about it, but to the geologist it is exciting because it is full of fossils – indeed it is one of the most fossiliferous of the older rocks of the world.

C.W.

New Red Sandstone

Sandstone disintegrates easily, so that the surface breaks into soil, and gives rise to the cosy, well-fleshed countryside of the Carlisle plain and the Eden valley. Much of the former was covered with the old Inglewood Forest, and it is still better wooded than the rest of the country.

The crumbling of the stone has its effects on buildings, too, especially barns and old walls which are left uncared for. The stone rots into soil in crevices and crannies, and ivy-leaved toadflax roots there, mouse-ear hawkweed and the cresses. The buildings are integrated with the landscape. Even the squat, grim streets of miners' cottages at St Bees and the villages nearby have a sombre glow of their own. The rooms are small, but the walls are thick and will not easily fall down. Wigton is built almost entirely of sandstone, and so is the fine market town of Penrith, and most of the older part of Carlisle.

The soft nature of the sandstone, however, has one great defect. Because of its workability, and because, perhaps, it has a warm, religious look, it has become the main stone for ecclesiastical building. Carlisle Cathedral, the abbeys of Calder and Furness, and nearly all the churches, old and recent, are built of sandstone. And the stone has crumbled sadly. In particular the ornamentation has been damaged. On the east end of Carlisle Cathedral the stone has worn and then flaked off, so that the figures have lost their faces, and sometimes the front of their bodies, as if they had been hacked off with an axe. Decorations of lesser relief – like the carvings round the door of the northern front of St Bees Priory – have been mumbled and half-smudged away. In the same way, the many Norse and Anglican crosses up and down Cumbria have suffered badly.

C.W.

The Coal Measures

For more than two centuries coal was the rich black heart of West Cumbrian economy. How many pits there have been is hard to say, but over 1,200 shafts are known. In 1986, the last deep pit to close was the Haig Colliery at Whitehaven, and that seemed to be that. Today coal is scraped from the surface in giant opencast workings at a number of Cumbrian sites, and a new deep adit has started in the St Bees Valley.

The upper rocks of the carboniferous series are the coal measures. We cannot claim that they form a ring round the district, for only about a quarter of the circle is found, just outside the strip of limestone which runs from Egremont to a little east of Caldbeck. The coal area is rather wide from Whitehaven along the coast to Maryport, and thence curves in a thin rim through the mining villages of Dearham and Aspatria and peters out before it reaches the Eden valley, though there are beds of coal in the Ingleborough and Hawes districts. The mid-Lancashire coalfield may be considered perhaps to be part of the southern edge of the ring, and even – though this is stretching it too far! – the Durham and North Yorkshire coalfields part of the eastern edge. As the surface stone on the coal area is mostly a dirty-looking sandstone, the traveller tends to connect it with the scenery of the Permian rocks rather than that of the limestone. It is a dark, dusty, blackberry-and-apple landscape.

C.W.

The Changing Scene

Because of the immense ages of time which have gone towards the shaping of the landscape as we see it today we are inclined to think that change belongs to the past. We speak of the unchanging hills and think of the apparent permanence of nature as distinct from the transitoriness of man. But – except for the glaciers – the forces of change are still at work today – frost, rain, wind, sun and rivers. The landscape is not dead nor static, a mere relic of the past: it is a living thing, at every moment changing and developing before our eyes.

Perhaps the most obvious changes are those taking place in the lakes and tarns, all of which are steadily silting up. Scores, perhaps hundreds, of tarns have already been filled and are now peat bogs on the fellside. In Kentmere a whole lake has disappeared, the process having been helped on by drainage. At the head of practically all the lakes which still remain there is a large stretch of flat land formed out of the mud washed down by the main river of the upper dale. Haweswater is an exception merely because here the water-level has been artificially raised. At Coniston, two considerable streams flow into the head of the lake – Yewdale Beck from Tilberthwaite and Church Beck from the Old Man. Both of these pass near old quarries or mine workings, so that both have brought down immense amounts of rubble, soil and quarry dust, until they have built up acres of stony delta between the village and the jetty. Parts of the water edge are so deep in ooze and so thick with ten-foot reeds that you can push a boat into them and find yourself completely caged in a jungle of brown and green blades. If the process continues, then we may find that the top end of the lake, opposite Tent Lodge, may be detached from the rest and become a small tarn like the Priest Pot, above Esthwaite Water.

Sometimes, too, a large and powerful beck enters a lake half-way down its course. Then, if there is no strong current, the delta which forms is likely, in the end, to cut the lake in two. Such multiplication by fission has already taken place in the case of Buttermere and Crummock and also in that of Derwentwater and Bassenthwaite, both pairs of lakes being more or less reunited in times of flood. In the second example, the intervening delta is now just as big as either of the remaining lakes, since the original Derwent-Bassenthwaite-water was assailed on either flank by a stream of considerable carrying power – Newlands Beck on the west and the Greta on the east.

P.L.

The Coming of Man

The Last Catastrophe

The landscape of the Lakes was shaped largely by a series of catastrophes – volcanic eruption, earthquakes, inundation and glaciation – and the last catastrophe was the coming of man. He came, like the ice, in a series of invasions.

Of the people of the past who came to the district, whether to stay or not to stay, many left memorials on the surface of the land – cairns, monoliths, crosses, castles, churches. Others left few visible signs, but their influence is felt in the speech and way of life of those who came after them. All of them, in one way or another, helped to make the Lake area what it is.

The levelling tidal wave of modern civilization is sweeping over the Lakes as over the rest of the world, washing away landmarks and depositing foreign wreckage. Soon the special character of dale life may be obliterated and half-forgotten. But as yet something of that character remains, and the true local accent can still be heard, though it is becoming fainter and fainter.

P.L.

The Early Britons

The Lakes and Furness were a backward part of the country, still stuck in the Ice Age when primitive man was living in the South, and persisting in Bronze Age ways when the rest of England had advanced to Iron. The poverty of the area meant that old practices were not easily discontinued or old possessions thrown away. When miners in Furness broke into the Old Men's workings, they found two stone axes just as they had been left two thousand years ago – Stone Age tools to dig out Iron Age iron!

Furness seems to have been comparatively populous in the Bronze Age, with camps or settlements at Aldingham, Walney, Scales and elsewhere, and an important village near Urswick, at what is known as

46

Urswick Stone Walls. There was another pre-Celtic village not far away, near Devoke Water, on the western slopes of Black Combe, with hundreds of burial cairns scattered round it, and there were settlements in other parts of the district, often in wild and bleak places such as the fells above the upper valley of the Calder. These pre-Celtic and early Celtic tribes were very poor. Though copper was available in the hills they were very slow to turn from stone to bronze. The valley bottoms were mostly sumps of bog and peat, and the valley slopes were thickly wooded with oak, chestnut, hazel and birch, so that the people were forced to make their home on the barer hillsides, where they could rear their half-wild stock animals, and grow a little grain when they could scrape together enough soil to plant it in. The camps were often four or five hundred feet above sea-level, exposed to the western winds, with the sea-mists rolling up the dales and the clouds hanging over the fells like a grey thatched roof for days on end.

P.L.

The Romans

The power of the Roman Empire left its mark, clear and ineradicably, on Cumbria, but its lasting influence was not great. All the other races who settled among the fells were assimilated into the common stock. The Romans were never assimilated – they remained always foreigners.

Hadrian's Wall and the country of the wall belong in no way to the Lakes but it was behind this defence that the Roman occupation of Cumberland and Westmorland was carried out. The lakes themselves offered little. Carlisle, in the north of the county, had become a considerable town, while around most of the larger forts on the wall and at Old Penrith on the main road there grew up villages of shopkeepers, traders and camp-followers. The Roman soldiers frequently married British girls, who lived close to the forts and adopted something of the Roman way of life.

The Lakes, however, had none of this. There was little chance for trade, and the country, from the Roman point of view, did not look inviting. Their policy, therefore, was that of policing rather than of colonizing – of keeping the peace and making the miserable hill-farmers pay as much as they could towards the army's upkeep.

But in spite of little hope of profit the Romans took a lot of trouble over this part of the province. From Ambleside (from whence they may have had a rough connecting track along High Street to Brougham) they built a road to Ravenglass on the coast, with a fort at either end of the route and one midway at Hardknott. None of the Border forts has a site to compare with that of Hardknott. It stands on a triangular plateau at the confluence of the valley of the upper Esk and the gill up which runs the track to Hardknott Pass. On the two seaward sides the drop is almost sheer. Standing just outside the north-west walls, a Roman soldier could have spat into the river, 400 feet below, if the wind were behind him. And if he turned, and looked updale, he could have seen the main leap of the Esk Falls, white and steady as a pillar of salt. Here the valley opens like a split in a tree-trunk among some of the highest country the Romans ever saw in Britain – Crinkle Crags, Bowfell and the back of the Scafell Range.

On the third side of the triangle the land rises comparatively gently for three or four hundred yards, giving enough room for a parade and exercise ground, and then tilts in another steep rake to the peak of Hardknott Hill. It was a site almost impregnable by the military standards of the second century – but who was going to try to take it in any case? For the men at Hardknott were among the loneliest in the whole Roman Empire, desperately short of company, and relying almost entirely on the port of Ravenglass for their supplies. Even the local girls must have been very scarce.

P.L.

The English

In the centuries which followed the Roman occupation the people living between the Clyde and the Mersey were gathered into the kingdom of Strathclyde. Little is known of this kingdom, though one of the Celtic tribes which lived in the area – the *Cymru*, or Welsh – gave its name to Cumberland. Some early form of Welsh, indeed, was the language of Cumberland when the Romans came and remained long after they had gone, so that you might expect to find a good deal of the Celtic vocabulary embedded in the Lake landscape. In fact, there is very little. A few towns, such as Carlisle and Penrith, retain mainly Celtic names. So do one or two of the fells, such as Helvellyn and Blencathra, while quite a number of the rivers still keep on murmuring in Welsh, including the Eden, the Derwent, the Esk and the Leven. But in the villages, the farms, the clearings and settlements, and in the work and speech of the people, the old Celtic tongue is almost entirely forgotten.

The kingdom of Strathclyde began to disintegrate in the seventh century, by which time two small Anglian kingdoms were established on the north-east coast – Deira round about the Yorkshire Wolds and Bernicia from the Tyne to the Forth. From Bernicia the English infiltrated into Cumberland along the lines of the Eden valley, and established many settlements on the coast. The western industrial area is full of places with Anglian names: Workington, Harrington, Frizington, Parton, Hensingham and so on. From Deira they spread into South Westmorland and on to Cartmel and Furness, planting their names in such places as Pennington and Aldingham. Because they were primarily an agricultural people they kept mostly to the lowlands, leaving the fells and the dales to the last remnants of the British. For this reason they are about the least interesting of the early settlers, giving to the people only what they had in common with the rest of England. The true Lake character came not from the English but from the Norse.

P.L.

The Norsemen

The race which made the Norse crosses was the last to invade the dales in large numbers, and it was in many ways the most important of all. It has left its names hacked on the fellsides and scotched along the walls of the dales. It has left its language still alive in the dialect. It has left a dale way of life which remained unchanged for centuries. Yet oddly enough this invasion is almost unrecorded. There are a few vague references to Cumberland in the works of early Scandinavian historians and that is about all.

Evidence, none the less, is to be found in place-names. Throughout the ninth and tenth centuries the whole of the north of England endured Scandinavian raids, but the raiders were Danish rather than Norse. The Danes harried the north-east coast and settled in Lincolnshire and Yorkshire. From thence they pressed north into Tyneside and ranged across the country into the British kingdom of Strathclyde, and they are reported to have sacked Carlisle in AD 875. In Cumberland and Westmorland, however, the place-names for the most part are not Danish but Norse. There are many places in Norway today the names of which are very similar to those of places in the Lake District and the resemblance is even stronger in the case of Iceland, which seems to be because in Iceland, as in Cumbria, the invading race tended to call the settlements after the chief or warrior who took possession. A great number of place-names in the Lakes contain a Norse surname as part of their etymology.

The Norsemen were much influenced by the Celts, with whom they had mixed and married, and from whom they had learnt some of the gentler arts of civilization and also, probably, something of Christianity. They were no longer merely raiders or barbarians. So that when they looked east from Snaefell on the Isle of Man across the thirty miles of sea to the Cumbrian skyline, they were thinking not of loot but of a country to settle in. And when eventually they set foot on the Cumbrian coast, they found a land of narrow dales, divided one from another by high ridges, well suited to the life of small individualistic communities such as they were used to. It was on a smaller scale than Iceland, but less severe, and in each of the dales there was a strip of land potentially far

Farmhouses at Troutbeck Valley above Windermere

more fertile than the barren acres of the subarctic.[1] It was a cosier, more friendly country. They must have felt at home almost at once.

Nor is it likely that they met with great opposition. The English were settled in the lowlands along the Solway, but there were not many of them south of St Bees Head. The British tribes which still remained in the hills had been dwindling for centuries, though north of the Duddon they had made an alliance with the Scottish lowlanders and revived the old kingdom of Cumbria or Strathclyde. In AD 945, however, this came to an end when the Cumbrians, under the command of King Dunmail, were defeated by the Saxon King Edmund. Tradition points to Dunmail Raise, the pass between Thirlmere and Grasmere, as the field of battle and the site of the king's grave, though, in fact, he died at Rome thirty years later.

We cannot be certain what happened to the Cumbrians after this. Maybe some of them emigrated to Wales; maybe the survivors were allowed to linger on among the mountains. Certainly they would be in no state to offer much resistance to the Norsemen. By the twelfth century we may take it for granted that the dales were inhabited by a mixed race, predominantly Norse in blood and custom, and speaking a Norse dialect probably incomprehensible in the rest of England.

P.L.

The Statesmen

These yeomen farmers were small freeholders or customary tenants. For a time, at least, they were a strong social group in Cumbria.

In every dale there developed a number of small family farms, each owning its couple of hundred acres or perhaps much less. They were in communication with one another, but they were independent, and with certain modifications many of them remained independent until as late as the eighteenth and nineteenth centuries. The men who farmed them, the statesmen, cultivated their own fields, passing them on from father to son, and grazing their sheep in the fells.

In many ways, the dalesman remained a Viking for centuries. He kept much of the grit of his old tongue in his dialect, for long a seeming-barbarous language, quite unintelligible to the southerner. Even today he speaks with a grating, clattering grutch, which is as indigenous as the sound of the wind in bare sticks or a stone slithering down a scree. His vocabulary is as Scandinavian as a lemming, and he has stamped it on the landscape till you cannot think of it in

---

[1] It is possible, however, that in the ninth century the climate of Iceland was warmer than it is today.

Anglo-Saxon. Even an Englishman must learn the language of the native when he visits Cumbria.

The independence of the statesman was maintained only with a struggle during the years which followed the Black Death. He still kept his old love of individualist sports – wrestling and the fell race – but he found it hard to make a living. By the time of Wordsworth, many of the dale farmers must have been very poor, and the sons were not looking forward to the family inheritance.

In the case of the Lakes, the rise of the tourist trade was due as much to the wish of the inhabitants as that of the tourists themselves, as much to conditions inside the Lakes as to fashions outside.

The old statesman would have had nothing to do with the travellers: there was a fierce independence about the Norse farmers which had little use for foreigners. But the statesman had been in decline for centuries and, indeed, by the end of the Middle Ages he had already begun to look outside his farm for extra livelihood. The boom in the cloth trade, which transformed so much of the English countryside in the fourteenth century, made its mark even on the Lakes. Kendal and, to a larger extent, Keswick both became centres for collecting wool and manufacturing cloth. By Tudor times Kendal was famous for its coarse woollen products. In this district there was not only wool from the fells but water-power for the fulling-mills, so that soon trade became so prosperous that it spread from Kendal into the lower valley and over the hills to Windermere, Ambleside, Grasmere and Langdale. Here, in the villages, the fullers and dyers set up their mills, but the early stages of manufacture, the spinning of the thread and weaving of the cloth, were still carried on in the cottages by the housewife and her husband. The statesman, home from his few fields or his heaf on the fell, would turn to his loom in the evening, while mother and daughters worked at the spinning-wheel. Many cottagers who had no land at all took on full-time piece-work from the village mills, and soon the valleys held a population much greater than that which could have been maintained by agriculture alone. Langdale, in particular, had far more people than it has today.

Then, in the reign of Elizabeth, the trade began to decline. Kendal was able to keep going by supplying cloth for the negro slaves in the American colonies, but the trade largely disappeared from the smaller villages. And on top of this, plague came to the district. Tradition says that it was particularly severe in Langdale, while it is recorded that 2,260 died in the parish of Penrith and 2,500 in the parish of Kendal. The valleys were now left half-derelict. Desperate attempts seem to have been made to plough a few extra acres at the dale-heads or on the flanks of the fells, trying to wring a bucketful of oats from the grudging rock.

L.

The Drift Away

Real poverty came to the dales in the seventeenth and eighteenth centuries. The statesman had been ready to do spare-time work for the factories, but he was too proud to hire himself out to work on another's land, so that, in spite of unemployment, we find that wages, especially wages for casual labour, remained as high as (or higher than) those in South Lancashire and the Midlands. But without supplementary work, the farms were too small and too primitive to yield a reasonable living, so that the younger people began to drift away. The little farms became empty and rotted into piles of grass-covered stones, while Wordsworth's story of the Ruined Cottage, in the first book of *The Excursion*, is typical of what was happening to those who depended entirely on casual jobs. In *Michael*, too, the poet gives a picture of one of the old statesmen, struggling with an inheritance which was already mortgaged before it came to him. By a lifetime of hard work he has paid off the debt, running the place entirely on his own – tilling the fields, herding the sheep, building walls and byres, repairing implements, and, in the evening, carding wool for his wife to spin. But his son Luke, who was to follow him, has no liking for the dale life and takes the first chance that comes to get away from the district. The old man waits, year after year, carrying on the duties of the farm as well as he can, but without the heart to continue with the plan of improvement and modernization symbolized by the projected sheep-fold. There is a splendid bareness about the lines as well as considerable social significance:

> His bodily frame had been from youth to age
> Of an unusual strength. Among the rocks
> He went, and still looked up to sun and cloud,
> And listened to the wind; and, as before,
> Performed all kinds of labour for his sheep,
> And for the land, his small inheritance.
> And to that hollow dell from time to time
> Did he repair, to build the Fold of which
> His flock had need. 'Tis not forgotten yet
> The pity which was then in every heart
> For the old Man – and 'tis believed by all
> That many and many a day he thither went,
> And never lifted up a single stone.

L.

The Changing View

Up to about the middle of the eighteenth century the Lakes belonged to the people who lived there. It was they who made the dale villages and towns and the dale way of life. They were obviously fond of their home, but it is doubtful if they ever considered whether it was beautiful or not. Perhaps some did and some didn't, but certainly they never expected anyone to admire the mountains. To us nowadays this seems a lack of perception, but to the countryman, the country is his home and his livelihood. Mountains are barren blocks which grow nothing and hinder communication. It was only when there developed a larger urban population that people got into the habit of seeing the country not as an environment but as a spectacle. Today, in the minds of many, production seems to belong to industry and the country is largely a collection of pretty scenes, or an inhabited park. Such people will often carry to absurd lengths their preference for barren scenery, and will sign petitions that ploughland or forest be let return to waste, and drained fields to swamp. In the eighteenth century the dales folk noticed with surprise that people were coming from London and other parts to look at the lakes and fells. The first travellers never went far from the main road, kept as much as they could to lake level, and clearly preferred the gentler scenes – Derwentwater, Grasmere, Rydal and Windermere. 'Beauty lying in the lap of horror' expressed their usual reactions.

C.W.

Landscape with Figures

In early prints of the Lakes it is common to find the people treated as merely part of the scenery. Raiders in Highland dress light bonfires beside Derwentwater; bandits or robbers assemble on Kirkstone; vague, draped figures, melancholy as the mist, pause and ponder over the sands of Morecambe Bay. The landscape becomes a landscape with figures, but it would not do for these to be the solid, shrewd, independent people who could be met at every farm and in every inn. Such people did not really suit the scene as the tourists saw it. They required figures less substantial, more shadowy. They were in search of the sentimental primitive, of simplicity and innocence, and they preferred a simplicity that was rather obviously naîve, and an innocence that was easily betrayed. For, while they enjoyed searching for a lost Eden, they did not really want to find it. They would contemplate with pleasure the *idea* of Eden, of a rural community free from the vices of the town, but they did not really want this idea to disturb their pride in their own urban way of life. Eden, like Sunday school, was charming, but essentially for the children, and they themselves, they felt sure, were completely adult.

L.

Along the Coast

Marsh People

My grandmother grew up beside the River Bela between Milnthorpe and Arnside. At night, as a girl, she would gaze across the blackness of the sands or the blackness of the tide and try to spot a single light shining through the mists of Foulshaw Moss, and years later I learned from her that the loneliest of the Lake dwellers of the past were not the people of the hills but the people of the marshes.

P.L.

Across Morecambe Bay

The number of cross-bay travellers grows year by year and between May and September exceeds 5,000. Parties of two hundred or more set out with the guide to brave the quicksands, where the danger is real enough. A guide is essential for the quicksands and the fast-moving tides are still claiming lives.

In Morecambe Bay we have a coastline which has lifted itself *away* from the sea. So that instead of a between-tide margin, 200 or 300 yards in width, we have a vast area which, at one time of the day, is an arm of the sea, half as broad as the English Channel, and, six hours later, is a sub-county of sand-banks, skears, mudflats, saltings and marsh. Above Greenodd at the meeting of the Leven and the Crake, and along Rusland Pool, the Eea, the Gilpin, the Kent and the Bela, the high tides push so far among the mosses and meadows, that the sea-birds can be seen feeding only a few yards from the chickens in the damson orchards. Conversely, the fells are encroaching on the sea, for the sands and banks of the estuaries are made up largely of silt washed down from the eroded rocks of the fells. Look at Morecambe Bay when the tide is out, and you are looking at the mountains and hills brought low.

The bay has played an enormously important part in the human history of southern Lakeland. First of all it was a barrier, dividing the area from the rest of England. Then it was a line of approach, especially for the Vikings. Finally, it was a line of communication, a highway, linking Lancashire to West Cumberland and the Lakes.

It is this latter aspect which means most to me, for my grandfather came from Cartmel beside the Eea, my grandmother, from Milnthorpe beside the Bela, and both settled at Millom beside the Duddon – which, though it is not on the bay, is just beyond the northern tip of it, and shares the same weather, the same limestone and the same industrial history. It was the bay which brought them together, brought them to Millom and brought me into being.

From early times the cross-bay route was a matter of both profit and danger. In 1322 the Scots, under Robert Bruce, came down the Cumbrian coast, crossed the Leven Sands to Cartmel – where they spared the priory but stole cattle and burnt farms – and finally crossed the Kent Sands to Lancaster, where they sacked the town and castle. Other travellers often spent the night between tides at Cartmel Priory, where the Austin canons were responsible for maintaining guides across the Kent, just as the lesser religious house of Conishead, near Ulverston, had a similar responsibility for the Leven. (The guides, who are called carters after the first family to hold the office, still carry out their duties from Kent's Bank and Canal Foot, Ulverston. They are appointed by the Duchy of Lancaster, and draw their salary of £15 a year from a charity trust, which, however, is finding it difficult to raise the money to pay the guides and maintain the guide houses provided for them.) According to West's *Antiquities of Furness*, the Conishead monks used to say mass for travellers on Chapel Island, a small rocky knoll in the Ulverston Sands, about a mile from the Bardsea shore, but the tradition has little evidence behind it, and the building which you can see from the railway viaduct is that of a mock ruin set up by Colonel Braddyll who built the gothic-revival Conishead Priory in the early nineteenth century.

G.L.

Caught by the Tide

The shape of Morecambe Bay is roughly that of a capital M, the dip in the middle, made by the second and third strokes of the letter, being the Cartmel Peninsula. Travellers coming from the south used to embark at Hest Bank, a few miles north of Morecambe, fording the channels of the Keer and the Kent and touching solid ground again at Kent's Bank near the present-day Grange-over-Sands. There they often rested between tides, perhaps spending a night at an inn in Allithwaite, Flookburgh or Cartmel, or at Holker Hall, if they had friends who could give them an introduction to the Cavendish family. The dangers of the journey may have been exaggerated, but the parish registers of Cartmel Priory and

Mud berths, Whitehaven

other bay-side churches are full of records of coaches overturned, small carriages stuck in quicksands, horsemen washed away, foot-travellers, fishermen and cocklers caught by the tide.

G.L.

Ann Radcliffe Crosses the Bay

Mrs Radcliffe, 1764-1823, was born in London and enjoyed considerable success as a romantic novelist. She delighted in long summer carriage-excursions and had a good eye for natural scenery.

No one could evoke better than Ann Radcliffe the tame terrors of her age – the shadow on the window, the silence in the ruined abbey. Yet when she came to the Lakes she left her ghosts behind her, turning instead to the tangible mystery of rock and tide. Her beautifully written account of the return crossing, from Ulverston to Lancaster, reminds one of an eighteenth-century chalk drawing:

> We took the early part of the tide, and entered these vast and desolate plains before the sea had entirely left them, or the morning mists were sufficiently dissipated to allow a view of distant objects; but the grand sweep of the coast could be faintly traced, on the left, and a vast waste of sand stretching far below it, with mingled streaks of gray water, that heightened its dreary aspect. The tide was ebbing fast from our wheels, and its low murmur was interrupted, first, only by the shrill small cry of sea-gulls, unseen, whose hovering flight could be traced by the sound, near an island that began to dawn through the mist; and then, by the hoarser croaking of sea-geese, which took a wider range, for their shifting voices were heard from various quarters of the surrounding coast. The body of the sea, on the right, was still involved, and the distant mountains on our left, that crown the bay, were also viewless; but it was sublimely interesting to watch the heavy vapour begin to move, then rolling in lengthening volumes over the scene, and, as they gradually dissipated, discovering through their veil the various objects they had concealed – fishermen, with carts and nets stealing along the margin of the tide, little boats putting off from the shore, and, the view still enlarging as the vapours expanded, the main sea itself softening into the horizon, with here and there a dim sail moving in the hazy distance. The wide desolation of the sands, on the left, was animated only by some horsemen riding remotely in groups towards Lancaster, along the winding edge of the water, and by a mussel fisher in his cart trying to ford the channel we were approaching.[1]

L.

[1] Ann Radcliffe, *Observations during a Tour to the Lakes* (1795).

England's Loneliest Road

As the route across Morecambe Bay increased in popularity, the strange case arose that here, on the loneliest road in England, it was never possible to be alone. For when the tide receded there were often forty, fifty or more carts, chaises and gigs, with foot-travellers, horses and dogs, all waiting on the shore for a carter to guide them across. The sands, for the most part, were firm and smooth – hard as 'stucco', as one writer says,[1] 'upon which the horses' hoofs scarcely make an impression' – and many people enjoyed the swift, easy, silent motion of the carriage, though others were disappointed because they could see so little of the shore. In winter, especially, with the light half-gone and a heavy mist scarfing the marshes, it must have been very like flying blind in an aeroplane. Yet even to the least imaginative traveller, there were incidents to break the monotony of the journey. The crossing of the main channels, for instance:

> 'Now,' said my sister, 'we must either go back or swim over.' But judge my surprise, when we drove right into the stream; I own I felt afraid, for a moment. But my sister's vivacity soon dissipated my fears. A more picturesque, grotesque, *touresque*, or whatever other *esque* you may think fit to call it, I think I never saw.[2]

It is a subject that would have suited the watercolourist Thomas Rowlandson – dozens of carts and traps toppling over the kerb of the channel, flopping down the short steep chutes of wet sand, splashing in the water; horses floundering on the opposite bank; riders up to the thighs; dogs swimming, or barking and running in circles; wretched foot-passengers begging a lift or at least a hand-hold on a cart or carriage; men wading and swerving as the floor shelved deeper than they expected; women shrieking and pulling their skirts about their knees. Yet all around them was the endless disregard of the sands, under a damp cuticle of reflected light. What danger there might be was easily forgotten in the bustle, and even the discomfort was well paid for by the sight of others in a worse fix, and it is hard not to think of the crowds who would enjoy the same sort of mock-perils and horseplay among the big-dippers and helter-skelters which later were to be built along the shores of the same bay.

L.

[1] The Hon. Mrs Murray, *A Companion and Useful Guide* (third edition, 1810).
[2] John Briggs, *Letters from the Lakes*, etc. (1825).

Piel Island

The castle, which is in the care of English Heritage, and the Ship Inn, which is let to a landlord, are owned by Barrow Council. The old pilots' cottages have become holiday homes.

Even apart from the castle, Piel is a fascinating place. It is so small – smaller, in fact, than Belle Isle in Windermere – that you can walk briskly round it in a quarter of an hour. Yet it is by no means featureless. The cliffs on which the castle stands rise twenty to thirty feet above the shingle, and, at its highest point, the island rears up to forty feet, which looks quite a mountain above the flat sands when the tide is out. The channel between Piel and Roa is fairly deep, and can be rough enough to cut off the island for days at a time. Yet its shores are gentle, the pebbles knitted together by many of the flowers of the shingle – sea-kale, sea-campion and the yellow, horned sea-poppy. Inland, if you can use such a term, there are thickets of gorse and ragwort, and even a bordering of reeds and marsh plants round the little tarn or pond in the centre of the island. It is hard to believe that there can be so many changes and variations of soil and habitat in so small an area.

Yet with all this to look at, you still find your gaze turning continually to the castle ruins. It is not often that I grow enthusiastic about castles, in ruin or not, but Piel is an exception. For one thing, it was never the centre of feudal oppression or military power. It was not the home of a usurping Norman family, nor, indeed, of any family at all. It was built in the mid-fourteenth century by the monks of Furness Abbey to protect the abbot's legal trade in wool and his probably more profitable illegal trade in smuggling. Some people have presumed that it must have been intended as a protection for the abbey against Scottish raiders but it seems hard to see how this could have been so. The huge size of the outer courtyard, however, suggests that, at the time of the raids, it may have been a place where the people of Piel and Walney took refuge with their cattle and other stock until the raiders had moved out of the district.

This outer courtyard, set in the extreme south-east corner of the island, has the shape of a quadrilateral – a square with one side cut short by the angle of the shore. It was once surrounded by a wall, with towers at the four corners and a moat on the two sides away from the shore. The south-east tower and most of the walls on the south and east have been swallowed up by the sea, while the walls on the west and north were left unfinished or, possibly, were filled in with a wooden palisade. Inside the south-east quarter of this outer courtyard is an inner court, again with moat and wall and corner towers, but, this time, with a drawbridge over the moat leading to a gateway with tower above.

The keep stands in the inner court – a massive three-storey building, divided on each storey into three compartments. It is this internal plan, quite unlike that of the ordinary baronial type of Norman castle, which suggests that this was really a warehouse, a fortified storehouse, occupied only by a small garrison of soldiers, with no resident lord.

After the Dissolution of the Monasteries, Piel Castle fell into disrepair, though there was some talk of restoring it during the invasion scares of the reign of Queen Elizabeth. Nothing much was done, however, until 1920, when the Duke of Buccleugh presented the castle to the mayor and corporation of Barrow, who were also able to buy the eight cottages on the north side of the island.

The attractive, old-fashioned inn still caters for the hungry and the thirsty, but it has become known, chiefly, for an absurd ceremony, much drenched in beer, by which visitors are dubbed Knights of Piel.

G.L.

Neither Land Nor Sea

The ironworks at Millom no longer sails out into the Duddon estuary (here named Dunner). The works closed in 1968, was carved up and sold, leaving a desolate landscape where for a century the smoke had shown which way the wind had blown. And whichever way it blows, wrote Norman, it's a cold wind now.

In front, the saltings and sands reach to Furness, but there is no sign of the sea, for the peninsula of Odborough New Town stretches half-way across the mouth of the river, blotting out the western horizon, with slag-banks and chimneys. From the summit of Scafell and Coniston Old Man the ironworks can be seen sailing out into the estuary like a great battleship, smoking at all funnels. This decayed edge of the marsh, wedged between the gasworks and the Dunner Banking, seems to belong neither to the land nor to the sea. The tide arrives only three or four times a year, and in summer it is burnt dry as concrete. Yet the salt has laid its savour here, and the smell is the smell of rotting seaweed, fish, and the excrement of sea-birds. At the bottom of the railway embankment it is the salt plants that grow among the pumice-like crumbles of washed-up slag – sea plantain, sea purslane, sea milkwort, and thrift. The mud flats are mauve and brown, not yet responding to the spring, but in the gulleys the leaves of the scurvy-grass are green as spinach and thickly frosted with white cress-flowers. The tide is rising fast and will be one of the highest of the season. Very little of the marshes is covered as yet, but the water is flowing off the drains, and seeping into the pools and creeks that lie among the turf. The Rotting Pool, which usually runs five or six feet below the surface in its deep moat of mud, is now full almost to the brim, and scum and bubbles and gull's feathers drift upstream on the thrust.

P.P.

A High Tide

Today the sea is claiming its own. The wind which all night blew from the north-west, banking up the water on the far side of the estuary, has now veered to the south-west, and is driving the tide across the threshold of the village. The Oatrigg Pool – which because of the freak of the Ice Age carries all the drainage of the south side of Black Fell – is dammed back by the tide and has overflowed on to the road. There is a crowd of Odborough boys at the edge of the water. A hundred yards away, by the Primitive Methodist Chapel, where the tide is held by a rise in the road, Oatrigg boys wave and jeer. Some of the Odborough tribe try to dash through the flood on bicycles, unaware of the little dip that lies opposite the poolside cottages. They advance, their spokes churning the water like the paddles of a river steamer, when, suddenly, the front wheels nose downward and the pedals slap into the water. They brake, and find themselves skimming along like ducks. They cannot turn, cannot put out a foot to gain their balance. Desperately they clutch at the railings at the side of the road and hang there like shipwrecked sailors. The ranks of Tuscany cannot forbear to cheer. Others, climbing on the middle rung of the railings, side-step along until they are poised on stilts above the broadest stretch of the water. A car coming round the corner refuses as a horse refuses a jump, and turns back again. A hearse makes its way down Harbour Street, while those mourners who come late, raise their hats on the other side of the tide. At the doors of the poolside cottages, wives and grandfathers watch the tide sniffing around the gates of their small gardens. The bottom of nearly every gate is sealed with sandbags and clay, so that little can seep through, but where the householder has not taken this precaution, the water is wriggling up the shingle of the path. Already one or two women are beginning to block up the bottom of the front door. They are not unduly anxious, however, for there is no real tide here, only the back-flowing of the pool. But beyond the Primitive Methodist Chapel, in Sea View and Marine Terrace, the sea really does invade the streets. There many a man, fighting with brush and bucket to keep the tide out of his backyard, has turned to find it rippling through the kitchen, having entered the house by the front door.

Here old Sam Burrows caught a fluke in the parlour and Bill Salt, the fisherman, dug his bait off the front-room oilcloth. Here the ducks have been seen swimming in and out of the Harbour Hotel, and the landlord swears he found a plover's egg in the straw of the spittoon. Violet

Moss's mother, who was born at Oatrigg, remembers how her father had bailed water out of the pianola. The people of these houses are as wary of the sea as their ancestors were of the Scots. They are ready at any hour to bolt themselves in their pele towers and board up doors and gateways. The yard doors have a double flap, at the bottom, which can be stuffed with clay or sacking. The front gardens often have a boarded fence over which you have to step as over a low stile. All the men and women of this little Holland know the tide-tables off by heart. They can estimate to an inch the combined effect of a high tide and a westerly wind. They have much experience of soaked carpets, damp and slime in the walls, and the floors a wet, stinking slush of salt, sand, scum, oil, tar, shells, weed, and bladder-wrack. Yet someone is caught out every time; someone has forgotten or been lazy or has not noticed the direction of the wind. This is the hope that draws neighbours as the hope of a crash draws crowds to a speed track. The lovely, preposterous catastrophe brings heads to every window and a rush of small boys in wellingtons wading down the thrust of the tide. A pram stands above the wheel-tops in the water, while the baby leans over the side and grabs at floating feathers. The news tom-toms round the village: 'Ma Bosanco has had it in. Bloody great crabs as big as tortoises walking round the kitchen. She wouldn't come downstairs till we'd thrown her a pair of clogs up to the bedroom window.'

The sea rolls up in a bludgeoning swell, continually skirmished by the wind. Because of the curve of the foreshore, the waves approach it at two angles, and each pair of waves, meeting, amalgamates into a bore that pushes along the channel of the pool, and then – at the same point every time – leaps the rails into the streets. The water froths against the slate porches of the chapel, and the freestone doorsteps and low window-sills, and concrete slabs of the company terraces. Gulls rock like buoys in the centre of the street and oyster-catchers skirt past only a foot above the dogs that are chasing them in a frenzy of frustration. The highest swells are lifting over the rise by the chapel and trickling into Harbour Square. Give it another six inches, and two-thirds of the village will be flooded in no time. But already the tide is on the turn. The ripples no longer reach to the limit of the wet. The water slinks back into the pool. The houses stand ugly and unconcerned as ever, their feet in a tide-mark of slop and wrack and rubbish. The sun gives the wet streets the dazzle of tinfoil. The dumped sand, drying quickly, is whipped up by the wind into a brown, gritty smother. The cats return to the pavements.

P.P.

The Shore

It is not so much that the tide goes out as that the sands come in. For half an hour or more after the time of high tide the water seemed to be hesitating, slipping back and then edging up again, and the whole Oatrigg shore, from the wall to the dunes, was whinnying with ripples and gulls and children. Now, the sand has heaved itself up like a man waking from sleep, and the tide runs back off its ribs and shoulders. The children are left paddling in foot-sized quicksands of their own making; the beachcombing birds hurry back to business.

Immediately the water-traffic, which had been silent under the flat-iron of the tide, begins again. Little stranded pools wriggle to get back to the sea. Runnels nose this way and that along a Hampton Court maze of ribbings. And from between the boulders of the wall unsuspected becks and backwashes appear, each with its own four-inch-deep channels that not even the stormiest sea can obliterate for long. At the same time the tide of man flows inward, towards the land. The children settle down to sandcastles or run back to family picnics in the dunes. Young girls – shy as a fig-leaved Eve about their own bodies – unselfconsciously strip and dry their younger sisters in full view of their boy-friends. Mothers gather up baskets and spades and begin to worry about buses. A few young men, out early from the Works, run down the sands to catch the tail-end of the tide, but for the most part the beach is empty.

For Oatrigg, at any rate, the shore is shut up for the night, and only visitors stay on after tea-time. The Oatrigg children clatter sulkily up the Main Street, with the air of having had enough of the beach. The women bring chairs and knitting on to the pavement. The men stand around the Harbour Arms or sit on seats by the bus-shelter, their backs turned solidly to the sea.

P.P.

A Coastal Strip

Many visitors to the Lake District are disappointed with the Cumbrian coast. It depends, I suppose, on what they expect. They may be looking for cliffs and headlands, but there are no rocky cliffs south of St Bees or Nethertown. Or they may be looking for sea-lochs and estuaries where the tide nudges high among the fells, but the coast from Haverigg to St Bees is a gently bending curve with only the one large inlet at Ravenglass. Most of all, I think, people are disappointed because they find that the mountains do not come down to the sea, but are divided from it by a two-mile-wide strip of rather ordinary-looking farmland.

There are reasons for all this. To begin with, the rock beneath the shore is not one of the slates of the fells, but the red sandstone of the Carlisle plain, though it shows itself so rarely in the south of the county that it is very hard to credit this. Secondly, the whole shoreline has been shaped and shaved by the glaciers which moved across the Solway during the Ice Age. Before that, the fells must have sloped gently and evenly from summit to sea-level, but after the ice withdrew the western flanks were sliced away almost perpendicularly. Look at Black Combe from Walney Island and you will see that it takes the shape of a bowler hat, with a rounded, flattish crown, and, on the seaward side, a steep drop to the brim.

Yet the ice did not leave the coast planed flat like an ironing board. It dropped huge dollops of sand, clay and gravel, heaped up into ridges that, in places, reach a hundred feet in height. Behind these the natural drainage was blocked and silted up, so that at least five streams – the Ehen, the Irt, the Esk, Annaside Beck and Whicham Beck – shy sideways when they are within smell of the sea, and dawdle about until they find a place to break through the clay ridge.

As a result of this, there is often a swampy dip between the shore and the lower slopes of the hills. To modern road-engineers this would not matter, but in the early days, when most travellers would drive their carriages up Scafell rather than face mud, the roads swung inland, to go bumping over the drier foothills of Black Combe.

G.L.

Sea and Fells

There is one spot on the Esk-Irt dunes where you can still enjoy the emptiness and freedom of the coast, with the sea on one side of you and the fells on the other. Go to the old Eskmeals station, either from Waberthwaite at low tide, or from Bootle shore if the road is flooded. When you reach the railway viaduct, look inwards. At high tide this is a sea-loch, and at low a tongue of slithering mud-sand, purple with sea lavender and sea aster. And above the shore, are the granite hills of Muncaster, much spiked with conifer, and the tiny, old, box-pewed church of Hall Waberthwaite, just visible among its sycamores. But turn round, go under the viaduct, and make your way, at right angles to the flow of the river along the side of the fence, and you will cross, first of all, a few hundred yards of rather squelchy saltings and then come to the dunes which are here about half a mile wide, though they seem, when you get among them, to be as vast as the Sahara. The sand is bare and loose, in twenty-foot-high swells and waves scarcely restrained by the marram. The hollows are not turfed over, as at Haverigg, so that these dunes are rather less interesting to the botanist, though I have found sea-buckthorn (*Hippophaë rhamnoides*), which, so far as I know, is not found elsewhere on this coast. Instead of turf, you get flat, saucer-like salt-pans, strewn with cobbles, or dark green in the damp places with sour marsh plants. Through gaps in the ridges you look

Sandstone cliffs, Fleswick Bay

across the channel to the Drigg Haws, with their almost perpetual umbrella of dipping and screaming gulls. Otherwise you are cut off from the rest of England as if you were on an island. But if you clamber to the top of the dunes, the Wasdale and Eskdale fells bludgeon themselves into your notice, and, above all, the blunt-headed instrument of Black Combe, and you will be reminded that you are in the heart of the Lakes.

G.L.

Salt Marshes

The salt marsh pushes its fingers surprisingly high into the fells. In Dunnerdale you come down the daffodil woods below Stickle Pike, and then at Duddon Bridge with the river among the boulders, and hazels, cherry and spindlewood all round you, you notice the salt only a few yards away. Below Muncaster, the marsh is wedged up among the granite hills of lower Eskdale. Moreover, before the land had settled to its present level, the tides were twenty-five feet higher, which must have made the sea stretch well into Westmorland along the Kent, and as far as Woodland up the Duddon estuary.

C.W.

St Bees Head

The stranger will probably say that St Bees Head is the one feature along the whole shoreline which looks just as he had expected. Yet St Bees Head has its surprises. Thomas Carlyle, remembering it from the Dumfriesshire hills, called it 'that sapphyre promonotory', and it is only when you begin to get close to it that it looks red. When you get closer still, you see that it is green almost as much as red, for huge swathes and drapes of turf hang down from the top wherever the cliff eases back. At the bottom, however, the rock is bare as a ship's hull, plated, slabbed and riveted against the sea, with a defensive breakwater of blocks and boulders that the sea itself has piled up. The slabs have been rounded and moulded by the tide, rough to the touch but smooth to the eye, with the ripple of the waves still on them and pools standing in dubs and salt-cellars. At other places the face of the rock is pitted and pock-marked by the spray as if an abstract sculptor had been inventing a design with a blowlamp.

The little bay to the south of the headland used to be one of the most attractive spots on the Cumbrian coast, but it now gets so crowded at summer weekends that the council has tidied up the foreshore with stepped concrete kerbs, a car park and a caravan site behind. The result could, in fact, have been worse, but it is enough to tame down the wildness and roughness which once belonged to the bay.

You can still find all this, however, if you climb the cliff-edge path which takes you to the top of the headland. And here you will get your second surprise. For St Bees Head is not one headland but two. The head which Carlyle saw from Dumfriesshire was not the one we have seen from Seascale. The two heads, in fact, are about two miles apart, and half-way between them lies the enchanting Fleswick Bay.

The cliffs here are almost perpendicular, of beautifully striated rock, greeny-pink as an under-ripe strawberry, and tufted with thrift and sea campion and the white crochet-work tags of earth-nut and hogweed. But at a point about half a mile beyond Tomlin (the hill overlooking the South Head), the rocks are folded inwards to let a little beck enter the sea, and it is in this indentation that the small sickle of a beach is exposed. The sea-edge is of a dark red rock, worn so smooth that it looks like toffee cooling in a pan, while the beach, seen from the top of the cliffs, seems to be made up of greyish glinting shell-sand. The few bathers and fishermen who reach the beach by the long track from Sandwith find themselves in an enormous, eliptical walled garden, one half of which is laid open to the sea. Peeping Toms will have to peep from the Isle of Man. Friends who have descended to the beach say that it is the most private and the most paradisal spot of almost any they know.

The cliff-walk goes all the way from St Bees to Whitehaven. It is a clearly marked path, with stiles between fields and a fence running along the edge, though it is quite easy to step over this if you want to. The whole distance is about four miles.

G.L.

The Solway

The greatest of all the Cumbrian marshes are those which border the Solway. The Solway is a county of its own. No one who has not lived beside it (and I have not) can see it except as a stranger. Yet even a stranger cannot deny its personality. As soon as you round the northern point of St Bees Head there is a new vista. You see the sea sweeping inwards almost to Carlisle, and, beyond, the hills of Kirkcudbrightshire and Annan, with Criffel dominating them. This is the land of enormous mud-flats and sands; of the tide which comes in like a galloping horse (as Scott describes it in *Redgauntlet*); of moss-troopers and smugglers. Here are the little ports – Allonby, Silloth, Bowness and Port Carlisle; here were the war-time aerodromes. Not far from Maryport (the name is modern) Mary, Queen of Scots, landed after her flight from Scotland; at Burgh-by-Sands Edward I prepared to subdue the Scots and died there before he started.

C.W.

Lakes and Dales

Valleys

In the Lake District we have dales with steep, bare sides, below which a flat strip of fertile land runs right up into the heart of the mountains. From the upland slopes, they appear as green corridors lying below the brown, grey, purple and blue of the fellsides.

When the ice carved away the sides of the valleys it left what had been smaller tributary valleys hanging in the air like an upstairs landing in a half-demolished house, leading to nowhere. Such broken-off valleys give us some of the loneliest spots among the fells – a desolation of stones and bracken, walled off by massive cliffs of silence. The becks, as if still surprised not to be taking their pre-Ice-Age course, plunge to the valley bed, and if the rock of the cliff face is particularly hard, or if the rock on which the water drops is particularly soft, then we have one of the typical Lake District waterfalls – a thin stream of water falling uninterruptedly for sixty feet or more, or perhaps taking the drop in two consecutive leaps. They may also be caused by the deflection of the beck from its original course, and may coincide with faults in the rock.

P.L.

The Central Dales

I call them the central dales for convenience, but the long hollows which hold the lakes of Thirlmere, Grasmere, Rydal and Windermere are not true river-carved dales at all. Instead, they lie along the line of the Lake District's main geological fault, though, like the river-dales, they were enlarged and deepened by the action of the ice.

The northern section of the fault is, admittedly, very like a normal dale, and must have been still more so when Thirlmere was narrow enough to be bridged in the middle. By now, of course, the lake has been dammed, the water-level raised, and a slag-heap of detritus tipped along shores shamefacedly screened off by conifers. Manchester has a conscience about Thirlmere. There have been well-intentioned schemes to give more access to the public and to save what can be saved of the lake's still considerable beauty. But it remains – as does Haweswater – a dammed and damning example of what must not be allowed to happen to any of the others.

Yet once you get above the dark green tide-mark of trees you begin to see what the early tourists saw in Thirlmere, once called Wythburn Water or Leathes Water after a local landowner. It was dale-like, undoubtedly, with a rather dainty and river-like lake in the bottom, but from the little Wythburn Church to Legburthwaite it ran straight as a street. None of the dales proper is nearly so stiff. Indeed, the Thirlmere – i.e. the 'fault' – side of Helvellyn is perhaps the most solid, least fractured wall of volcanic rock in the whole district.

This rock spreads over the Raise, too, so that the small, reedy lakes of Grasmere (the grass lake) and Rydal (the valley of the Rye) are cupped like a thistle head in a calyx of green and spiky fells. But just below Ambleside the volcanics fall away and give place to the gentler Silurian rocks, and the effect is as if the fault had widened out to include the whole of the central southern area, Coniston and Esthwaite as well as Windermere.

The importance of this geological fault in the history of the Lakes is enormous. From the very beginning it offered what was obviously the best line of communication. By the end of the Middle Ages it had become the main route for the wool trade; in the eighteenth century it was the way by which the tourists discovered the district; and today it carries the heaviest road traffic in the Lakes. And when the eighteenth-century tourists followed the route they found not just lakes and mountains but a string of towns and villages – Kendal, Bowness, Ambleside, Hawkshead, Grasmere – whose existence, from the beginning, depended on sheep.

G.L.

Thirlmere

This reservoir has undergone great changes since Norman wrote the following passage. For the first time this century visitors have been allowed access to its shores. Sailboats, canoes, rowboats and dinghies use the lake, though not powerboats. And miles of paths have been opened to walkers. Some good has come to Thirlmere in other ways, for over the years broadleaf trees, partly because of the exclusion of sheep, have seeded themselves naturally, conquering some of the barest slopes. Long-term forestry plans are to replace much of the spruce, firs and larch between the road and the water with natural broadleaves and Scots pine.

We must allow no more major valleys to be flooded: there is just not enough of the Lake District left to throw any more of it away.

On the other hand, the reservoirs we already have are here to stay. No one is going to pull the plug out of Thirlmere or Haweswater. They are permanent or nearly permanent in a way that plantations are not, and we had better accept them and get along with them as well as we can.

We have to admit, first of all, that they are by no means ugly. The smaller reservoirs, indeed, are often lively and attractive, adding the sparkle of water to dull, humped moorland. Tarn Hows, for instance, one of the most notoriously pretty places in the district, is an artificial lake, though not – admittedly – a reservoir. Nor is Thirlmere ugly, if we forget what it used to be. The trouble with Thirlmere, is not that it is a reservoir, but that it is a municipal park.

On the Helvellyn side it is bordered by the busiest road in the district. On the western and less frequented side, Manchester set a carriageway winding among conifers, and edged by walls neat as a stone fireplace. The effect is paper-planned, so prim, that you expect to find a public convenience behind each screen of trees.

P.L.

Windermere: A Period Piece

Windermere was once the queen of the Lakes, but she abdicated long ago. Of course, to people from cities, so used to cars and crowds that they scarcely notice them, Windermere may still seem both pretty and peaceful; but to one brought up as I was, in the country of Black Combe and the Duddon, it seems not so much a part of the Lake District as an ambitious park, with drives, walks, seats, kiosks, sailing-boats, rowing-boats, regattas, long-distance swims and tame ducks.

Yet it is still a pleasure to cross the lake by the ferry, sliding close to the oval, Georgian house on Belle Island, which was named after Isabella Curwen of Workington, whose husband, John Christian Curwen, bought it for her as a wedding present. A pleasure again to turn off just before you reach the ferry on the Cunsey side, and drive through the National Trust property beside the lake. Here, with the two umbrageous little islands called 'Lilies of the Valley' between you and Belle Isle, you are in a placid backwater with a floating suburb of houseboats. Any southcountry man should feel thoroughly at home.

A northcountry man, however, had better push beyond the metalled road into the woods, where the view is fragmented into tiny bays and scoops, with becks and sykes dripping into the water every few yards. The banks are chock-full of the wild and half-wild flowers of planted woodland: creeping Jenny, tutsan, enchanter's nightshade, and pink purslane (*Claytonia alsinoides*), a native of North America, and the small yellow balsam (*Impatiens perviflora*); the huge Himalayan balsam, so common beside the canals of industrial Lancashire, is also beginning to invade the dales.

But perhaps the best way to see the lake for the first time is to take a trip on one of the pleasure boats, from which you see it at the right speed, neither too fast to miss much, nor too slow to be bored. And if the boats seem rather archaic, that is all the better, for Windermere is now a period piece. *G.L.*

*

To sail on Windermere is like going on a child's paddle-boat in a park. There is a promenade at Bowness, with a putting-green nearby; there are hotels and large country houses dug into the wood-slopes like badgers' setts; and, already, motor launches and speedboats have created a traffic problem on the lake itself. One would not be surprised to learn of *Merrie England* or *Rose Marie* being performed on Belle Isle, with the audience moving backwards and forwards on the ferry.

Windermere was the Victorian bridgehead to the Lakes. It belongs to a time when most visitors came by train and did not move very far. The result, at Bowness, is a holiday town – an inland watering-place, with neither the elegance of a spa nor the boisterousness of the seaside. Yet there are places only a few miles from Windermere which are even less frequented than the more remote dales. The eastern shore of the lake is given up to the villa and the parked car, but to the west and south there are homely valleys which have little of the self-consciousness and eye-to-business of more celebrated places. There is the Woodland Valley, south of Coniston; the Rusland Valley, south of Windermere; and the valley of the Winster, lying between Windermere and the Kent. Here and there, the land heaves itself into middle-height moorland, neither craggy nor savage, but with saucer-shaped dips and indentations where you can sit alone for hours, even at the height of the holiday season.

P.L.

Esthwaite Water

Esthwaite Water, between Coniston and Windermere, is the most park-like of all the lakes. With its little peninsulas, two on either side, it looks on a large-scale map like a gap in an otherwise finished jigsaw puzzle. It was created, in the first place, by a side-loop of the Langdale–Rydal–Troutbeck ice, and the entire lake has the character of a gravelly, waterlogged glacial moraine. At both the top and bottom end there is a dub or large pool, cut off from the main body of the water by a hundred or so yards of silt. In fact, with its shallow, reedy shores and

The Gondola and the Coniston fells

the cows grazing in the waterside fields, it resembles one of Capability Brown's lakes, an embellishment in a country seat.

This is not intended as disparagement. Esthwaite preserves an eighteenth-century, pastoral beauty and is one of the most lived-around of all the lakes. If only it were less accessible – if, perhaps, it were in another part of the district – it would surely be counted a spot of special charm. As it is, Beatrix Potter's rabbits have left droppings of sentiment all round its shores, though it is not the little books themselves which are sentimental but the readers. Esthwaite, in fact, like Hawkshead and Near Sawrey, would be none the worse for an outbreak of literary myxomatosis.   *G.L.*

Tarn Hows

Those who fear that afforestation and its accompanying industries will ruin the Lake District should go to see Tarn Hows near Hawkshead. Here, the centre of an afforested area, is a little lake which has become very popular with cyclists and motor tourists. It is certainly a gem, almost a trinket, almost too pretty and not quite in character. It is a double lake, figure-eight-shaped with islands, and fir trees round it and on the islands, spiky or feathery. It is tiny, but to scale. Across Tom Heights are Coniston Old Man and Wetherlam, and, farther round, Langdale Pikes, familiar and homely, and, still further, Helvellyn and the Ullswater fells. If you climb to the top of the rise above the tarn you see Windermere and Esthwaite Water, and in the distance the sea, and there is one exciting view, through a wood, of Coniston Water, end-on like a long curved knife.

Yet not only are the trees due to the forest industry, but so is the tarn itself, for it was formed by damming a stream in a swamp to give water-power to the saw-mill in Yewdale below. The overflow from the reservoir skidaddles down Tom Gill in a long string of Skeltonics that include at least one waterfall poised like a champion diver.   *C.W.*

Rusland Valley

Rusland, lying to the east of Coniston Lake, is really a double valley made by two parallel streams, Colton Beck and Rusland Pool, both of which flow into the estuary of the River Leven between Haverthwaite and Greenodd. Colton Beck is only a few miles in length (its lovely upper stretches can be reached by the rough road from Nibthwaite Grange), but Rusland Pool is considerably longer, and above Rusland Church it is split into two tributary streams, Force Beck or Grizedale Beck and Dale Park Beck.

The roads in Rusland take the form of a capital H. The left downstroke, coming from Hawkshead, follows Grizedale Beck to Satterth-waite, passes Whitestock Hall (a tile-hung, Georgian mansion, grey-yellow beside beeches) and meets the main Barrow road at Greenodd. The right-hand stroke comes from Esthwaite Water, down Dale Park to the Haverthwaite crossroads. And, about the middle of the valley, there are a whole scribbling of little transverse roads which make up the horizontal stroke of the letter.

I have given all these precise and perhaps rather prim-sounding directions because Rusland is a valley which has to be searched for. You can't just drive your car straight at it, as you can at Wasdale, knowing that, if you don't fall in the lake, you are bound to reach the dale-head in the end. It is not, of course, in the least inaccessible, but it has the luck to lack most of the features which would have turned it into an obvious tourist target. It has no lake, and its streams are mostly enclosed in farmland or forest. It *has* a waterfall – a beautiful asymmetric arrangement of delayed drops and dawdlings at Force Mills – but this so discreetly screened that many people drive past without noticing it. Rusland has none of the higher hills, no crags, not a great deal of open fell at all and, in fact, not many views in the picture postcard sense. Yet it is a dale which has retained much of the look and tone of what southern Lakeland must have been before the tourists discovered it.

This does not mean that it has not changed. Nor does it mean that it is uninhabited or untouched by man. In fact it has very much the look of being lived in, which is the look these valleys have had for centuries. Today, no doubt, the dale people are not all country people, for Rusland is handy enough to Ulverston and even to Barrow to house men from the Glaxo works or Vickers. But the townsman has not yet completely taken over the place. The half-a-dozen little villages are still almost entirely unselfconscious, with only a few infestations of lilac doors, Venetian blinds and ornamental ironwork among the whitewash and brown-wash, the slate roofs and milk-churn stands, the weed and mould and lichen colours of barn, farm, cottage and church.

Most of the villages are more scattered than one expects, but Bouth, in the lower dale, is compact, with a pub, a post office, crossroads and even what might be called one or two streets. All round about there is a monkey-puzzle of narrow roads, some of them single-track. Here, and round Oxen Park, Bandrake Head and Colton Church, you have the feeling, rare in the Lakes, of sneaking into the villages by the back way, running between stone walls and shippons and through orchards with the washing hung out. Here and there, as you climb above the 200-foot contour – the land is never much higher – you come into rough pasture with the bracken fighting it out with the grass, and with bluebells in spring, harebells in summer, and patches of gorse in bloom practically all the year round.

G.L.

Wrynose bottom

Coniston Water

Coniston Water (once called, more attractively, Thurston Water, after the Norse name Thor) looks rather dull when seen from the village side, with a backing of shapeless moors now cardiganed in conifers that do little either to improve or to harm the view. But once you cross over to the Monk Coniston side, the lake takes on another aspect altogether, with Old Man and Wetherlam giving it a backing as dramatic, almost, as Wastwater's, while Coniston Old Hall, with its enormous cylindrical chimneys, diversifies the middle distance, as the eighteenth-century travellers might have said. The eastern or Brantwood side has become a popular motor-run in summer but at other seasons is almost deserted. I remember especially one brilliant February day, when I drove between shining banks of snow among sugar-stick trees and dead bracken frosted to white paper doilies. The lake was frozen, the ice covered with a thin layer of snow, and footprint, skate-print, dog-pad, bird-track and even tyre-tread showed how it had become a new kind of thoroughfare, though a greener shade in the centre marked the edge of danger. It seemed warmer than on many a day of August, yet the sun had already set for cottages at the foot of the Old Man, and the refrigerator door was beginning to swing close for the night.

G.L.

The Langdales

It may seem odd to count the Langdales among the Western dales, since they run almost due east, yet in substance and character they belong with the Wasdale, Eskdale and Coniston fells, and have little in common with the Windermere country towards which they look.

I came to Little Langdale for the first time when I was a boy, having pushed a bicycle from Dunnerdale up what was then the gravel road of Wrynose Pass. I was not thinking of what I would see when I got to the top, for, since Cockley Beck, all my thoughts had been fixed on the source of the Duddon. For fifteen years I had lived beside that river, at the point where it ends and empties into the sea, and now I was going to find the point where it began. I did not find it, of course, for above Cockley Beck the river divides into half a dozen becks and tributaries, any one of which may reasonably be called the source of the Duddon. So that when I got to the top of the pass, I had a feeling of anti-climax. There was the Three Shires Stone, marking the place where the old counties of Cumberland, Westmorland and Lancashire met, but otherwise there was nothing much to look at – no view, only rough grass and bog-holes filled with a plant which I did not then know to be buckbean. I pushed my bicycle, rather grudgingly, for another hundred yards or so, and then, suddenly, Little Langdale opened before me like a crevasse – the deep grove of the upper-dale, the tree-less tarn, the little knoll of Birk Howe hiding the village, and, further off, Windermere and the fells beyond. I found I could not ride down after all, for the road was steeper than on the Cumberland side of the pass, and the surface little better than that of a stone wall pushed over. But that hardly seemed to matter. I reached the village and stopped for a glass of cider at the inn, then called the Tourist's Rest, but later imaginatively re-named the Three Shires by a relative of mine.

'You'll fall off your machine,' said the innkeeper, and gave me a non-alcoholic imitation.

Since then the track over Wrynose has been well surfaced, though anyone who crossed it a few days after the storm of 13-14 August 1966 could see it much in its old rough state. At that time in a matter of hours a huge reservoir of rain poured down a small area centred around the heads of Dunnerdale, Borrowdale and the two Langdales. Damage in Borrowdale was estimated at £100,000 and farmers reckon that some of their fields have been lost to cultivation for ever.

In Dunnerdale damage was less extensive, though the beautiful Birks Bridge, which normally stands about thirty feet above the river, was snapped in half, the walls on one side being swept away with only the arch left standing. Above Cockley Beck cart-loads of boulders were tipped four feet deep on the water pastures, beck-side walls were tossed away, and huge scallops bitten out of the river-banks. All the little fell springs seemed to have erupted, pouring out lava-like gushes of clay. Other spots looked as if a rake, twenty or thirty yards wide, had been scraped down the fellside, leaving long sores of raw, blue scree. At one farm in Little Langdale the water poured in one door and out of another, dropping the debris of the Ice Age on the fitted carpets. And those of us who live only a dozen miles away thought of it only as a rather wet night!

In ordinary summer weather, however, the only blockage on the Wrynose–Little Langdale route is likely to be from the eruption of cars, in spite of which I hope the planners will not be tempted to 'improve' this road. For Little Langdale is one of the most perfect of the dales, where a way of life that took centuries to evolve can be sensed from the relation of house to house and house to rock – the village with inn, post-office, the old school (with a church-room upstairs), the beautiful, largely seventeenth-century farmhouses of Birk Howe, Bield and Fell Foot, merging into the fellside as if they had grown out of it, the quarrymen's cottages and the quarrymen's bridge, called Slaters Bridge, which is a combination of the typical hump-back of the Lakes with the clapperstone of the Pennines. Driving a full-size motor road up this dale would be as senseless as laying a tarmac footpath through Westminster Abbey.

Great Langdale, too, has been threatened with a wider road, and, though I hope it will not happen, I admit that it would be less disastrous than in Little Langdale. For Greater Langdale lacks the privacy of its smaller neighbour. It is more of a corridor than a valley, so that as you ascend all you notice is the magnificent twin-tower elevation of the Pikes like the west end of a cathedral.

G.L.

Kirkby Moors

The Kirkby Moors are bare to the point of being indecent. They have no shape, except in the way a stretched-out pig has shape. They only just top the 1,000-foot contour, yet they raise themselves into such a cold air that the snow often lies thick on them when Black Combe, twice their height, is quite clear. They are of all the hills west of the Kent, quite the dullest to look at from a distance, yet, once you are among them, they have a powerful, almost hypnotic attraction. I like country like this – country that takes no notice of man, that is stripped of all prettiness and never condescends to order itself into a view. The views are what you see *from* it.

You can approach Kirkby Moor from the south by roads from Ulverston, Pennington and Marton, all of which converge at the farm called Horrace. This was once the home, in retirement, of a forgotten poet, Edmund Casson, who endeared himself to me, years ago, by telling a friend that he had heard there was a young man, just over the Duddon, who was writing rather well. At Horrace there are immense views backwards, across the bay and down the line of the peninsula to Piel Island and Walney. And then, beyond Horrace, you dip into the heart of the hills, where there are no views at all. All distances are blocked from sight by the shapeless heavings of moor, black and ochre, most of the year, but in August suddenly smouldering up to one of the greatest conflagrations of heather I have ever seen. It is also one of the best places for bilberries. The peat, sometimes cut and stacked, swells up about you like a half-solidified, oily sea. There are sumps and squelchy patches, with lousewort and bog asphodel growing there; and if you drive slowly in a car, a brown grouse may cock its red eyebrow at you. And beside the small beck which drains this upland valley, there is a track which leads along the moor tops to the Burlington slate quarries of Kirkby. (Its real name is Kirkby Ireleth, to distinguish it from all the other Kirkbies, but in practice the name of Ireleth is kept for a village on the hill above Askam.)

When you move out of the dip of the moor on to the northern slopes, you look down on the Duddon estuary and what to me, is the greatest view of Greater Lakeland: Black Combe, Dunnerdale, the Scafell and Coniston ranges, the sands, Millom and the sea; Skiddaw slate,

Borrowdale volcanics, Kirkby Moor flags, limestone; fell, valley, farmland, and marsh. I could write a whole chapter on this view. I could write a whole book on this estuary. I *have* written a book[1] on the town.

G.L.

Dunnerdale

The long beautiful dale was a favourite with Norman, especially its river, the Duddon. When he was still aspiring to do that most difficult of all things for a Cumbrian writer – to come to terms with the greatness of Wordsworth – he faced up to the problem with a number of poems, including 'To the River Duddon', which, like the following passage from his Portrait of the Lakes, *reveals a lifetime's knowledge of the dale. The Duddon, perhaps as much as anything else about which he wrote, showed him on his own distinctive path as a poet and writer.*

There is no better example of a lakeless dale than Dunnerdale. It is narrow, compact, self-contained, and does not dwindle away at its foot, as does Langdale, nor splay out like the lake valleys of Wasdale and Borrowdale. Wordsworth, in his Duddon sonnets, followed the river from its source to the sea, but it is better to track it in the opposite direction.

At Duddon Bridge you have the salt marshes of the estuary just below you, and the jaws of the dale ahead – High Duddon, muffled in rhododendrons, on the old Cumberland side of the river, and Bank End on the former Lancashire side. The main road climbs up Bank End so that you enter the dale, as it were, from above. On either side are steep scars of woodland, swilled with green in spring, and in autumn as fiery and challenging as a red-haired girl. Down in the valley bottom the river seeps off under cover of hazels among banks of shingle, wild garlic and daffodils. It is a flittering, twittering, rippling, restless, hunting, dodging, never-still world of longtailed tits, dippers, water-rats, weasels and otters. It is also a world of ants – millions upon millions of them, turning all the leaf-mould into one huge ant-hill and even covering the branches of the trees like flies.

But up on the main road you are already on the open moor. The walls have been got rid of, and the former Lancashire side of the dale is steep and rough, with black junipers among the screes, and the old, unused pack-horse road to Broughton Mills cobbled like a causeway up the crack of a dried-up gill. Dunnerdale is probably the best of all the dales to visit in late autumn or winter, for it faces due south, so that the low, midday sun pours straight into it. If you are facing updale there is not a

[1] *Provincial Pleasures* (Robert Hale, 1959).

shadow to be seen: the bracken is on fire up miles of fellside. The dead birch leaves, the little conifer shapes of the mosses, the chips of quartz in the rock, all gleam in every detail as if they were on show in a jeweller's window.

At Ulpha Bridge the river is confined for a few yards between narrow rocks. It is very deep here, and green as bile, but below the church it widens out, and someone has planted a row of conifers, well spaced and elegant. For the first mile and a half above Ulpha the scene is surprisingly docile, and the valley bottom is as tidy as a strip of Cheshire. Then the road leaves the river and wanders off to meet the big beck which bounces down from Seathwaite Tarn. Wonderful Walker's church stands in Seathwaite and some distance above this, years ago, I first saw the signpost pointing simply to

THE LANGDALES

In fact, it points to a fracas of rock and rowan and rough pasture through which the road winds like a sheep-trod across a scree.

This is the point where a track swings to the right into the one substantial tributary valley of Dunnerdale, and then curves past Holling House, out on to the open fell and over Walna Scar. And it is from the lower slopes of this pass – a kind of side-entrance into Dunnerdale – that you can get the finest vantage point for viewing the dale as a whole. Below you is the small, tureen-shaped valley of Tarn Beck, divided from the main dale by a low hump. Upwards, the valley pushes past the hirsute cone of Harter Fell to the three-fold camel-humps of Scafell, Scafell Pike and Great End, which look as if they belong to the head of the Duddon instead of to Eskdale and Wasdale. Downwards, the dip of the river takes a long left turn beneath silver, civilized woods, until the heave of Hesk Fell and the back of Black Combe block out the rest of the view.

Turning updale at the Langdale signpost we soon find ourselves back beside the Duddon which had been hidden from us in the cleft of the Duddon Gorge where it batters its way through rolled and tumbled boulders. This is the romantic country of mid-Dunnerdale, bright as a border ballad, prickly with larches and brindled with heather and rowan berries, where the river is in a continual jingle of what Wordsworth called 'would-be water-falls'.

At Birk's Bridge there is another chasm – the narrowest and deepest in the dale – and the river runs under a tunnel of oaks and alders, beneath which the leg-rock sits perpetually soaking its corns. Then the country changes and the dale-head opens out, hollow and bare, and soon we come to the outdoor study centre of Hinning House (from the Middle English Haining – an enclosure), with close beside it the houses built by the Forestry Commission and appropriately screened by trees.

For yet another quarter of a mile or so the dale-bottom is as flat as the seashore, and the river runs among hay fields and glacial gravel. This is the combe or corrie, the rounded dale-head, very characteristic of glaciated valleys, where the top end of the glacier has bitten back deeply into the rock. Then, at Cockley Beck, the dale is really over and the river swings to the right, towards Wrynose Pass, and splits up into many small becks any one of which may claim to be the source of the Duddon.

P.L.

*

Along the road from Corney, once you have crossed the ridge you round a little swelling in the moor and suddenly look right down into Dunnerdale. To the north is the hindside of the Scafells, and across the valley the great mass of the Coniston group. All around is the sour moor, dabbed with the dark green of juniper bushes, which most people mistake for flowerless gorse. But you hardly notice any of this, for your eyes are drawn to the valley, the narrow aisle of cultivated land running up between the fells. There are cottages, farms, a church, fields, woods, and on either side is as rough a sea of crag and bracken as any in England. Even today it is not hard to sense the centuries of stubborn back-breaking work which have gone to making this valley habitable and homely. You are looking, however, at only about one fifth of the dale – the stretch between Ulpha and Seathwaite. Behind Wallabarrow Crag, which, from this viewpoint, seems to plug the dale like a cork, there are another five or six miles of meadowed riverside before the sheep take over completely at Cockley Beck. But if you want to understand the self-contained, ingrown, almost insular type of society which persisted in the dales until about the middle of the eighteenth century, then this view will help you more than any other.

Of all the dales it is the most completely and consistently dale-like. Dunnerdale does not peter out. Stand on Duddon Bridge, looking upward, and you are in the jaws of the valley, with steep, wooded hillsides jutting up on either side. Turn round, and only a couple of hundred yards away you can see the beginnings of the tidal marshes. The buildings of the eighteenth-century ironworks hidden among the trees of High Duddon mark the meeting-place of dale and sea, for the charcoal for the furnace came from the woods and the ore was brought up the estuary at high tide. The buildings themselves are as compelling to the imagination as those of any medieval abbey – vast and solitary. Today, thanks to the planning board, they have been carefully restored, and some reroofed, and we can see how the steelworks of Barrow and the ironworks of Millom lay latent in that old furnace like a tulip in a bulb.

G.L.

Black Combe

*The combe features often in Norman's writings. Shadow of Black Combe,
Black Combe White, Cloud on Black Combe – the long humped-up hill
which he called the Maes Howe of Cumberland yielded him much
material. It was one of the few mountains that he ever conquered on foot,
his punctured lungs thwarting him from his early TB days. Even now the
combe does not draw hordes of walkers, but to Norman at least it was
always home ground and mountain enough.*

Black Combe is the wart of the north-west coast, a protuberance that
catches the eye from Scotland as far south as Wales. From the south, in
particular, it looks as if it were erupting right out into the sea, indeed, at
high tide it is surrounded by salt water on three sides. And since, on its
fourth side, there is only the low, slovenly moorland around Devoke
Water, Black Combe looks isolated, left out on its own, an island of a hill
joined to the lake archipelago by the causeway of Birker Moor. It has its
own weather, too. When you can see Black Combe, we say in Millom,
it's going to rain; when you can't see it, it *is* raining.

'Grim neighbour, huge Black Combe', Wordsworth wrote from Bootle
in 1811, to Sir George Beaumont, '… In his own storms he hides himself
from sight.' Or as the Lancastrian poet of *Sir Gawayne and the Grene
Knight* put it 600 years ago:

> The heven was up halt   bot ugly ther-under;
> Mist muged on the mor   malt on the mountes,
> Ech hille had a hatte   a mist-hakel huge.[1]

In Millom you just can't get away from Black Combe. There are some
streets where the view was once blocked out at one end by a slag-bank
and at the other by the combe, and on a misty November day there was
not much difference between the two. So that to me, as a child, Black
Combe was *the* mountain – the others were just names. Then, in my
early 'teens, I became worried by the ridiculous notion, still held by
some people, that a mountain, to earn the name, has to be 2,000 feet
high. And Black Combe was only 1,969. I even thought of going up
every month or so and tossing a few more stones on the cairn until it
had gained the extra thirty-one feet. Later years have shown me that this
is quite unnecessary, for if any hill in the Lakes deserves to be called a
mountain, it is Black Combe, and as far as I am concerned, 1,969 feet is
as near as dammit.

The combe is one of the Skiddaw slate fells and the barest of the lot.

[1]The sky was lifted up, but ugly beneath; mist drizzled on the moor, melted
on the mountains; each hill had a hat, a huge cloak of cloud.

Scarcely a tree grows on it anywhere above the 200-foot level. It is not only bare but round as an egg, with, it would seem, hardly a fold or a corrie to break the monotonous smoothness. That, at least, is how it looks from a distance. When you get closer, it begins to reveal its more private character. If you approach from Thwaites or the Duddon Bridge end of Whicham Valley, you will first of all see the flanks of the combe on your right, public as a shop-window. On the left is the broad, flat bottom of the rift-valley, and across the valley, the ridge of Lowscales, the most southerly splinter of the Borrowdale volcanics. If you cross the valley (by the little road that passes the amusingly-named Po House[1] and comes back on the main road near Whicham church) you will get a close look at the miniature crags and screes, the gorse and heather stair-carpets of this lovely rock; and you will also see that the bluff Black Combe has its own homeliness, its crooks and nooks.

G.L.

Devoke Water

Devoke Water on Birker Moor is the least seen of all the lakes, though the bridle path to it is clearly signposted at the side of the road. From the signpost you have to walk about 500 yards before the lake comes into sight. One wonders whether to call it a lake or a tarn. In size it is as much a lake as, say, Grasmere or Rydal Water, but it has the bareness, the dreariness, the essentially upland character of a tarn. The water looks as if it has been trapped there since the Ice Age, the last meltings of the last glacier. And apart from one half-ruined fishing lodge, built for the owners of Muncaster Castle, the place can have changed very little since then. If you go down the slope and squelch along the shore, the scene begins to look more cheerful, with the brown grouse revving up in the bilberries. The water, too, from here, has a glint on it and was once famous for its trout. But it is in the black of winter, when the night wind from the Irish Sea blows over my roof straight on to these fells that I think most often of Devoke. There are stories of tramps breaking into the fishing lodge, lighting a fire in the iron fireplace, and spending the night there, wrapped in their rags. The men of the Bronze Age, living in stone huts at Barnscar, not very far away, would scarcely have had cause for envy.

G.L.

Eskdale

Most people arrive in Eskdale at about mid-dale, and the middle stretch,

---

[1] I am told that collectors keep stealing the signpost!

from Eskdale Green to Boot, which cuts Eskdale into two parts, is comparatively populous and built on. This is mainly the result of the Eskdale narrow gauge railway which, in the days before the motor-car, made Eskdale the most accessible of the western valleys. When I was a boy a ride on the Ratty was summer's special treat, and, once the train had arrived at the terminus, nearly everyone set off, past Dalegarth Hall, for Stanley Gill and the waterfall. The hall, at the foot of the gill, is one of those manor houses, not quite pele towers, that were nevertheless fortified against possible Scottish raids. Its chimneys are fine examples of the huge cylindrical structures which are the Lake District's own special contribution to English domestic architecture.

Above the Woolpack Inn, where for centuries the farmers have held their shepherds' meet and where I spent my honeymoon, the dale becomes barer and bonier. The river accompanies the road for about two miles and then swings left, by Brotherilkeld and Taw House, and eats its way like a woodworm into the core of the mountains. The track which runs beside it is surely the most private, overhung, utterly-locked-off right of way of any in England, though you can get an outsider's view of it from just beyond the walls of the Roman fort half-way up Hardknott Pass.

Hardknott is on the Roman route from Ambleside, via Little Langdale and Wrynose Pass, to the Roman port of Clanoventa, at Ravenglass, which, though the point has been disputed, is thought to have been the place from which the Romans planned to invade Ireland. The walls of the fort are now in the care of English Heritage, and have been treated to the same kind of restoration which has roused so much controversy at Hadrian's Wall, and though I feel much sympathy with those archaeologists who argue that the ruins should be left as the Romans left them, yet I cannot forget that the Romans did not, in fact, leave them as ruins.

But Hardknott is not only a Roman road, it is on the line of the Lake District's most celebrated obstacle race – in fact, the twists and nearly one-in-three gradients of the pass make what is said to be the most severe classified road in Britain. At a busy weekend, one bad change of gear can force a long queue of cars to begin nervously reversing round precipitous bends, and on bank holidays the village children take their tea there to enjoy the fun.

G.L.

Wastwater and Wasdale

Wastwater, more than any of the other lakes, looks like a Norwegian fjord. There is little of the usual margin of silt, willows and shingle between fellside and water-edge, while on the screeside the water cuts clean along the drop of the rock.

The view from this point is so familiar, even to those who haven't been there, that there is no need to describe it. An inventory will do as well. In the foreground, the lake; on the left, Seatallan, Yewbarrow and Kirk Fell; in the centre, the pyramid of Great Gable; on the right background, Lingmell, Scafell Pike and Scafell; on the right foreground, the screes. It is one of the few views in the Lakes which looks as good in summer as in the other three seasons, for it is so much a matter of shape, proportion and balance that even the drab green of August does not smudge the effect.

But because the landscape is so very still, it is seen at its best when the air is moving, either in a storm, or in those times, between successive depressions, when moist clean air blows in from the Atlantic carrying foam-balls and tatters of cloud. Then, changing minute by minute, one peak will be blotted out and another in bright sunlight, or a huge waterfall of cloud will pour down the cleft between Kirk Fell and Gable, while the top of the latter floats like an island above the tide.

Wasdale is wonderfully typical of the landscape of the Borrowdale volcanic rocks which make up the centre of the district and include all the highest peaks, except Skiddaw and Saddleback, and at least half of the lakes. These volcanics are still slate in the common use of the term, but they were formed, not of mud, like the Skiddaw rocks, but of the lava and ashes thrown up by ancient volcanoes. And this mixture of material that went to their making has produced rocks that vary greatly in degrees of hardness – the lavas, on the whole, forming rocks of greater durability, and the ashes, rocks which easily crumble. The result is often a terraced effect, of steep laval cliffs and gentler ash slopes. Where the volcanic ash has been subjected to pressure, however, it may turn as hard as iron; at other times it will split along the line of the cleavage and weather into mere scree.

This is what gives rise to the continual variation in the landscape of the inner ring of the Lakes – a restless swirling turmoil of peaks, crags, pinnacles, screes, gills, clefts, tarns and waterfalls. One side of a valley will be as hairy as Harris tweed; the other will be glabrous as leather, with a dark green mould of moss in the creases. At one point in its course a beck will be oozing blackly through peat and bilberries and glacial clay; and, five minutes later, it will be head-over-heeling down a gill, through a fracas of dumped boulders and arthritic rowans. The most dramatic of all such scene changes is that of Wasdale. At one end of the lake there is the enormous west drop of Scafell; at the other end are the screes, the biggest geological ash-heap in England, where a whole fellside is slithering away like the brick and plaster of a bulldozed slum-clearance area.

Because it has been photographed so often, Wasdale seems to be more

Pillar Rock and the fells above Ennerdale

of a view than a real place. The familiar image of the lake, gathered from calendars and picture postcards before you ever go there, comes in between the eyes and the real thing. So that if you want Wasdale to become its true self, you should walk away from the picture-frame and see it from a less posed position. First of all go to the foot of the lake. This used to be the private estate of Wasdale Hall, but was bought by the National Trust, which opened a public footpath along the shore of the lake and turned the hall, a pleasant nineteenth-century building of pink Eskdale granite, into a youth hostel. From here you look square at the screes, only a couple of hundred yards away across the water. In the morning it takes the sun a long time to slant over this skyline, and, while all the fells of Copeland Forest are swimming in sunshine, the lake remains black in shadow. And in the evening, when the western shore is settled into dusk, the screes reflect the glow of the sky, volleying it down into the water, which glimmers dark purple and lilac and red long after the fells have lost all trace of colour.

G.L.

Calder Valley: An Oddity

Between Ennerdale and Wasdale lies the small valley of the River Calder which conceals one of the oddities of the Lakes – a snip of the general pattern printed on a different material. From Ennerdale Bridge you leave the River Ehen and cross Cold Fell to Calder Bridge. As you climb out of the valley there is one fine backward view of Ennerdale Lake, but afterwards you move across a rather formless landscape of a kind not often found so near the high fells. You pass, on the left, a partially reconstructed stone circle, marking a burial site, and find that you are running round the side of a huge smooth hump of hill-land, that seems to have been modelled in clay, for there is next to no sign of rock.

It is when you drop to the river at Calder Bridge that you first notice the change in colour. Here – as at Lamplugh, Beckermet and Gosforth – the walls and farms, the church and the older houses are all built of sandstone. But if you look over the wall by the church, you will see that at Calder Bridge this is not an imported stone, for the river runs through slabs and mouldings of red rock, smooth to the eye and rough to the touch. Sandstone is common enough in the northern parts of the county and give us some of our best river scenery. But the upper Calder valley is the one place where this rock wedges itself right up among the mountains. You can sense the difference as soon as you leave the village by the road which runs past Calder Abbey. There are drystone walls, as in other parts of the Lakes, but they seem to be made of huge slabs of gingerbread, greened and mildewed with age. Even the farmers have joined in the wish to be different, for some of the field-hedges are planted with laburnum, which hardly seems the right tree to keep the sheep out, though it looks pretty as a birthday card in spring.

G.L.

Ennerdale

Here as in other parts of Lakeland, felling and replanting have been taking place, with more open spaces left towards the dale-head.

The view from the foot of Ennerdale Water is a famous one, and since there is no motor road up the dale, it is the only view most people see. Instead of dwindling to river-width, as most lakes do, the bottom end of Ennerdale Water broadens out into an almost circular basin, about a mile in diameter. Above this basin, the lake narrows, pinched in between two out-jutting rocks – Bowness Knott on the left, and Angler's Crag on the right – each with a backing of still higher crags and fells. In sunless weather they make a black, forbidding front curtain, which, for theatrical effect, is not excelled even by Borrowdale. The upper half of the lake bends out of sight, behind Bowness Knott, but above it, six miles away, is Pillar, looking like an end-stop to the valley, though, in fact, the river and the track swing round it and beyond.

The upper dale is the country of the Ennerdale granophyre, a beautiful, pinkish, igneous rock, very like its near neighbour, the Eskdale granite. It is a rock usually seen at a distance, as crag and peak. To see it close at hand, you should make your way from Croasdale to the beginning of the forestry road along the northern shore of the lake. There is a right of way for walkers to the top of the dale, and farther if you like, by Scarth Gap to Buttermere or by Black Sail to Wasdale. And all this way the granophyre will be round about you: in the walls, in the cobbles, and in the cuttings made by the becks as they bustle under the track on their way to the river.

Mention of forestry, however, brings us into the area of controversy. I did not know Ennerdale before the trees were planted. Those who did have complained that the valley is smothered by firs, or say that from the tops it now looks like a bath half full of dirty green water. What must once have been one of the barest and most Icelandic of the dales has now largely disappeared from view at river level. Yet what has come in its place seems strangely attractive. Indeed, by counteracting the erosion which was quickly turning all these western fellsides into barren scree and bracken, afforestation may help to restore the land to something like its former fertility. It would be better, of course, if the trees were oaks or chestnuts rather than conifers, but even the latter protect the soil from wind and frost and, above all, from the sheep.

The question of the effect of planting on the Lake scene had better be left until we come to the areas where it has been carried out with some imgination. Ennerdale is not one of these. There is little variety in choice of tree, the upper line of the plantation is angular and mostly unrelated to natural contours, and the woods can seem monotonous if you insist on walking through them, mile after mile. Yet, if you are prepared to stand still or potter about, you will have no need to complain of monotony. The Ennerdale plantations for the most part are of Christmas tree evergreens, full of robins, blue tits and the blue jay, which, flashing among the boughs, always looks fawn and white, like a little flying deer. Chinks of birdsong glitter beneath the shadows. At every turn and dip in the track you can see Pillar or Steeple, spiring up above the dale, and, because this is not a public highway, you are not fenced about on either side, but enclosed by old stone walls or merely by grass verges.

G.L.

Buttermere: The Secretive Valley

Others besides Norman have been impressed by the closed-in nature of this dale, including Nicholas Size who kept the Victoria (now the Bridge) Hotel and wrote The Secret Valley, *a fictional account of the struggle between the forces of the Norman William II and descendants of Norse settlers.*

Buttermere Valley is enclosed and secretive. Even at the height of the holiday season the visitor feels something of a trespasser. The valley includes two lakes, Buttermere and Crummock, together with Loweswater in a tributary side-valley, and each seems set in a roughly circular, unbroken basin. It is hard to see where the water can flow out. The fells stand round about – Mellbreak, High Stile, Fleetwith Pike, Robinson – sloping so easily from base to summit that you scarcely realize how high they are. It is only when some high-up, measurable object catches your eye – a cairn, maybe, or a bush of broom – that the mountain comes into perspective. Then you feel the mass of it towering above you like a boot above a beetle.

At Gatesgarth, beyond Buttermere, the road bears left over Honister, but this is not the true head of the dale. Bear right, at Gatesgarth, along the track that leads to Warnscale Bottom between Fleetwith Pike and Haystacks. Almost in a matter of yards you will find yourself blocked out from the world – the beck running dead-straight along the flat pavement of upland pasture. There are drains cut in the peat, and broken-down walls, and sheep with their late lambs, all in a corridor not much wider than a football pitch between the enormous prison walls of the fells. The silence is so solid that you would need a pneumatic drill to bore through it, yet only a couple of hundred yards away the cars are trailing one another on the sharp turns of Honister.

P.L.

Borrowdale

Borrowdale is 'the dale of the fortress' (Old Norse *borg*), the name coming from a fort which is thought to have stood near Castle Crag. It is beyond argument the most theatrical of the dales. Derwentwater itself (the Derwent is the river of the oak), has none of the river-like character of, say, Windermere, but is more like a wide forestage to the backcloth of the upper dale. Again, though the peaks round about are not on the whole as high as those of the western dales, they manage to look even higher. For everywhere the scene seems to have been touched up and exaggerated by a romantic artist – if any view at all in the Lakes resembles an eighteenth-century landscape print, it is surely that of Borrowdale.

The Lodore Falls, for instance, near the head of the lake, are neither particularly high nor particularly precipitous, but, after rain, the water comes gushing down as from a burst dam and can be seen from Portinscale, three miles away. As for hills, Castle Crag, above Grange, is less than 1,000 feet in height, but it juts up like a wigwam, making even Skiddaw look lumpy in comparison. And almost opposite Castle Crag, on the other side of the road and river, is the Bowder Stone, typical, one might think, of the many such boulders left by the retreating ice. But, while the rest are found mostly on remote fellsides or in the coastal farmland, far away from any road, here is the biggest of them all, only a few yards away from the bus-route, and perched on one corner like a performing elephant on one leg.

North of Rosthwaite, the valley branches into two: Borrowdale proper and Stonethwaite, from whence tracks lead over the passes to Wasdale, Far Easedale and Great Langdale. This is walker's country. But the road along the other tributary dale, that of Watendlath, the waters of which flow into Lodore, is often jammed with cars, while the view from Ashness Bridge is probably the most photographed of any in the district. For Borrowdale, like Keswick, has taken the full brunt of the crowds. Go there for solitude, for rural peace, for Wordsworthian tranquillity, and there's little hope of your finding them, or not, at least, in the holiday season. Instead, you will find parked cars and the riverside around Grange Bridge staked out by picnickers – tartan rugs spread on the rocks, transistors squeaking above the sound of water, children snaring tiddlers, and tubular chairs set up round the gas stoves.

If you want to find quietness in Borrowdale, in summer, you must get up very early in the morning before the cars beam out from the town like starlings from the night's roost, or else walk beside the lake in the late

Back o' Skiddaw

evening after sunset. Then the fells are black cut-outs against the green of the sky, and the trees are huge haystacks of shadow at the foot of which the water gleams and flickers.

G.L.

Barest Lakeland: Back o' Skiddaw

Back o' Skiddaw (pronounced Backer Skidder) is the barest country in the Lakes. Mungrisdale and its small white-washed church look snug enough, with the phantom-haunted Souther Fell to the west, but once you get out of this valley you are travelling on a plateau open to all the winds from Scotland. On your left are the empty Skiddleback moors; on your right the mean-looking, inhospitable, middle-height upland that stretches to the edge of the Carlisle plain. It is not bare as the moors are bare, for the land is partly cultivated, and there are birch woods and bushy wind-breaks along the side of the military-straight main road which runs from Penrith to Wigton. Yet it looks as un-homely as the tundra. Such villages as there are, Caldbeck and Sebergham, seem sunk below ground level in little dug-outs of valleys. Caldbeck is famous as the home of John Peel, and there is a hideous gravestone in the churchyard with the heads of hounds nosing out of the stone as if their howls were going to haunt him through the after-life. The church itself, on the other hand, is of great beauty, set back from the road among trees. As with the rest of the village it is built of sandstone which is what makes both Caldbeck and Sebergham look different from the villages of the dales. The latter are one with the rock about them, man and nature working together. But Back o' Skiddaw, nature is less co-operative and man has to fight hard for comfort, building his defences of the warm stone of the plain. At Sebergham, two miles down river, where the hill country finally peters out, there are some of the fine Georgian farm-houses which are typical of the Carlisle plain; one, near the bridge, has two clipped evergreens in the front garden like an enormous pair of timpani. This village, though less known to the public than Caldbeck, has a better right to fame, for it was there, in the eighteenth century, that the curate, Josiah Relph, wrote his dialect poems while coughing his life away in the raw, fellside winters. Relph's *Pastorals*, after the classical model, were probably the first attempt in English to use the dialect for serious poetry, and his little book of poems 'embellished with the *Picturesque Engravings* of the ingenious Mr *T. Bewick*, of Newcastle' is a volume any Cumbrian should be delighted to own.

The road from Carlisle through Dalston and Uldale, which approaches the Lakes from the north, misses Caldbeck and Sebergham and also Ireby. Very few visitors to this part of Cumbria find Ireby at all, though it has the look of having once been the capital of Back o'

Skiddaw and the place where the fell farmers met the men of the Solway hinterland. It still seems quite tucked away and off route, though a whole starfish of roads spikes out from it – one of them, to Torpenhow, so narrow that if a motorist puts out his hand to signal he is likely to put it right through the hedge! Ireby has its little moot-hall and a butter-cross, and the whole village has the air of being comfortably unconcerned whether anyone finds it or not. It is well below the bilberry-line, yet still seems to belong essentially to the fells.

G.L.

Ullswater and Patterdale

Patterdale (Patrick's dale) is the only dale – apart perhaps from Little Langdale – which should be approached from the head rather than the foot, for by far the finest scenery lies between the lake and Kirkstone Pass. If you come from Pooley Bridge you have a long drive through rather ordinary waterside parkland, and it is not until you get nearly to the turning for the Cumberland Troutbeck that the curtain begins to go up on the highly effective last act of the lake. If you come from Kirkstone, the tributary dales begin to open out, one after the other, as soon as you reach Brotherswater – first, Dovedale on the left; then Hartsop with its village on the right; then Deepdale on the left. The fells begin, surprisingly, to close in as you get nearer to the lake, which keeps tantalizingly out of sight most of the way. Patterdale village and Glenridding are both truly home-grown, with scarcely a stone anywhere that has not come out of local quarries, yet they are now so given over to the holiday trade that they have a forlorn look in the off-season.

Patterdale, in fact, after having once been one of the out-of-the-way valleys, has now become one of the main tourist centres. Visitors come by car from Windermere, by coach from Keswick, Carlisle and even Newcastle, and every now and then the steamer calls at Glenridding Pier, and a batch of usually elderly people moves slowly over the lakeside gravel to cups of tea and postcards. The still-narrow road swarms like an open-air market – children rushing for ice-creams, fathers trying to find a car park or a lavatory. Where the road comes close to the lake, girls wade out into the water, and transistors drop their little bags of aural dye into the once-clean silence. On patches of grass between the birches mothers spread rugs and groundsheets, and set up folding chairs and tables, and soon, I fancy, they will bring portable gnomes and bird-baths to make the lakeside look still more like the back-garden lawn.

Yet, somehow, all this is the kind of cheerful family clutter that can be put away at bedtime. Go along the same road in the late evening, and you will find a heavy impasto of stillness on the lake – the surface like a breathed-on mirror, moist and steely, with the eastern, roadless shore rising out of the water, black and fjord-like. Or go, at almost any time of the day, into any of the by-valleys or gills on either side of the lake – Martindale, for instance, on the Howtown side, beyond which you can push on to Boredale and Bannerdale, two hidden-away, north-looking valleys, where in winter the sun scarcely even knocks at the door.

Ullswater is a spot which supplied everything that could be asked for by the eighteenth-century travellers in search of the Picturesque. They sailed along the lake as if they were circumnavigating unexplored Africa, fired brass cannons to set the echoes pealing and amused themselves listening to stories of the Mounsey family, the so-called Kings of Patterdale. On the western banks of the lake the Duke of Norfolk built a hunting lodge, called Lyulph's Tower, in the form of a fortified china cabinet, and Wordsworth obliged with a poem beginning 'List, ye who pass by Lyulph's Tower,' the style of which adequately matches that of the architecture, though it has done his reputation much less harm than the hackneyed O-level piece on the daffodils of nearby Gowbarrow.

                                                                      G.L.

Haweswater

It was once two small lakes, High Water and Low Water, but in the 1930s Manchester Corporation turned them into a reservoir, drowning the village of Mardale, an event that Lakelanders never forget, and some never forgive. The last service was held in Mardale church on 18 August 1935; the bodies were removed from the churchyard and buried at Shap and elsewhere. Before the dam had been completed the buildings had been demolished, leaving only drystone walls and Chapel Bridge visible whenever there is a drought.

The change of character at Thirlmere from lake to reservoir is even more obvious in the case of Haweswater, which does not look as if it had ever been a lake. The water lies trapped unnaturally in its drowned valley. The shores are almost dead straight and lined with what at a distance looks like a huge concrete kerb. There is no village, there are no farms and there is only one hotel. The only road runs up the Swindale side, and is strictly blocked off from the water-line, offering no temptations to picnickers. Visitors who come by car have really to go out of the Lake District altogether in order to get here, passing through the scruffy, powdery limestone country around Bampton. The road runs for three or four miles between the steep, lumpy, almost cragless sides of a dale which is surely the most monotonous of any in the district, and then, at the water-head, it stops dead.

And at this point you begin to wonder whether Manchester Corporation may not have saved this valley by damming it. For ahead of you is a magnificent dale-head, surpassed only by that of Wasdale. The crags of Harter Fell bludgeon themselves into the over-dale air, while the track divides into two, passing, on the one side of the peak, to Longsleddale and, on the other side, to Kentmere. It is a tremendous display of violent, empty landscape, with not a single intrusive building and not a fag-end littering the turf.

Yet you feel that something is wrong. It is not just that the village of Mardale is below the waters, its church sunk too late to have gathered legends of ghostly bells. It is not that the shore-line of detritus disfigures the view, since at the top end this is not much to be noticed. It is rather that the transition from open fell to closed water is too abrupt. The marginal quarter of a mile or so is missing. We have neither the characteristic dale-head delta of burnet meadows, shillough and willows, nor the upland tarn fringe of mosses and reeds. So that what we see is not a dale with a lake in it, but a group of fells plunged up to the waist in cold water.

P.L.

A Glimpse of Eden

For much of its course, the Eden is a surprisingly secluded river that buries itself out of sight, like a mole in an open field. Between Armathwaite and Kirkoswald, it is so muffled up in thick woods that it is completely hidden from the roads on either side of it, so that to follow it you have to leave the road and take to the track along the celebrated Nunnery Walks.

It is quite possible for those who are short in wind or limb to get a most satisfying glimpse of the Eden woods – though without actually seeing the Eden – by stopping at Nunnery, two miles south of Armathwaite. The nunnery of today is an eighteenth-century mansion built on the site of the old Benedictine convent. You pay at the house, circumnavigate the gardens, and walk about a quarter of a mile across fields into a wood. Choose, if you can, dry weather in spring, for the path is slobbery after rain and in a ferment of flies in the heat of summer. The woods are less dark in spring, too, and the path is marked out and enlivened by many tufts and bunches of little white flowers, the common and the lesser stitchwort, and also the meadow saxifrage, which I have not, in fact, found very common in our parts.

You come now to Croglin Beck, a tributary of the Eden, flowing down from the Pennines. Here the beck, which has dropped 1,500 feet in five miles, has drilled into the rock like a brace and bit. There is a gorge quite unlike the splintery, bouldered-cluttered gills of the Lake District – e.g.

Aira Force, which is not very far away. Instead, the water has bored deeply and smoothly into the rock, making a chasm narrower at the top than the stream which has cut it. Further down, at water-level, the rock is scooped back into caves and hollow basements, out of sight from above. The waterfalls – there are more than one – drop sheer, like water poured from a bucket, in the manner of the falls of the millstone grit. And the whole scene is scaffolded and girdered with trees – beech, oak and rowan. In spring, before the leaves are too thick, the varying greens glint and click together, and the light infiltrates right down to the lower dungeons of the chasm, flashing on water that continually turns over on itself.

We have penetrated, now, to the secret heart of the sandstone country, or, if that sounds too romantic, to its bowels, which, after all were once regarded as the seat of compassion. Let us be still less romantic and say that here we see the internal plumbing of the sandstone country – the water flushing and circulating; the rock scoured and swilled. Everything seems to be of the same element. The mud is sandstone watered down; the dead ferns are mud drawn out into a pattern. Much, too, is of the sandstone colour – not red, for there is not enough light to bring out the red, but rather a rich moudly-brown, mossed over with green or lichened with grey. We have dug down to the growing root of the landscape.

G.L.

Longsleddale and Bannisdale

Longsleddale is a farming valley. You can look into it from one point on the Shap road, above Garnet Bridge, where it has the appearance of a long narrow trench dug right into the foundations of the hills. This, indeed, is what it was in danger of becoming when the Manchester Corporation wanted to lay a pipeline from Haweswater to run down the whole length of the valley. The pipes would have gone underground, but it was estimated that 70,000 tons of soil would have had to be shifted, and that 200 lorries a week would have used the dale road while work was in progress. It is hard to see how contracts on that scale could be managed without leaving the road hacked and widened and the face of the landscape scarred in a way that would take years to mend. A government decision of 1965 saved the valley for the time being, but one cannot feel altogether confident about the future.

The threat to Bannisdale was even greater, for here Manchester wanted to build a dam and turn the valley into a new reservoir. This scheme, too, was dropped, though every now and then there are warning signs that the watermongers are still in business. It is true, of course, that if Bannisdale were to go under not many people would miss it. There is no metalled road along the valley, but only one that enters it about mid-dale, near Dryhope Farm, and then succumbs to mud and gravel at the little bridge over the beck. From above that point, Bannisdale is a backwater in time – a shallow hollow lying between fleshy, muscled hills with here and there a sparse, fluffy beard of oaks, blond in autumn and black-stubbly in winter. There is no village, no church, no pub, no tales of the Kings of Bannisdale; nothing, in fact, to rouse romantic nostalgia. Yet this is not one of the deserts of England. It is a valley that has been lived in and worked in for centuries. Every meadow and intake, every wall and barn is the result of many generations of toil, struggle and grim persistence. As I said when the controversy about the proposed dam was at its height: if you drown Bannisdale, you drown history.

G.L.

Shoot and Stem

Bracken

The relentless bracken is still spreading. Yet if it is useless in agricultural terms, to the foresters at least it does indicate deeper, better soil, usually the site of old woodlands.

As we come down the slopes, round about 1,500 feet, or even as high as 1,800, the bracken appears. It is usually rather thin at the top, but on the lower slopes it makes a thick jungle, waist-high, or even shoulder-high. It is exhausting to force your way through it in mid-summer, when the flies buzz round your head and you cannot see where you are putting your feet. Then you realize the toughness of the stalks, and the sharpness of their edges if you happen to run your hand along one of them. But the bracken is surely one of the best of all mountain coverings. It does not go into dead black for half the year like heather. Only for one month at the height of the summer is it dull – before that it is the quick green of larch, and afterwards it mellows through yellows, browns, reds and purples, and even keeps on smouldering under the snow, so that the green of spring comes up among the brown of the previous year. In many of the fellside farms the bracken was cut for bedding, and as it lay to dry it flamed almost as yellow as the gorse, and then, when carted away, it left a sober patch of stubbly turf, making the fellside piebald.

C.W.

*

Many people think of bracken as part of the natural scene in the Lakes in contrast to the 'unnatural' changes and modifications brought about by man. In fact, the spread of bracken is due almost entirely to man. The old dale smallholder, struggling to scratch a living from two or three upland fields and a few acres of fell pasture, had to scythe and dig and burn to get full use from every square yard of his land. The farmer of today simply cannot afford labour for this sort of work. So, since the time of Wordsworth, the bracken has gone unchecked and has invaded miles and miles of middle fell-land, often skirmishing below the fell-walls to colonize fields which were once under cultivation.

Yet the spread of the bracken is a sign of the problems facing the hill-farmer. If oaks were the climax vegetation of the dales, then bracken is the anticlimax. Much of the Lake District, especially the more exposed flanks along the coast, is turning into an eroded landscape of bare rock, scree and bracken, splendidly photogenic, but barren of human meaning.

P.L.

Among the Berries

There are the heathers, too, spreading indeed from shore level to the tops of the fells. And there are the berried plants – bilberry, cowberry, bog whortleberry and, much lower down, cranberry. The stone bramble also grows among the hills. Of all these the bilberry (*Vaccinium myrtillus*) is by far the most common. It seems to choose not the steep slopes, but flat terraces and combes, and peat bogs, where, perhaps, old tarns once stood. There, in summer, it is a dark, rather bitter green, with the berries, like purple pearls, hidden till you move the leaves. But in a good season you can sit and fill your pocket with berries without moving from one place.

C.W.

Mountain Pastures

Of all the Cumbrian flowers those of the mountain pastures are the most exciting. It is hard to say how these differ from the flowers of the fells or of the lowlands, yet they do, and you cannot mistake the new character of the plants the moment you turn away from the lowlands or step down from the mountains. This character is the same wherever the mountain pastures are found – in the dales, in the lake country around Coniston and Windermere, and in the little valleys around Kendal.

It shows itself even in the grass, which seems dark green, wide-bladed, cool and sappy, fed on the mists. And among it you find orchises of many kinds, and cow-wheat, betony, lousewort – all half-secret plants, of dark, brooding colours, rich orange or purple. Typical, too, are the marsh marigolds growing as common as buttercups in the damp fields. They are usually a mountain variety (*Caltha palustris*, var. *minor*), with flowers of a darker yellow growing close to the ground – there are acres of them to be seen at Torver beneath the cliffs of Dow and Old Man. Another of the Ranunculus tribe common in the dales if the beautiful globe-flower (*Trollius europaeus*), with huge yellow sepals

Beyond Martindale

enclosing the flower like the rind of an orange. Frequent also is lady's mantle, not very conspicuous, but making a flat green covering still darker than the grass.

Even the flowers which are also common in the lowlands – wood-sorrel, dog-violet, sweet violet, bluebell (which, as in Scotland, is usually called the wild hyacinth), moschatel, with dog's mercury, primrose, and enchanter's nightshade at the edge of woods – seen here have a darker, richer look. They all have that rather intense appearance of flowers which feed among thunderclouds, or of the orchises which look as if the grass were sweating blood.

C.W.

Around the Farms

Around the fellside farms are to be found many of the flowers which have escaped from the gardens and manage to fend for themselves. The yellow Welsh poppy is one of the commonest, and you will also find Solomon's seal, lungwort or Adam and Eve, snowdrops and daffodils. Perhaps the daffodils are really wild in parts. No doubt many of those which grow beside the rivers have spread from bulbs washed from cottage gardens, but in some places, as near Broughton Mills in the Lickle valley, there are fields of them, growing as thick as corn – small, pale-flowered blooms on short stalks.

P.L.

Flowers of the Limestone

To me the greatest delight of the Orton area is finding myself once again among the flowers of the limestone. I speak not of rare species, interesting primarily to the botanist, but of the obvious, showy, abundant flowers which dress up this landscape for anyone who has eyes at all. First, there are those which one has already seen in the limestone of southern Cumbria – huge masses of meadow cranesbill and the large scabious. Then, in the hedges around Brough, you can see marjoram and the giant bell-flower; and in those west of Appleby, the white flowers or the red berries of the wayfaring tree; while the purple chimneysweep's brushes of the greater knapweed grow actually on the grass verges of the A66.

But for me one flower above all typifies the Orton limestone: the bird's-eye or mealy primrose (*Primula farinosa*), a flower not so rare that I dare not mention where it grows, yet one that few people will see in the whole course of their lives. It is a flower specially associated with Teesdale, but it also grows in places to the west of the Pennines, and, in particular, around Sunbiggin Tarn which can be reached by car from

Orton, or from Newbiggin-on-Lune. The tarn itself is quite unlike the tarns of the Lakes. It is a shallow pool, sunken into peat, half filled up with reeds, and surrounded by an enormous waste of dreary, anonymous moorland. But close to the tarn, and all along the sides of the road from Raisbeck, there is, in June or July, a faint fume of colour, like a pink-mauve ground-mist among the sundew, the tormentil, the stone bedstraw and the heathers. The flowering time is short and varies from year to year, and you are lucky if you have, as I have, a friend who will drop a postcard telling you when the flower is out. Gardeners may perhaps not be over-excited about it, finding it only a smaller version of the primula they grow in pots or in the herbaceous border. But to me, the small but very lovely blooms evoke curlew-cry and plover-creak and the loneliness of those in-between lands that are neither mountain nor valley. And, even if the flower is not in bloom, there is still the pleasure of discovering Sunbiggin itself.

G.L.

Dune Plants

The dunes for the most part lie in the south-west of Cumbria, since the rivers of Morecambe Bay are without them, and there are only miserable mole-hill-high specimens along the coast further north. But on both sides of the Duddon and on Walney Island, and again around the joint estuary of the Esk, Mite and Irt, there are great savannahs of sand stretching for miles. At Haverigg, behind a thirty-foot-high and fifty-yards-solid sea-wall of dune, the sand is rolled out level and overgrown with green. This is a dune-turf land, where the marram grass is replaced by a tight-knit jumper of thyme, tormentil, heartsease, heath and dog violets, bird's-foot trefoil, hare's-foot trefoil, the small yellow clovers and the white Dutch clover, biting stonecrop, devil's-bit scabious, hemlock storksbill and a dozen species of cresses and hawkweeds. To one who recognizes even half these flowers, the names give out a scent of herby turf, sprinkled with salt and sizzling with lark-song. On the former Lancashire side of the Duddon, at Askam and Roan Head, the sand is darker and redder, more mixed with soil. There is burnet rose, here, with its bleached white flowers and ebony-black hips, and I have found the yellow dune-pansy – a seaside relation of the mountain-pansy of the fells, which, however, is more often blue than yellow.

P.L.

A Dyke Top

The thorns which run along the top of this dyke have not been trimmed for years. Already they have become not so much a hedge as a row of stunted trees. Each rises on its black trunk and creaks round the chapel, like an umbrella blown inside out. A tatter of black leaves still adheres to the fingertips of the branches, yet along the twists of the wood there are everywhere tight warts and pimples of bud. The ashes, mingled with the thorn, kick into the air their long, clean colt's legs, each with a black hoof at the end. The elders, too, are clean, being bent and brown and brittle as if made of pipe-clay. Even a hazel appears here and there, its inch-long catkins a stiff bright green. While the catkins of the one decrepit alder – its top snapped off for a bonfire – are purple and bunched and curved like a bird's claws.

None of these, however, is exclusive to spring. Buds and catkins belong as much to autumn, and are a commonplace of October in any country lane. Yet the eye knows for certain that the year is new, that something has changed since last it looked at this spot, three or four weeks ago. It is not easy to be sure what this can be. The hedge-bank looks fresher, brighter – but this might just be the effect of the sun. It looks cleaner – but this might be the effect of last week's rain. It looks greener, too – but that is due, not so much to the coming of greenness, but to the tearing away of the old year's rag-mat of brown and black and yellow.

Yet this is not all: for along the hedge-top in among the trunks of the thorn, and up and down the sods among the stones, there is a hint and frill of leaves no bigger than confetti, scattered in the black soil. A month or two may reveal them as belonging to a score of species: goosegrass, speedwell, celandine, moschatel. But now they are still anonymous, still indistinguishable each from the other, yet as intent and purposeful as a hatching of insects creeping out of their cracks in the early sun.

Here and there is a recognizable plant: chickweed, as green as Ireland, with its small, mean, jealous eyes, that will never shut so long as there is a peep of light; ivy-leaved toadflax with its little purple snapdragons draping itself over the lumps of slag as if it were in the window-box or greenhouse from which it originally came. And there are also the red dead-nettle, the daisy, common groundsel, and even a dandelion. But these are just flowers that don't know what time of year it is.

P.P.

Daffodils

The daffodils have a timetable of their own in Odborough. In January they appear only in wreaths, sickly and dying among the evergreen. In February they are seen in shops and parlour windows, making little splashes of sulphur all along the grey of the street. In March they begin to shoot up in orchards. A shudder of yellow runs under the apple trees and the washing whenever the wind blows. But April is the month for the garden narcissi. Then they bounce and see-saw in every allotment and lawn – yellow trumpets and white, large cups and small ones, bunch-flowered and doubles – Pheasant's Eye, Cheerfulness, Beersheba, Scarlet Elegance, Texas, King Alfred, and Mrs E.H. Krelage. They stand, now, on this Good Friday, in the churchyard beside the drive, in garden-party clothes, dithering in the cool wind. The yellow orchard daffodils warm the breath like brandy, but these make you cold to look at them. The season is not ready and we are not ready for the season.

P.P.

Gardens

Gardens are partly the work of God who makes the country and partly of man who makes the town. But in Cumbria God does more than his fair share. I am thinking not of the gardens of the great houses of the lowlands, Lowther Castle, Rose Castle, Sizergh Castle and the rest, with their lawns, rose beds, and topiary art, but of rough-and-tumble, half-wild gardens of the lower fells and the dales.

First there are the farms, small, square and perhaps whitewashed, with half an acre or so of fellside walled off from the rabbits. Often the ground is steep and rocky, with only a few apple trees planted there. The blossom on the apples tosses in the wind like foam and the trunks creak in stockings of whitewash. Perhaps there are damsons, too, as in the Lythe valley, where thousands of trees flower every spring. White is the colour of the fellside farms, bright white in spring against the grey and green; white of whitewash, and of blossom and of washing too, tugging and twirling on the clothes-line stretched from tree to tree. And earlier there is the white of snowdrops. Then the daffodils: not white, of course, but having something of the same Easter cleanness and freshness. It is in these orchards, not in fields or by the riverside, that the daffodils look their best, when they strain and rebound in the winds.

Lower in the dales, and around the shoulders of the mountains, and especially in all the low hills around Coniston and Windermere, there are larger gardens, but still shaggy and half-wild. Here are the small manors, often fortified at one time against Scottish raiders, and the country houses built in the nineteenth century for settlers among the lakes. They are mostly dark, these gardens, with firs and monkey-puzzles throwing shadows over the roofs, and the crags in a great wall above them. There are hollies, too, grown into trees, and yews and other dark-leaved trees and shrubs, and the pale Solomon's seal, hanging its white chessmen under the leaves.

But the dominant plant is the rhododendron. Many people do not like rhododendrons. They belong to the Asiatic mountains, but if they are at home anywhere in England it is surely here. They grow into huge bulks, scarcely shaped like trees, but solid as rocks. They bulge around the houses in waves, sometimes overtopping the chimneys, so that the roofs look half-submerged like the farms of a drowned valley. The steep gables and dormers of dark green slate jut out among the darker green leaves. In spring the bushes flower, and the most common of all the colours is a dark, stained-glass red, glowing intensely among the almost black leaves. The blackbird nests there, and the mountain thrushes and all birds whose songs flash and flicker in the evening dusk.

C.W.

Weeds

Norman relished his defence of weeds. They come, as he wrote elsewhere, without invitation; and they don't take the hint when you want them to go. He appreciated the value of roadside verges as reservoirs of wild plants – long before such ideas became common – and could name rare varieties of weeds as easily as he could mountain plants.

Nevertheless, the real spring flower, the first flower of the front-end, is already in bloom. Move up Jubilee Hill, from the chapel of the Brethren to the church of the Establishment, and you will find a curiously prolific and persistent weed. It spreads all over the bank that divides the drive from the vicarage garden in among the trees, right up the slope towards the graveyard – nearly a quarter of an acre of it. Digging and burning has not the slightest effect on it, for below the surface is an entanglement of roots, tough as barbed wire. God knows how long it has been there. Church people know it as a familiar nuisance. Those who visit the churchyard only for funerals and Armistice Day processions notice it without knowing they have done so, and carry its green as part of the image of corruption and decay. Thousands of mourners, passing up the drive, have had their attention diverted for one second to its rankness – a sprawl not of the resurrection but of cold endurance. Those who return to Odborough after an absence of many years are astonished to recognize the weed, so long forgotten, growing unchanged in a town of changed faces.

Few people have ever seen it in flower. All they have seen is the wilderness of leaves – leaves very like those of coltsfoot, but of a brighter green; flat, heart-shaped leaves, the size of pancakes, that curl at the edges and are veined, puckered, and crinkled like human skin. Yet there *is* a flower for those who know where and when to look for it: a tallish spike bearing a dozen flower-heads, each surprisingly like mauve coltsfoot heads, and the whole very like butterbur, or wild rhubarb. It is a stiff unprepossessing bloom, somewhat resembling those brushes which are used to clean lavatory bowls. Yet, gathered, it has a faint honey fragrance, unique among the winter flowers, because of which, no doubt, some vicar's wife planted it years ago.

The present vicar hates the plant. He has seen the flowers and has recognized them for what they are – winter heliotrope, *Petasites fragrans* – but he feels that it makes the neighbourhood of the church porch look too much like a rubbish-heap. Nothing he can do seems to discourage it – nothing short of digging a six-foot trench and filling it with solid concrete. He has nightmares in which the weed seems to be the only green thing left in a hydrogen-bombed world – persistent, flourishing, and drawing a new vitality from the radioactive air.

P.P.

Lake Woods

The dale country is not a country of forests, with greensward and undergrowth and great trees. Its typical woods are more like spreading thickets, with some chestnut and oak, but more often slender-trunked trees. There, as by the streams, the birch grows, and the hazel, on steep slopes, with bramble, and tutsan tangling round the roots. There is not much soil, and the roots grip the stones, where the little becks scour them clear of moss. Here in early March there is a time when the hazel catkins are hanging and yellow, but still, not flicking their pollen about. The sky is often grey, and the grass still dark and the bracken brown, so that the catkins glow with a pale light of their own.

Later, when the catkins are dropping, it is the gean, the wild cherry, which is the most handsome tree of the dale woods, frequent but not clustered, blue-white, the colour of skimmed milk, above the still-brown bracken.

The woods are full of tits of all kinds, and the rocks are whiskered with fern. Sometimes they descend to lake-level, and even when they don't there may be a long line of trees along the lakeside. Coniston, Windermere, and particularly Ullswater in parts, are bordered by trees which curve over the edge, making a little tunnel along which you can walk on the rough slate beach. There scarcely seems to be any soil, and the slates squelch under your feet and the driftwood branches crack, but still the trees can find something to feed on. Perhaps the dead rats and birds, and sometimes sheep which float to the shore, help to provide animal manure. This is the lakeside landscape of Beatrix Potter's *Squirrel Nutkin* and other stories.

C.W.

The fells above Eskdale

Rowan and Juniper

The rowan on the whole prefers the smaller becks, where it is often the only tree. And though it lives in wild enough spots it is a meditative tree, not particularly graceful, and with rather drab leaves. It is only in early autumn, when the bunches of orange or red berries weigh down the branches, that it is as romantic as its name.

The rowan is also a tree of the fellsides, where only the juniper grows at a greater height. Round waterfalls it rises to 2,000 feet. Elder also climbs high alongside the becks, and hawthorn, each giving a crop of white blossom, the one in June, the other in May. The juniper may sometimes be seen in the lower dales as a tight dark flame of a tree, but more often it belongs to the desolate fellsides. Here it does not grow tree-like, but straggles as a thick bush, from a distance looking like gorse when kissing is out of season. It is then a shrub of the damp slopes, where the mist hangs in it, bunched over the branches like muslin over currant bushes. Then it seems a bitter, sullen green. Yet when you look closer, its leaves have an under sheen of blue, and the spider-webs are laid all over them, gleaming with the wet. You forget its shapelessness then, because of the patterns of spine and web and water.

C.W.

Inglewood Forest

Cumberland once had three great forests, two in the north – Inglewood and Allerdale – and one in the mid-west – Copeland. Inglewood was well wooded and famous for its timber.

The forest laws made Inglewood a far from jolly place to live in. The forest may be said to have lain, roughly, between the Eden and the Caldew, though it stretched further west as far as the present Carlisle-Thursby road. The southern boundary ran just below the Sebergham-Penrith road, reaching the River Eamont south of Penrith. Penrith, therefore, was within the forest, as were Dalston and Great Salkeld, while the name still persists at Hutton-in-the-Forest and at Hesket-in-the-Forest, or did until Hesket dropped the 'forest' in 1934.

This, however, was by no means the full extent of Cumberland's forest area. To begin with, there was the smaller forest of Allerdale, stretching to the west of Inglewood as far as Wigton and the River Waver. Then Henry II afforested or 'put in regard' (i.e. subjected partially to forest laws) a vast new area: on the west, the whole of the land between the Derwent and the Solway, and on the east, the land from the Eden to Geltsdale and the slopes of the Pennines, making this one of the largest hunting forests in all England. Not all of this was woodland or heath. There were manors, cultivated land and privately owned woods within the forest boundaries. Indeed, Inglewood as a whole was a well-managed royal estate, and the Crown collected a good revenue from grazing rights for cattle and pannage for swine, from fishing rights (especially in the ballad-sung Tarn Wadling) and from the sale of dead wood and of bark for tanning, though, significantly, no tanner was allowed to set up business within the forest.

Owners and tenants were subject to rigid restrictions. They were not allowed to put up adequate fences in case these trapped the deer, which therefore continually strayed on to farmland and damaged the crops. It was an offence, also, to fell a tree or cut down a bush which might give shelter to the game. No undergrowth could be cleared (ridded was the word often used, hence the number of farms called Riddings) nor could land be brought into cultivation without a licence. No one was allowed to set up a mill within the forest or even put up a hut or shed – such rulings will sound not unfamiliar to anyone living today within the boundaries of the National Park.

It was strictly illegal, of course, to kill a deer or a wild boar, though certain officers of the forest, such as the Foresters in Fee (an hereditary office usually held by members of the Boyvill family and the Huttons) were allowed to hunt lesser game, such as hare, fox, wild cat, pine marten, badger, otter, squirrel and wolf. Of the deer, all three, red, fallow and roe, were found in Inglewood, the red being the commonest and the roe, as in most northern forests, the scarcest. From accounts of kills, it would seem that the fallow kept to the north and the east of the area, preferring woods and undergrowth. Certainly, game was plentiful enough at the time of Inglewood's greatest fame, and there are accounts of some tremendous hunts. It is said that when Edward I visited the forest in the eighth year of his reign, he hunted for four days, and on the first day alone killed 400 harts and hinds. Even as late as the reign of Henry III, the Pipe Rolls show that 200 harts and 200 hinds were taken in two successive seasons.

Penalties for breaking the forest law were extremely severe, but F.H.M. Parker, the author of the comprehensive study[1] of Inglewood to which I owe much of this information, insists that they were not carried out nearly as vindictively as tradition and the ballads would make us believe. The deer-stealer, by the time of Edward I, was fined heavily, imprisoned for a year and a day if he failed to find surety for the money, and was liable to be banished at the end of that period. But, of course, the nobles and rich tenants readily paid up. Moreover, there was no social discredit attached to poaching. Charges of breaking forest law

[1] Printed in Volumes 5, 6, 7, 9 and 10 of *The Transactions of the Cumberland and Westmorland Archaeological Society*, New Series.

were made, not only against the nobility, but against the bishop, the prior of Wetheral, and several clergy, though the bishop and the prior may not have been personally responsible for the acts of their servants. In fact, poaching was so much taken for granted, that Adam Turp, lord of Edenhall, near Penrith, and a repeated offender, was later made into an official verdurer with the task of administering the law he used to break.

The laws pressed more heavily, however, on the common people. Henry II made it an offence even to be found carrying a bow and arrow within the forest, which meant that the poor man lost most of his chance of picking up a rabbit or a wild duck which was often the only fresh meat he enjoyed from one year's end to the other. The lawing of dogs – a cruel practice by which three toes were struck off the forefoot with an axe – was another particularly unpopular measure. Though the ballads may have exaggerated, there is no doubt that the forest laws gave rise to centuries of resentment and to a hatred of officialdom and outside interference which has not yet quite died out among the people of rural Cumbria.

G.L.

Creatures Great and Small

Sheep

The number of Herdwick sheep in the county, excluding lambs, is about 100,000 and fairly static. About 25,000 are on many of the eighty-five or so fell farms owned by the National Trust, which is a strong supporter of this astonishingly hardy animal. Nowadays sheep tend to be marked with scourable fluid because stains and tar result in the wool being downgraded. The identification tags Norman mentions have not proved totally popular, for they can tear the ear and fall out. The majority of farmers keep to lug marks, which rustlers find nearly impossible to disguise.

The native sheep of the dales is, of course, the Herdwick. I say 'native' somewhat cautiously, for though there is no truth in the local legend that the breed first came ashore from a wrecked ship of the Armada, there does seem just a slight possibility that it may have been brought to the county by the Vikings. More probably, it was evolved by them out of an indigenous breed which they found in the dales when they first arrived.

No animals look so much at home on the fells as do the Herdwicks, not even the fell ponies. They are small sheep with rather grizzled faces – lithe and hardy, able to climb like goats and leap over any but the highest wall. They are lean about the legs and flanks, though the wool which covers them like upholstery often hides this. It is only when they are allowed to laze about and fatten in the riverside meadows that they put on flesh and give the sweet mutton they are famous for. In the past, much ewe-milk cheese was eaten in the dales and hams of mutton were cured like bacon. When the sheep have been clipped in summer they look naked and white, but usually their wool is long and grey, with bits of dead bracken and thistle and dung stuck to it.

It is hard to think of the Herdwicks as domestic animals. They seem to belong to the land rather than to the farmer. The flock is often rented with the farm, and when the tenant leaves he has to make up any

Sheep farm, Dowthwaite Head

121

deficiency in the numbers and may take the benefit of any increase. Each flock has its own 'heaf' or pasture on the fells where it spends the summer and autumn, and the sheep often know their own heaf so well that they will return to it from a long distance. Yet some of them stray, mingle with flocks not their own, so that, by a long tradition, the farmers meet twice a year to exchange foundlings and stragglers.

All sheep look very much alike and identification is made possible by an elaborate system of markings. First the sheep are smitten on the body with red ruddle,[1] or sometimes with blue or green staining. The marks are usually in the form of stripes, pops (i.e. round blobs) or letters, and are placed on different parts of the body. In addition – though this practice has diminished – the ears are cut or marked in some distinctive way, or, sometimes, the horns are burned. Each farm inherits its own lug marks which may go back far in history. The ears may be cropped (i.e. the end of the ear is chopped off), or forked, or ritted (slit). They may be fork-bitted (i.e. a V-shaped notch is cut out of the side of the ear), or key-bitted (a square notch). And as there is a top and a bottom side to every ear with two ears to every sheep, the number of possible permutations and combinations is very great.

In 1817 J. Walker of Martindale compiled *The Shepherds Book*, which catalogued the lug marks and smits belonging to the fell farms west of the Eden. Several revisions were made and books brought out to cover other parts of the district, and one of the most comprehensive of these volumes, Gates's *New Shepherd's Guide*, was published by the *West Cumberland Times* in 1879. This has nearly five hundred pages, with an engraving of the same two prize sheep repeated three times a page. On each engraving the smits are stamped in black and red, while the lug marks are indicated diagrammatically, and there is added a technical description of the marks and the name of the farm and farmer to whom each belongs.

From the pages given to the parish of Whitbeck beside Black Combe come the following:

John Grice, Far End; cropped near, upper halved far, stroke down near lisk, pop on tailhead.

---

[1] In the west coast district the ruddle usually came from small veins of haematite ore, the discovery of which in some cases led to the opening-up of the early iron mines.

William Thompson, Barfield;
cropped and ritted near,
stroke from shoulder blade
on near side over back,
and to lisk on far side.

James Robinson, Hall Foss;
cropped near, ritted far, three red
strokes down far shoulder in the form
of a crow's foot, J.R. on near side.

George Kirkby, Beckside;
cropped and under key-bitted near,
under halved far, three short
strokes over back.

The practice of cutting the ears began giving way to the use of metal identification tags or studs, though some of the more old-fashioned farmers still kept to their lug marks. I can hardly think that the change was greatly regretted by the sheep.

But another practice which survived until about the beginning of this century must have worried them much less. This was the habit of counting the flocks in a set of Celtic numerals which had come down from the British tribes of pre-Viking Cumbria. The numbers are grouped in twenties so that when a shepherd had counted to a score he put a finger up and started again. When all five fingers were up he had reached the hundred, whereupon he put a pebble in his pocket or scratched a mark on a wall. The numerals vary a little in different parts of the district, but here is one version:

Yan, taen, tether, mether, pimp;
Teezar, leezar, catterah, horna, dick;
Yan-dick, tan-dick, tether-dick, mether-dick, bumpit;
Yan-a-bumpit, tan-bumpit, tedera-bumpit, medera-bumpit, gigot.

Sheep-farming has coloured the dalesman's language, his pastimes (the popularity of fell-hunting is due in good part to the need to protect the lambs), and even the way he builds his farms and cottages. Some of the latter, for instance, have spinning-galleries where the wool could hang out to dry in various stages of home spinning and weaving – a very good example can be seen at the farm just beyond High Yewdale Bridge on the Coniston-Ambleside main road and another outside the Fisherman's Arms at Spark Bridge. Again, during the wool boom of the sixteenth and seventeenth centuries, it was the Herdwick which began the prosperity of towns like Kendal, Ambleside and Hawkshead.

P.L.

The Debt to Sheep

At the last count there were more than 2,600,000 sheep and lambs in Cumbria, five or so for every person in the county.
The Herdwick is no longer the only sheep to be seen in the dales, the Swaledale and various cross-breeds having almost superseded it in some parts. Yet the dalesman still owes much of his social life to the sheep, whether the Herdwick or any other breed. Straying sheep have often been at the bottom of arguments and quarrels, but they are also the reason or the excuse for some of the happiest events of the dale year – the shepherds' meets, at which the strays used to be gathered together to be sorted out and claimed by the owners, with proper exchange and recompense. Nowadays, a farmer who finds a stray will probably look at the lug mark and telephone the owner right away, leaving him to collect it in his van, but the shepherds' meets still go on, a ripe Cumbrian mixture of business, gossip, song, drink and tatie-pot supper.

G.L.

Trapped by the Tide

The sheep in this incident near Millom escaped: the tide was already on the turn.

And now, suddenly, the sheep find that their bank is flooded and the water nearly up to their bellies. Some of them try to escape, but immediately begin to plunge and flounder in the deeper water on the edge of the gullies. The others stay still, and merely raise their heads reluctantly from cropping and begin to baa. The sea is unrippled, grey, dull-shining as pewter. Reflections appear on it blurred but undistorted, like a view seen through a dirty glass window. The whole range of the ironworks and slag-banks lies upside down on the grey of the water, the posts of the breakwater running up the chimney-stacks like scaffolding. The slab-banks slant down in underwater cliffs or grottoes, and the smoke whirls and whitens as if a school of porpoises were blowing below the waves. What ten minutes ago was an inch or two of dampness, oozing across the marsh, is now a lake as deep as the sky. The tide is alive with the shadows of sea-birds, chasing the real birds three feet above them. Quick black-and-white oyster-catchers and ring plovers are flung out to sea like a handful of pebbles at every turn and flick of the wind. Gulls are few, having already congregated in their colonies among the dunes. Shelduck are in pairs and will soon fly off to the moors. Curlews gargle; peewits creak. An engine on the ironworks line eases its safety valve, and a jet of pure white steam descends like an inverted whirlpool deep into the depths of the tide.

The sheep now are growing more alarmed, for the water has mounted their backs and they crane upward with their necks, keeping their heads above the surface. They are baa-ing pitifully, but no longer dare move, for every step threatens to drown them. The dozen or so heads jut out inexplicably above a sea that looks deep enough to swamp the ironworks chimney-stacks, and the air is filled with the wailing of mermaids. Timothy turns apprehensively to his grandfather.

'No sense in it at all,' says the old man. 'They should never have been left out in these tides. No sense in it at all.'

P.P.

Sheep-dogs

It is impossible to think of the Herdwicks without thinking of the dogs which herd them. The fell sheep-dog is not at all like the collie which wins prizes at shows. The value of a sheep-dog depends on its ability, not its looks. The dogs, indeed, are rarely pure in breed, and it is not unusual for them to have quite a strong mixture of foxhound. If the dog lives at a remote farm, it is often suspicious of strangers, regarding the whole fellside as his own backyard. If, however, it lives at a farm by the roadside, where it is used to passers-by, it is more likely to be very friendly, so friendly that it may seem to be fawning, especially if it has been taught to creep.

The sheep-dog is indispensable to the shepherd. The skill of the dogs is known to everyone, and is demonstrated at its highest in the sheep-dog trials held at Eskdale and elsewhere. The ordinary shepherd asks only that his dog shall manage the sheep quietly and intelligently, working over rough country and long distances. He will stand on a rock and with whistle, shout and wave of the arm will direct the dog over operations which may cover a good many acres. I have known a farmer send a dog on an errand which involved its being completely out of sight behind a bump in the ground. He could tell by the movement of the sheep whether the dog was working as hard as it ought to, and when it began to slacken off he would blow on his whistle to encourage it.

There are many stories of the wisdom of sheep-dogs. One – and I am assured of its truth – pleases me greatly. A farmer from Ulverston (I have altered the place names) sold some sheep to a farmer from Kirkby Lonsdale. The buyer, noticing that the Ulverston man had a very good dog, asked for the loan of it to help get the sheep home, and promised to send it back by passenger train. When he got to Kirkby Lonsdale, however, he shut up the dog, hoping that it would eventually settle down in its new home. To inquiries from the owner he said that the dog must have gone astray on the railway journey. One day the dog broke out, had a look round the farm, picked out the sheep which had belonged to his real master, separated them from the rest of the flock and drove them back along the roads to Ulverston. And the Kirkby farmer could say nothing about it, as he should not have detained the dog!

C.W.

Deer

More than 600 red deer are estimated to be in the Lake District today.

The deer were once the wild aristocracy of the Lakes. The native deer is the red deer, which roamed the mountains and dales at the time of the Romans, giving not only their flesh for food but their horns for rough drinking cups and the like. Fine herds of red deer lived in Ennerdale, Wasdale and Eskdale as late as the seventeenth century, and their antlers are continually being found in the sands of the estuaries. Direct descendants of these herds still live in a wild state at Martindale, beside Ullswater, and wander over Helvellyn and also in other parts of Cumbria.

The Romans may have introduced the fallow deer to the Lakes, or perhaps it did not arrive until later. It was once very common, especially in south Cumberland and around the lower reaches of the Leven and the Kent, where, as in other parts of the country, it is still preserved in parks.

C.W.

Birds of the Fells

The characteristic birds of the upper fells are the birds of prey. And of these the raven is the patriarch. Ravens must have been common once, as you can tell from the many crags and hills named after them. There are not so many of them now, but they are holding their own on most of the central fells. I have watched one soaring (appropriately) over Raven Crag in Yewdale, high above the dale, circling lackadaisically, not seeming to be searching for anything, but merely taking a stroll through the air.

The golden eagle might also be seen. It nests in the eastern fells and has done so for twenty years. The smaller birds I know better. Chief among them is the wheatear, which flicks ahead of you as you walk, always keeping an eye on you but never flying too far off. It makes its call, clacking little stones together, and bobs its white rump, and though it lives quite high up the fells it is also common along the dunes on the coast. Two other birds which range from coastal level to the tops of the fells are the skylark and the meadow pipit, both of which tend to leave the highest reaches during the winter. The skylark is practically the only song-bird to be heard on the tops, and sometimes you have the unusual experience of seeing and hearing it flying *below* you in the air. As you get a little lower down the fellsides, where gorse appears and small thorn trees and rowans, there are more birds. The stonechat, so familiar in similar localities in the south downs, is not common, though you'll find it among the gorse of the dunes. In the hills this bird is replaced by the whinchat, a quieter, less dapper bird, which watches you with a supercilious, white eyebrow.

C.W.

Touching All Senses

The dipper belongs to about the same river sites as the grey wagtail. Its most characteristic appearance is on a stone or shingle in a quick-flowing beck, when it puts down its shoulders and butts into the water like a rugby player going into a scrimmage. It is also seen very often flying across lakes and tarns only a few inches above the surface.

There are also the game birds, red grouse and partridge, but the latter are restricted to cultivated land; and the plovers, the lapwing and the beautiful golden plover, especially on the limestone. All these belong more to the lower moors than to the fells. So too does the curlew. Its long note, like water gurgling from the mouth of a medicine bottle, is one of the loveliest of all sounds on the black moors above the coast. It is a sound that touches all senses – ear, eye, nose and skin – one with clouds and mists and the smell of young bracken. Curlews and lapwings are two of the birds which share winter and summer residence between the coast and the fells. In spring and summer there is nothing more characteristic of the moors and the scraggy fields below them than the creaking of the lapwing and its contortions in the sky. As you walk along the turf one pair after another begins to fratch and feint as you enter the nesting territory. But in winter the lapwing loses its love of solitude, and congregates in large numbers on the salt flats of the estuaries and in the marshy fields.

C.W.

The Gulleries

The most spectacular breeding places along the coast are the gulleries on the dunes, of which the best known is at Walney Island where lesser black back and herring gulls nest in large numbers, together with eider ducks and terns. At the Ravenglass gullery was one of Europe's largest black-headed gull populations – once estimated at 50,000 – but for now the gullery is finished, officially due to predation, but probably caused by a combination of factors.

C.W.

Wild Fowl

The Solway is a great haunt for the wild fowl, and so, too, is Morecambe Bay. Here you find enormous numbers of geese on the salt marshes – the pink-feet and the grey lag. But there are other species: barnacle-goose, bean-goose, brent-goose, and rarer visitors. It is astonishing how a bird so large and distinctively shaped as a goose can camouflage itself on a marsh where there is no cover. A gaggle of grey lag have been pointed out to me and I have had to stare for half a minute before spotting them. Even then they looked more like a flock of sheep, having the dirty-wool colour of sheep in the winter light, when marsh, mud and sand, sky and the distant hills are all grey or grey-brown. Swans also come to the estuaries and many kinds of duck. Birds of the open sea occasionally visit or are blown in by storms.

St Bees Head is the most popular spot on the coast for the true sea-birds. Here there is a double headland, built of sandstone, in great slabs and buttresses which provide protection for the birds and many ledges and shelves for them to nest on. There are razor-bills here, and guillemots, herring-gulls and kittiwakes. Cormorants roost, but have not yet been proved to nest. But Fulmar petrels do, and so do puffins. Here, until the middle of the last century, lived the Cornish chough, that red-legged crow, which clung on like the memory of the Celtic tradition long after the Saxons and the Normans had driven away the language.

C.W.

The Weather in View

The Wettest Village

The agent by which many of the changes in the landscape are brought about is the weather, and in particular the rain. And there is certainly a lot of it. Wordsworth admitted it long ago: 'The country, indeed, is subject to much bad weather, and it has been ascertained that twice as much rain falls here as in many parts of the island.'[1]

Seathwaite in Borrowdale is the wettest village in England, with 140 inches of rain a year. The Sty, above Borrowdale, has 165 inches. A mean average rainfall of 80 inches is common in the western dales, but when we get out into the central plain the rainfall is not much greater than that of the Midlands.

Moreover, as Wordsworth says: 'The number of black drizzling days, that blot out the face of things, is by no means *proportionately* great.'[2] When it rains, in fact, it rains 'yal watter'. No doubt the advertising committees of the holiday resorts in the Lake District will be able to prove that these towns enjoy more sunshine than most, but I remember many summers on the Cumbrian coast when huge clouds rolled up from the Irish Sea, day after day, and hung about the tops of the fells. In the sultry days of July the matting of cloud hangs across the sky, not black or threatening, but never thin enough to let the sun through. The sea is grey, like lead. Looking inland, the fells look flat and small, like a canvas backcloth.

Nevertheless, it is the climate which gives the Lake District much of its attraction. The aspect of the fells changes as quickly as the atmosphere, and the varying lights, the unexpected colours and the never-repeated shadows invent a new landscape every day. To quote Wordsworth again:

  Days of unsettled weather, with partial showers, are very frequent;

[1] *Guide to the Lakes.*
[2] Ibid.

Seathwaite

but the showers, darkening, or brightening, as they fly from hill to hill, are not less grateful to the eye than finely interwoven passages of gay and sad music are touching to the ear. Vapours exhaling from the lakes and meadows after sunrise, in a hot season, or, in moist weather, brooding upon the heights, or descending towards the valleys with inaudible motion, give a visionary character to everything around them.[1]

So, early on an autumn morning, you will see a fellside above a lake draped in gauze like a ballet dancer. As the sun gets up the gauze rolls itself into coils, so that the flanks and the summit of the fell are bare, but bundles of mist still curl and twist in the combes and valleys. And earlier, before the sun rises, or rather when it comes to the edge of the horizon and the fellside is still in the slant of the shadow but the air and the trees are gleaming, then the light seems to trill like birdsong, and the air is unimaginably clear, and for hundreds of yards the gnats and midges become visible, little glints of light, rising and falling, with the swallows among them.

C.W.

The Best Time of the Year

When the guide-books consider the best time of year for visiting the Lakes, they nearly always recommend a rainy month rather than a dry one. The clouds, mists, and moving vapours gave to the landscape a softness and luminosity like that of wash drawings or an aquatint, and it was in the form of an aquatint that many of the travellers imagined their ideal landscape.

L.

Local Storms

The Lake District has its own stubborn way of clinging to rain and storms while the rest of England is passing through a drought. Often in times of good weather, a sudden squall will arise over one or other of the lakes, making the shore trees creak and the water rock, and scaring the life out of holidaymakers who have taken out a boat for some quiet fishing. Coniston and Ullswater are particularly notable for such storms.

A highly individual and famous example is that of the Helm wind, which is experienced along the Eden valley below Cross Fell. I have never seen a Helm, but it seems to be characterized by a heavy bank of cloud resting along the Cross Fell range, while three or four miles from the foot of the fell a long roll of cloud appears parallel with the Helm.

[1] *Guide to the Lakes.*

This is the Helm bar. Often the bar is joined to the Helm at the ends, making an ellipse with clear sky in the middle. The wind rushes down the side of the fell till it reaches a point below the bar, when it suddenly ceases. The wind is cold and violent, sometimes strong enough to uproot trees and overturn horses and carts, and makes a noise which has been compared to that of a railway train. Yet, however strong it may be, there is no wind at all beyond the Helm bar, or sometimes a gentle breeze blowing *towards* it, as if to meet the Helm wind.

The usual explanation is that a cold, wet wind blowing up the long peaty eastern slopes of the mountains suddenly meets the warmer western air on the crest of the ridge, and behaves rather like water falling over a weir.   C.W.

Gigantic Storms

Now of all Lake curiosities it was the weather which most obviously suggested terror and tumult. We may reflect, ironically, that it still does, but while the modern holidaymaker grumbles about the rain, the Picturesque traveller gloried in tales of gigantic storms, floods, water-spouts and prodigious winds. It was the mild and temperate William Gilpin who set the fashion. In his *Observations* he tells the story of two storms – one at Brackenthwaite in the Lorton–Buttermere valley, and another at St John's-in-the-Vale – which have since gone roaring and rumbling through journal after journal and guide-book after guide-book. That at St John's-in-the-Vale, in 1749, had already been described by a Mr Smith in *The Gentleman's Magazine* in a manner suited to this spot where the very crags took on the shape and similitude of a medieval castle – turrets, buttresses and crenellations materializing like a geological ectoplasm out of the bare rock.[1] There had been, he says, much thunder and lightning in the hills beyond Skiddaw and at last 'the cloud from which the tempest proceeded' came against the mountain, splitting on it like a wave against a rock. The cloud divided into two halves, one of which 'discharged a great quantity of water' on the Carlisle plain, while the other passed over Threlkeld into St John's-in-the-Vale. Here it broke into a violent thunderstorm, or cloudburst, which ravaged down the side of the fells, turning all the little becks into cataracts that swept rock, scree and debris before them, uprooted trees, battered down walls, crushed cottages, and tore up the valley bottom like a bulldozer run mad. 'The inhabitants,' says Smith, 'who were scarce less astonished and terrified, than they would have been at the sound of the last trumpet, and the dissolution of nature, ran together from under the roofs that sheltered them, lest they should be

---

[1] This is the foundation of Scott's poem *The Bridal of Triermain*.

beaten in upon their heads, and, finding the waters rush down all round them in an impetuous deluge … such of them as were able climbed the neighbouring trees, and others got on to the tops of haystacks.'[1]

L.

The Moss 'Irrupts'

The celebrated 'Irruption' of Solway Moss was an odd affair, and we are lucky to have a dispassionate account of it from Pennant, who visited the district in 1772, the year after it happened. The Moss, as he describes it, consisted of some 1,600 acres, most of it quagmire or peat, and according to his theory it was really an under-surface lake of water or liquid mud covered by a crust of turf and moss which had grown thin because of continual digging for fuel. Then, in November, after several weeks of heavy rain, the lake swelled up and the crust broke. The flood seems to have advanced in a great slow-moving wave of mud, like the slow spread of lava from a volcano. A farmer, who discovered it, at night, thought at first in the darkness that his dunghill was moving. Then he realized what it was and warned his neighbours. The disgusting black flood slimed itself over 400 acres, gurgling and growling as it crawled along, so that families trapped in their upper rooms were left bewildered and terrified until morning. No human lives were lost, though numbers of farm animals were smothered, and one cow was saved only after having stood for sixty hours up to the neck in mud. 'When she was relieved,' says Pennant, 'she did not refuse to eat, but would not taste water; nor could even look at it without showing manifest signs of horror.'

L.

Snow

If the summers are moist, the winters are mild. Average winter temperatures in the dales are about the same as those of London, and the latter has much greater extremes. Heavy snowstorms are not common in Cumberland. Only as we get nearer the Pennines, in the Cross Fell, Shap and Sedburgh areas, do we often have heavy and prolonged snowfalls. The road over Shap is frequently blocked, and we used to hear of lorry-drivers stranded at remote farms, and we still hear of sheep being buried alive for days. But in the western fells the snow rarely lasts long – perhaps the salty air helps to melt it.

When the landscape is covered with snow it takes on a new appearance. The change in colour is not hard to imagine. Upon the

[1] From William Hutchinson's *History of Cumberland*, 1794.

whiteness of the snow are cast deep blue shadows, and the sunrise is red and golden and green. But the fells seem to lose their perspective on a grey snowy day. They look bigger, yet flat, too, and less solid. If there is no sun, the usual lines of the ranges are lost, and they become vague and strange. There is a khaki-coloured light which descends in the late afternoon and merges fell and sky together, and the sky seems heavier than the rock. When the sun comes out on the snow, and there is warmth in the air but no thaw on the ground, a mist forms, which clings so closely to the shape of the fells that they seem to have swollen during the night.

The tarns and reservoirs are usually frozen for part of the winter, and sometimes the larger lakes, but it is not often that these will bear from end to end. Probably the greatest frost recorded was that of 1871/2, which lasted for sixteen weeks, when every stretch of water was frozen. Again, in 1896/7, Windermere was covered with thick ice, and the railway company ran skaters' trips from London for six shillings return.

C.W.

Town Snow

One is always surprised by snow. The streets themselves looked surprised, holding their breath in an anxious hush – a hush which is perhaps the strangest thing about the snow. As you look at the street, seeing movement and hearing none, you feel as if an unnatural deafness had come upon you. Your eyes and your ears do not co-ordinate; it is very much like the sensation of a fever. The chimneys are bewildered, the roofs, slippery and uncertain. Dormer windows prick up their ears like terriers. The birds flop in the snow, learning to ski.

But the snow itself is completely without surprise. I survey it from my bedroom window and everywhere it is quite at home. It lies on the slates, unmarked except by sparrows; it swells and balloons over the edge of the launders. The roofs have lost their straight-line geometry of slant and perpendicular. The chimneys, hung with white soot, jerk up from a Moscow of onion-domed attics. Starlings, blundering among the chimney-pots, precipitate small avalanches over their tails. Jackdaws, trying to settle on the watershed of a roof, find themselves top-heavy and fly away, clacking like nutcrackers. The sparrows alone, with their urchin adaptability, have found their snow legs, and know already that today the street-bottoms are as safe as the air and that they run no danger from dog or bicycle.

The 'lum hats' of the chimney-pots are padded with white felt on the one side. A three-inch ribbon of snow, sideways up, is balanced on the telephone wires until, now and then, a bird lets on them, and ten or twenty yards fall like droppings into the street. The spire of St

Autumn gales, Bassenthwaite lake

Kentigern's, seen above the Banks, carries one elongated isosceles triangle of pure white from base to weathercock.

I push open my casement windows, making two carvings of snow tumble from the attic roof into the little balcony above the shop-window. The snow-plough has not yet been round, but already the street is trampled by the men going to work. No school-children so far, but I can hear the first faint scrapes and slushing of householders beginning to clean their pavements, and the sound is strange and hard to recongize in the almost silent air, seeming as if it came from a long distance, a country sound in the wrong place. Old Sprout, the greengrocer, banging the door behind him as he comes out of his shop, loosens half a cart-load of snow, which skids off his roof and pancakes on the pavement, missing his head by no more than a foot.

'Glory!' he says. 'Greenland's icy mountains.'

Half a dozen of Chris Crackenthwaite's apprentices pass down the street just as the girls begin to arrive at the market hall factory. At once there is a parabolic storm of snowballs. Headscarves, bootees, mackintoshes, and woollen gloves are whirled and scrimmaged together. The air glistens with screeching. Snowballs explode like white bombs on doors and lamp-posts. Girls, caught by the arm, have snow rubbed into their hair like salt into a herring. Three of them, catching a youth who is trying to push a bicycle through a snow-drift, tip him into the gutter and stuff his shirt with snow. Faces red as holly berries, mouths in a bubble of swearing, they dip and revel in the snow. The market clock strikes eight. Shaking the snow off their hair and coats, the girls skitter up the back stairs into the factory. The sparrows once more take possession of the street.

P.P.

Churchyard Weather

Today, it is not so much a thaw as an apology. The snow has lost all its self-confidence. It shuffles back from the pavements; it yields the road to the traffic. It hems and haws off the roofs; it squirms away from the touch of water. John Dodder, from his window, sees the allotments a mottle of white and green like Gorgonzola cheese. Violet Moss, looking down Furnace Road on her way to the grammar school, sees the slag-banks striped like a zebra. Miss Burns in Balmoral Road, at the foot of the hill of Old Odborough, finds a single crocus spiking through the snow, filing it as if it were an old letter. On the grass of the Jubilee pleasure ground the snow lies in a cold and embarrassed squiggle. Not even a dog wants to play with it now. The small children – of whom there are many about, for the junior schools are closed for the measles – kick their way contemptuously through it, refusing to recognize it as last week's friend. The cricket field wears a football jersey – parallel bars of ooze and snow marking the line of the drains. In gutters and spouts there is a drip and sniffle as if the houses had a bad cold in the head.

For this is churchyard weather. Nearly every morning the Catholic funerals process from St Joseph's to St Kentigern's, and nearly every afternoon the Protestants take their turn. The slow bell tolls more often than the town clock. It is as if the lives of the aged, preserved by the frost like fish in ice, rot away when the warmer air gets at them. This is the month when the vicar meets parishioners whom he never sees for the rest of the year. He walks across the graveyard in his thick pneumonia jacket. Wreaths are piled high over Mr Snoot, died in his armchair counting stars.

The melting snow dribbles off the sour daffodils – flowers forced in Cornish greenhouses to die resentfully on the graves of strangers. The bitter, unnatural yellow burns like acid into the dark evergreen of box and yew.

Under a sky as antiseptic as a scrubbed enamel bowl, 'flu, colds, and measles brew and bubble. Old Odborough School, in the quarry-like playground dug out of the slope of the hill, is fretfully empty. Violet Moss, ordered back home after fainting in the gym, skids and stumbles through the dizzy Market Square, where her uncle is setting off to deliver the morning papers, four hours late. Old Mr Sprout is staying in bed – if anyone wants taties they can go and dig for them. Dr O'Brien moves along Albert Road like a canvasser, calling at every other house, letting himself in by the keys left in the doors. Old Postlethwaite stands outside the cash chemist's, wrapped in layer after layer of clothing like a water-pipe lagged against the frost, morosely counting prescriptions he won't have to dispense. Christopher Crackenthwaite's top-hat becomes so familiar to the jackdaws at St Kentigern's that he's afraid they will start to build in it. The grave-digger complains that he is being worked to death.

P.P.

Enjoying the Weather

As the Lake District is one of the wettest parts of England, presumably most of those who come there are prepared to put up with a few wet days. But too many still believe that they need clear, bright weather before they can really enjoy themselves.

I blame photography for this. The photographer must have a clear atmosphere for most of his effects; he looks out for bold shapes, for sharp detail, and contrasts of light and shade. And those who first learn about the Lake District from photographs come expecting the real thing to be like that.

The travellers of the eighteenth and nineteenth centuries, on the other hand, learned about the Lakes from paintings, engravings and prints. They looked, not for precise detail and hard shapes, but for hints and ambiguities, for dimness and shimmerings and the golden glow of Claude Lorraine. There was a lot of stock romanticism in this attitude, of course, but it did equip them to enjoy the Cumbrian weather. Thomas Gray, for instance, came in October, one of the best of all months in the Lakes, when there is a cloudy, Michaelmas-daisy sky, and all the reds and browns and purples are toned down as if under a smudge of wood smoke. And there are quiet, dark, drizzling days in the dead of winter, when the evergreens seem to ooze beads of water, and the bracken sulks a deeper and deeper red the wetter it gets, and the besoms of the broom glow with a dark, intense green. A view, then, would be a distraction.

G.L.

Views: The Art of Seeing

Many people have lost the art of seeing what the countryside really looks like. They enjoy the fresh air, the sunshine, the space, the freedom and the view, but they no longer have the knack of seeing those differences of rock, soil and vegetation, of contour and texture, of methods of agriculture and styles of domestic architecture, even of the ways of building a wall, which help to make one dale so different from the next. Drop a Lakeland man, blindfold, anywhere south of Windermere, and, though he may not at once be able to tell exactly where he is, he will know, almost before he takes off the bandages, that he is not in Wasdale or Borrowdale.

G.L.

Sea to the West

You turn off the road by Whitbeck church (where, as my grandmother told me, they bury only the deaf and dumb) and take the rough road behind the farms until you reach the old Whitbeck mill, where you can get out on to the fell. The best time of the day is early evening, when the sun skims almost horizontally across the sea right into the cupboard of the gill; and the best time of the year is perhaps late summer. August is not usually regarded as an ideal month in the Lakes because of the drabness of the greens, but there is one week when the ling is in full bloom and the second flowering of the gorse has just started, and down by the beck the rowans are already top-heavy with berry. In the evening sunlight, the purple and lemony yellow and deep orange-red give a Celtic richness of decoration. The fellside leaps up, dizzying in height, though, from here, you can see nothing above the 1,000-foot contour.

The waterfalls – so little known that they haven't even got names – face you squarely, one above the other, like receding flights of steps. The water splashes and gurgles in the mosses; kestrels climb and wheel; the light pings off the crags. It is a scene which defiantly refuses to be turned into a beauty spot – as bold, as bare and as exhilaratingly open as any in Cumbria.

Yet it is when you look outwards that the view becomes the most Cumbrian of all, for you look across the down-like swellings of the shore to the sea and across the sea into the past of the county. To the north, disjointed like islands in the distance, are Cairnsmore of Fleet and the prominences of Galloway, and straight across is Man, the Celtic boss of the Irish Sea, Cumbria's Hebridean island. That is where the Celticized Vikings came from – the men who made the county and left their language shouting all around from beck, gill, force, scree and fell. You can hardly find, in the whole of the Lakes, any spot that combines more of the essentials of the county. Yet, 200 yards below, the motorists can be seen speeding along the new level, blithely unaware that there is anything in this stretch of the road worth stopping to look at.

G.L.

The Most Famous View

The man who goes to the dales goes there for more than scenery. The views are magnificent when he can get high enough to see them, but it is not the views that really concern him. It is the feel and smell of the place, the living company of the dale – the little crags jutting up like gateposts, the redstarts in the bracken, the Herdwicks rubbing themselves against a stile, the farm children throwing stones at an old bucket in the beck.

Yet, if you want views, the volcanic rock can give them. Wasdale is perhaps the most famous, looking up from the lower end of the lake where a shelter has been made by building two walls in the form of a cross: Yewbarrow, on the left; Kirk Fell, half-hidden; Great Gable, plumb in the middle; the lower Lingmell as a foothill to Scafell and Scafell Pike; and the screes, screening the picture on the right. It is Cumbria's classic landscape, shaped and arranged as by an artist. Indeed, it is shaped almost too perfectly. For the mountains of Wasdale resemble the Forth Bridge in that when you see them for the first time you think, immediately, how like their photographs they are! And you think, a moment later, that the view is not really new to you at all. It is second-hand – a copy of the earlier image you received from book or postcard. It is hard not to be disappointed, not to feel that the landscape is somehow lacking in spontaneity.

So that to see through your own eyes and not through the lens of a camera, you should walk, as it were, out of the picture. Turn your back

on the famous view just as you reach its climax, and twist left, along
Mosedale Beck between Yewbarrow and Kirk Fell. And in about a
quarter of a mile you will find yourself on the floor of an enormous
wash-tub of a dale, with the broken rim of Pillar and Wind Gap 2,000 feet
above you. Compared to the emptiness of this scene, Wasdale itself
seems as busy as a holiday camp.

P.L.

And the Most Famous of All the Famous Views

Of the high fells, Bowfell is rather less exploited by the photographer,
though it is surely the most graceful of them all – slender, conical,
concave, with an edge to it as if it were gimletting the sky. It is also, of all
the central peaks, the one most visible from a distance. Walking through
the streets of Millom, you turn a corner, and there, between the
gasworks and the Roman Catholic church, is Bowfell.

Perhaps the most famous of all the famous views is that up
Derwentwater, from Friar's Crag. Choose to see it, if you can, on a
winter day, with snow in the fells, and hoar-frost lying on the dead
bracken till the woods seem to be ferny with ostrich feathers. There will
be a thin cellophane of ice around the shores, but the centre of the lake
will be open. The eye skids across it to Borrowdale. One crag opens
behind another, unfurling like a metal rose, and beyond are Great End
and the Scafell range against the sky. It is not so solemn nor so
sculptured as the Wasdale view, but it is richer and more intricate,
ravelling the sight in a monkey-puzzle of peaks. If you take the road
beside the lake to Grange and Seathwaite, you will pass volcanic rock at
its most flamboyant. It is almost like a stage show with everything a bit
over-sized – an untidy tossing-about of rocks and trees, the fat,
complacent Bowder Stone, and a waterfall that in wet weather can be
seen three or four miles away gushing like a burst reservoir. Castle Crag
– the conical, inverted ice-cream cone of a hill which so delighted the
eighteenth-century painters – may even be a block of lava which has
cooled in the bottle-neck of an old volcano. In summer this is the most
populous of the dales, yet even the hundreds of cars, the coaches and
the tents cannot quite diminish its perspective. It remains gothic,
grandiose, pinnacled and continually astonishing.

Then, if you swing round on your heels at almost any point on the
eastern shore of the lake, there behind you will be Skiddaw, Catbells and
the fells of Newlands – the rounded, sulky hummocks of the older
deposits. There is no more demonstrative contrast between the Skiddaw
slate and the volcanic rock.

P.L.

Way to the Dales

The Old Roads

Many of the dale roads must have kept to almost exactly the same route for centuries. Not many years ago they still ran between the same walls, skirted the same rocks, and wound through the same gates to the same farms, often actually passing through the farmyards. Today, the main roads up and down the dales have become well-used tourist routes. The surface is good, the narrower places have been eased out, and the gates have mostly been replaced by cattle-grids.

To get some idea of the old dale routes we must leave the metalled roads and go on to the tracks which are now the possession of the walker – Sty Head or Walna Scar, to take two of the better known. It is important to remember that these were roads and not just paths – the normal routes for shepherds and pedlars on foot and for gentry and visitors on horseback.

P.L.

Pack-horse Bridges

After the Restoration, traders began to come to the dales in greater numbers – wool-buyers and weavers, tin and copper miners, colliers, import merchants from Whitehaven and smugglers from Ravenglass. They travelled with strings of ponies along the west coast and over the dale passes, and it was largely for them that the dale bridges were built – generally, though not quite accurately, called pack-horse bridges. Usually they are stone bridges of one sharply humped arch, with walls on either side and a narrow track between. Some were merely a clapper bridge of slate slabs laid from boulder to boulder across the beck. Slater's Bridge, in Little Langdale, combines the two forms, being half of it humped and half of it flat flagstone.

Few of the bridges are older than the eighteenth century but they have the timeless look of the rock. When they cross a shallow beck, heaving up from flat fields, they seem rather lonely and lost. But when

Birks Bridge, River Duddon

they are flung across a rocky cavern – as with Birks Bridge in Dunnerdale or High Sweden Bridge in Scandale – then they are as lively as the beck itself. The stones have a thick green pelt of spleenwort, wall-rue and rusty-backs, and the flood water froths up to the chin of the arches – at Birks the walls have little perforations, so that the water may pass over the bridge as well as under it during floods.

There is nothing archaic about these bridges. When carriages and heavier traffic came on the roads, it was easy to develop a stronger and wider bridge of the same pattern – that by the mill over Whelan Beck at Boot in Eskdale shows the transition to the new type. In fact, the single stone arch might well be considered by modern builders whenever a small bridge is needed. There is a good twentieth-century example just below the National Trust property around the Duddon Gorge, where it has replaced an ugly wooden structure. Here the newness of the slate has worn off, and the bridge gives a grand view of the boulders where weasels run, and of the hazels, rowans and oaks which dribble down the steep river-banks, changing greens like the water. It is a thoroughly practical piece of local workmanship, and, anyway, those who do not like it can use the stepping-stones a few yards lower down.

P.L.

The Shap Route

From the Ice Age almost to the present day the Lakes have remained divided and isolated – a difficult spot to get about in and a difficult spot to get *to*. They were also, and still are, a difficult spot to get past, for until 1971 there were only two ways of circumventing them, except by going as far east as Yorkshire.

The first was by Shap – the more familiar route to outsiders and one of great historical importance. Prince Charles marched this way in 1745 and afterwards retreated, followed by the Duke of Cumberland. For many years it was the main route from England to Scotland, both by road and rail. The road, on the Kendal side, swings up through rounded, bouncing, deeply dented, Pennine-like country, and descends to Shap village down a featureless, even slope, scratched and dusted by limestone quarries and cement-works, like a vast concrete ramp only half-overgrown with weed. According to the map it lies entirely in the former county of Westmorland, but it is really a segment of Birmingham or Glasgow drawn into a long moving chain. Yet from a café window or from a lorry-driver's cabin you can look down into clefts and dales and hamlets scarcely ever visited by a stranger – places compared to which the better-known Lake District valleys are like little Blackpools or Piccadillies.

Shap probably gets less snow than Bowes Moor, between Brough and the Great North Road, but it is open to freezing winds, blizzards and mist, and has patches as steep as some of the Lake passes with a dizzy drop at the edge. Lorries could lie for days, like abandoned tanks after a military retreat, while at the same time the roads along the coast had not even a whitening of hoar-frost on them. In 1970, however, the M6 motorway was extended north of Carnforth to provide an alternative to Shap.

P.L.

The Coast Route

The M6 is really a gigantic by-pass, and it is the coastal route which is the main approach to the Lakes and has had the greater importance in the lives of the people. But it is a very slow route. The railway, too, offers a slow journey, with magnificent views up the river-mouths, but also with many stops and much doubling back and shifting of direction. A traveller going from Ulverston to the north will find the afternoon sun shining on his right hand when he sits facing the engine. A traveller from Millom to the south will find, after about an hour and a half, that he is not one mile nearer London than when he set out – at a point between Grange-over-Sands and Arnside where the railway line lies in the same latitude as Millom. Along the coast, between Sellafield and St Bees, there is only a single-line track, and trains often have to wait in the little dune-side stations for other trains to pass. Many people from West Cumbria prefer to travel to London by Carlisle, and the Furness people to approach Scotland by Carnforth.

Yet for centuries the main stream of life in the district has flowed along the coast route. The Romans established a port at Ravenglass and the Norsemen arrived on that same coast. Medieval pack-horse trains passed up and down, crossing the sands of Morecambe Bay and the Duddon estuary. In the eighteenth century, the route was regularly used by travellers on horseback and in carriages, and as late as the middle of the nineteenth century there was a public service from Ulverston to Lancaster. Even after the railway was built, carriers continued to cross the sands bringing goods and passengers of the poorer sort. Herds of cattle and sheep were brought over the border from Scotland, or shipped to the Solway ports from Ireland, and driven along the coast to the slaughter-houses of Lancashire. Many, no doubt – cattle, sheep, horses and men – never got across. The quicksands are notorious and do not always stay in the same place. More dangerous still is the incoming tide, for the water can rise in the channels, making coils and knots round the traveller, while he remains unaware, because it is hidden from his sight in the deep, steep-sided gulleys. But once the tide has poured over the kerbs of the gulleys it can cover acres of sand or marsh in a very short time. One minute the traveller is out on a huge plain, the flat, wet sands all round, the coast far away. The low limestone rocks on the shore seem to pile themselves surprisingly high above him, walling him off from the world in a huge hollow. The tide rises an inch or two, and at once he is a mile out at sea, floundering about up to his ankles, and looking like St Peter walking on the waters. Then, unless he is a strong swimmer, he will find it hard to get back to the shore, for the gullies and the firm sand are hard to distinguish under water. Indeed, it might be best for him to stay quietly on his ridge of sand and hope that the tide will turn before it rises above his neck.

Yet in spite of the danger, the crossing of the sands remained for many years by far the most popular prelude to the Lake Tour. The danger, in fact, made it still more popular, for it added adventure to the trip, helping the travellers to see the Lakes as a place apart, almost an island, remote and strange. They viewed the bay from the ramparts of Lancaster Castle, and saw the fells arranged in an amphitheatre – it was a word they loved – from Black Combe round to Ingleborough. Then they embarked on the sands from Hest Bank and moved off into an amphibious, ambiguous world of mists and ripples and broken light on pools and gulleys. It was a landscape of archaic browns and greys, and the enormous glowing skies of Claude Lorraine – the kind of ideal country which the painters of two centuries had been dreaming about. When they landed on the shore they would soon come up against the hard facts of the Lake rock, yet out in the bay they could live on in the artist's dream.

P.L.

Dodging (some of) the Traffic

The trouble, of course, is that during the holiday months Lakeland roads are not empty of traffic, and many of them become so packed with cars that from above they look as if they were over-run with a plague of vari-coloured beetles. Then comes the demand for the road to be widened, but road widening inevitably means more cars and possibly coaches, so that the last state, like that of the man with the seven devils, is worse than the first.

As yet, most of the dale roads have not been bulldozed into concreteformity, and can still be enjoyed by a motorist who comes out of season. Best of all, for the pleasures of driving, are the roads along the more wooded lakes – Ullswater, Derwentwater (especially on the Barrow Bay side), Coniston (on the Brantwood side), and Esthwaite (on either side). Most of these do not run along the water-edge, but dodge round knolls and copses, approaching the water and sheering off, nosing up, sniffing and bounding away like a courting collie. The road and lake are in league with one another, yet the road is not assertive, you do not see much of it at a time, and from above it is scarcely to be noticed.

It is useless to tell many people not to come to the Lakes in the holiday season since that is the only time they *can* come. Luckily, the idea that all the roads in the district are swarming with traffic is not always true. Especially away from the main tourist centres, there are miles and miles of minor roads which are rarely discovered by the visitor. I have sat beside such a road on a Whit Monday afternoon – among some of the most agreeable volcanic rock in Cumbria, with ten miles of open sea on one side of me and ten miles of open fell on the other – and counted two cars in four hours. You can find many such roads in the smaller valleys which run down to the west coast or to Morecambe Bay, and in the country north of Skiddaw and that east of Kirkstone. Even in the busiest parts there are often alternative routes. A glance at a map, for instance, will quickly show that there are four roads from Cockermouth to Bassenthwaite, one of which is usually about as packed as Blackpool promenade. Yet the other three, even at the height of the season, often carry little traffic and are only a mile or two longer.

But it is from the old 2½-inch maps that the motorist can really learn how to dodge the traffic. Here he will find scores of small roads running up the side-valleys to remote farms and houses. With the help of these even someone who can walk only a short distance can reach some of the loneliest and wildest country in the district. Then there are the roads laid down for the Forestry Commission, some of which are open to the public, and there are also private roads to reservoirs, quarries, mines and the like, for the use of which permission will often be given. Of course you do not use such roads if your car is as wide as a bus, or if you are not prepared to stop and back when you meet a farm tractor or works lorry. The roads, after all, were made for the local people, not for the stranger.

P.L.

Mountain Passes

There are three passes which lead from the valley of the River Derwent to that of Buttermere or Lorton: Honister, from Seatoller to Gatesgarth; Newlands, from Portinscale to Buttermere Village; and Whinlatter, from Braithwaite to High Lorton. Of these, Honister is perhaps the finest of all the motorable passes in the Lakes. You climb rather blindly out of Borrowdale, seeing nothing much but a blank fellside in front of you, until, at a sudden twist, you find you are already at the top, threading through a cleft you had not realized was there. The youth hostel is at your side, and the Buttermere green-slate quarries are high above you on the ridge leading to Fleetwith Pike. The road now slithers down below the shoulder of Honister Crag with its long running sores of purplish scree, so that, if you leave it and cross Gatesgarthdale Beck by any of its accidental stepping-stones, you will find yourself at the foot of a slow-motion waterfall of broken rock. Fragments of scree and an overflow of rubble from the quarries seem almost visibly to slide apart and together again in a kind of creeping avalanche. And everywhere, among the rocks, you can see the typical fellside flowers: yellow tormentil, blue and white milkwort, eyebright, golden saxifrage and the alpine lady's mantle, deeply palmate and silvery with down.

Newlands, the middle of the three passes and the least frequented by motorists, runs along what used to be called Keskadale – a narrow desolate valley, which has much the look of those waterless troughs you sometimes find in the Pennine limestone. At the top of the pass the land flattens out for a short space, and you can park your car and look up at the feathery water-slides of Moss Force. Once over the watershed, you drop quickly, but Buttermere is hidden at first behind the flank of the fell, and you look back, instead, up the gill-like valley of Sail Beck below the precipices of Whiteless Pike and the Eel Crag group. It is Sail Beck, of course, which has made Buttermere, by washing down the acres of silt that have cut off the lake from Crummock Water. The division between the two lakes is only a mile long and frequently disappears under flood after heavy rain, yet the moment you descend to Buttermere village, beside the almost too neat church, you feel that this lake, this upper-dale, is secluded and self-contained as no other. On the east, the Skiddaw slates swell up in a row of rounded fells, solid as huge potatoes – Robinson, Whiteless, Grasmoor and Whiteside; while the western side is craggier – Red Pike, High Stile, High Crag and Hay Stacks, making a jagged wall unbroken for four miles except for the dips between peak and peak.

The eighteenth-century tourists admired Buttermere above all the lakes. The 'butter' implies that the lake lies in green pastures, and, in fact, the tourists saw it as another Eden, complete with an unfallen Eve, Mary Robinson, daughter of the landlord of the Fish Inn.

G.L.

Taking to the Hills

The motorist in a hurry on the bucking-bronco of a road from Gosforth to Silecroft and Millom must be exasperated to see – often only a hundred yards away – the dead level coastal plain along which the railway now runs. The reason why the road avoids this seemingly obvious route lies back in the Ice Age, for the retreating ice deposited a long, broken ridge of boulder clay and gravel along the line of the shore, behind which there developed a parallel trough of swamp and mud. And, since in pre-Macadam days mud was the traveller's worst hindrance, the road took to the hills. Eighteenth-century tourists praised the Lake District roads precisely because they were steep and stony and free from mud.

P.L.

Railways

Apart from the main lines by the coast and the narrow-gauge line in Eskdale, there were only four railways in the Lakes – the Workington–Penrith line, which passed along the shore of Bassenthwaite; the Foxfield–Coniston line; the Ulverston–Lakeside line, linking with the steamers on Windermere; and the Kendal–Windermere line. The first three of these are closed, the fourth still operates, and the private Lakeside and Haverthwaite Railway runs steam trains along part of the Lakeside line to the foot of Windermere. The harm done by such closures is immense. It isolates villages, throws still more traffic on to the roads, obliges the bus companies to run services along unsuitable routes, and forces the highway authorities to make improvements on roads which had better have been left as they were.

In the case of the Coniston line it is odd, now, to think how indignant Ruskin was when the railway was first proposed, for this line is so unobtrusive, so skilfully screened by trees, that you hardly notice it. By means of it you could creep right into the heart of the Lakes without the least fuss or hurry or effort. For forty years it was my regular way of approach to the central fells – setting off at the windy, sand-side station of Foxfield, and moving as if in a shallow trench between rocks and woods until Coniston Water appeared on the one side of the train and the Old Man on the other. When I travelled on this line on the day of its final run, in October 1958, I felt that the true road to the Lakes had been fenced off, even though you can make the journey by the other road in just about the same time.

P.L.

A Trip on the Ratty

Perhaps the easiest way to inspect Eskdale granite is by taking a trip on the Eskdale miniature railway, the 'Ratty Railway', which has a gauge of fifteen inches and was laid down in the 1870s to carry ore from the mines at Boot. Later it provided transport for the people of Eskdale and Irton and, after 1922, carried granite from the quarries as well as being an extra attraction for visitors. As local transport it has been entirely superseded by cars and buses, and in the later 1950s it seemed more and more likely that it would have to close down. In 1961 it was taken over by a railway preservation society, and since then has carried a record number of passengers.

The line begins not in Eskdale but in Miterdale, the small valley which lies between Eskdale and Wasdale. The sea at this point makes a three-pronged flank attack on the fells. At Ravenglass, where the three prongs (the Esk, the Mite, and the Irt) are joined on to the main shaft of the estuary, you will see scurvy grass and sea-plantain growing beside the heather, and the fishing-boats are drawn up as if the foot-hills were docks. The railway runs beside the salt marshes of the Mite and then climbs the slopes of Muncaster Fell. This is real granite country. It is on a small scale, like the railway, but everywhere there are chippings and crusts of rock which sparkle in the turf. The children cheer as the train runs under bridges or across becks. They lean over the edge of the trucks till you feel sure they will fall out. They snatch at ferns and the white frilly flowers of keck or cow-parsley, and if they are careless enough to snatch at the bracken they are likely to get their hands slashed by the sharp stalks. The train slows down in places, chugging up the inclines, and the rowans bend over it, almost knocking the chimney off the engine. There are wild roses and golden rod among the fern, so that if you like to take a risk you can jump out, grab a handful, and jump back into the train again. At one place the line passes near the quarries and you can see artificial screes of the pink rock. At Eskdale Green it finds a dip in the hill and enters Eskdale proper at a spot close to the route of the Roman road from Ambleside. It arrives, as it were, by the tradesman's entrance, behind the walls and hedges of back gardens, and hustles to the terminus at Dalegarth. The children get out, many of them being met by their parents who have driven up from Ravenglass by car. The Victorian visitors went without fail to see the waterfall in the deep, unkempt chasm of Stanley Gill, romantic as an old wood-engraving. Present-day visitors, educated by television, are more likely to go to see the Roman fort at Hardknott.

P.L.

An Old Canal

The old Lancaster Canal, begun in 1792 had the aim of linking Kendal to Wigan, though, in fact, it got no further than Preston. It did, however, link both Kendal and Lancaster to the sea, by an extension to Glasson Dock, and for a time, beginning in 1833, it ran an express passenger service, from Preston to Kendal and back. The boat held about seventy people; the fares were from four shillings to six shillings; and the time taken for the fifty-seven miles was about seven hours, the boat being drawn by two horses, changed every four miles. It must have been a good deal more comfortable than a journey along the A6. Today the canal is one of the most peaceful places in Cumbria – a long, curving, engineered lake crossed by innumerable, hump-backed, limestone bridges. Perhaps the deserted motorway will look something like that when we all take to the air.

G.L.

Man's Mark on the Land

Walls: The Basic Unit

Drystone walls are as familiar in Lakeland as are the mountains. They climb steep slopes, bulge over crags and cling to fellsides where none might expect it. Wallers back in the 1840s were paid 5s 9d for every seven yards they built. Today interest in the craft has revived a little.

The stone wall is the basic unit of Lake architecture. Cottages, farms, manor-houses and even villages are stone walls set together at angles and roofed over in parts. The walls were built mostly in the eighteenth or nineteenth centuries when labour was cheap, and they are falling to bits in this twentieth century when labour is dear. The farmer and the forester find it both cheaper and quicker to set up a new stake-and-wire fence than to repair an old wall. And as the holdings merge into larger farms, the great boundary walls of the open fellsides are no longer of any use, and will soon collapse into long rigs of heaped scree, and the art of walling with the unshaped stone will be forgotten. The art of walling with the shaped stone, however, is still widely practised. Many of the new walls along the improved National Park roads are of this kind, and though the stone looks raw it soon weathers comfortably into the landscape.

There is also another type of slate walling, less often seen and confined usually to the valleys, which consists of a fence made of large slabs of slate set up on end like thin tombstones, the edge of one just touching that of the next. These slates are not bound or fastened together in any way, though sometimes a thorn hedge is built close enough to give extra support to the stones. Such fences are seen in the Coniston and Hawkshead districts and speak of a time when the local people cared more for their own intake or kitchen garden than for the wild, unrentable fell-tops.

P.L.

Fell Walls

The fell walls do not look as if they had been built at all – they look as if they had grown, like the gorse or the bilberries. How they stand is a continual puzzle, for the stones are held together only by the force of gravity; no mortar and no soil. Yet they keep their footing and balance on the steepest slopes, climbing high over crags, even when there is an easy way round.

The walls often look as old as the stone circles, of the breakings of which some of them were built. Some mark a parish or a landowner's boundary; others record merely a not very successful attempt to win a few more acres from the fell. Many seem to have no purpose at all or a purpose forgotten generations ago. There is a road over Bootle Fell, from Duddon Bridge to Waberthwaite, by which the traveller can cut ten miles off the journey round the south of Cumbria. I walked it as a boy, when it was a turf track across the grey-brown moor-grass. Today there is a line of tarmac with good passing-places for cars. The road climbs and scoops through the sour, indeterminate moor – country as little worth enclosure, it would seem, as any in Cumbria. Yet just below the spot where the old Bootle Workhouse road forks off to the left, you find that you are fenced in by stone walls, so ancient, unrepaired and broken down that they look like ruined foundations revealed in an archaeological dig. The walls begin without apparent cause – the one on your right, as you descend, keeping close to the road, the other dipping to the banks of Kimont Beck. They come together again, accompany you on either side as far as Buckbarrow Bridge, and then fall away as inexplicably as they began. In front, or behind, is the empty fellside, and you feel that you have been walking through a dead age.

P.L.

Two in One

At Wasdale Head you see a splendid exhibition of drystone walling. For the whole of this dead-flat upper dale is divided by stone walls into irregularly shaped fields, one of which, not otherwise different from the others, contains the church and the graves of fallen rock-climbers.

The earliest drystone walls were built not of quarried slate but of cobbles gathered up when a space was cleared for cultivation. The biggest boulders were then merely rolled to the edge of what was to be the new field and left there to become the base of the walls. When the long, wandering walls that mark out farm and grazing boundaries began to be built on the fells, the wallers opened small quarries in the fellside and brought down the slate in sledges. As each section of wall reached the level of the quarry, they opened another quarry, higher up, to avoid

Stones and walls, Wasdale Head

the labour of carrying the stone uphill.

A well-built drystone wall is really *two* walls, side by side, each made of stones carefully fitted one to the other, while the gap is filled with rubble and small fragments. It is this loose filling which allows the wall to settle and adjust itself to any movements in the ground beneath. To strengthen the wall, the builders laid a row of flat slabs that cross through from side to side, joining the two outer walls together. Often there are two such rows of through-stones in a wall, sometimes three, and they may project at the side, making a ridge running the whole length of the wall which people sometimes think is intended as a kind of stile.

G.L.

Cottages

Lakeland cottages were not built for the sake of the view; nor were they built to be looked at. They were essentially homes, built to give shelter in what then was – and on a November night still is – a bleak and inhospitable climate. They are therefore as inconspicuous as possible. The farms of the upper fells squat and cower in the dips of little gills or corries – (the home of Wordsworth's 'Solitary' near Blea Tarn is a well-known example) – or huddle like a sheep close to an over-hanging rock. They are hewn out of the rock and the people who live in them are still, in a way, cave-dwellers. The walls are thick, doorways and windows low and deep-set. On the edge of the sandstone districts the roofs were once covered with huge sandstone flags, sometimes four feet square, but these have mostly been re-slated with the green stone of Honister or dark grey Kirkby Roundheads, though Welsh slates are to be found in the nineteenth-century industrial towns round the rim of the area.

In the dales, the cottages often stand toeing the road, with not even room for a hydrangea between wall and tarmac. Sometimes, where the road has been widened, a cottage will jut out like a bus which has got jammed, while at the old vicarage of Seathwaite in Dunnerdale, part of the outer wall of the ground floor seems to have been carved off to allow traffic to worm round the corner. Drystone walls do not always stand up very well to the tremors of traffic, for which reason – as well as for extra protection from the weather – many are now plastered or rough cast and whitewashed or colour-washed. Some of the ice-cream pinks and blues which began appearing in the district proved about as pleasant to look at as a half-sucked lollipop thrown away in a hedge. But in the Coniston district there used to be a shade of dark orange, less popular nowadays, which settles into the landscape like the colour of autumn oak.

P.L.

Farms

The farms are of any shape. The house may be stiff and angular, with three windows up, two and a door down, and chimneys sticking up at either end like a dog pricking its ears. In the seventeenth century they were usually only one room thick, and there are still some farms remaining where at least one of the rooms runs the full depth of the house from back to front. Some of the eighteenth-century buildings hide a certain Georgian elegance on the inside, and some have their entire front elevation tile-hung with local slates, like a perpendicular slate roof – e.g. Hesketh Hall at Broughton Mills near Broughton-in-Furness.

Some, such as the magnificent Coniston Old Hall on the banks of Coniston Water, retain the massive round chimney-stacks of the late medieval fortified manors – almost as massive as the pillars of Durham Cathedral, though built to hold nothing up. Nearly all have a porch over the front door – usually no more than two foot of wall jutting out on either side, with a little peaked roof on top, or perhaps one flagstone laid level across.

P.L.

Inns

Many wayside inns over the years have been converted into houses – the Black Lion at Oxen Park in High Furness is one example; Haltcliffe Bridge at Mungrisdale another, and there are many more. At the latter, there was no bar; the landlady carried pints of beer into a sparsely furnished room and it was supped at the fireside.

The older village inns are scarcely distinguishable from cottages or farms, and until recently, many of them *were* farms. In the eighteenth and early nineteenth centuries, when most people passed through the district on foot, there were many small and miserable farm-inns where travellers could get a pint of sour beer, a slice of bacon or a pot of porridge, and maybe a bed for the night. Most of them closed down years ago – as did Wordsworth's Dove Cottage which takes its name from the inn it formerly was. But those which still remain now find themselves caught up into the new tourist prosperity. Even in some of the more remote dales you can find village inns which boast of their wine list and offer a menu in French. No one is going to complain about the improvement in the food, but catering of this kind is a cosmopolitan profession, so that many of the smarter inns and hotels are being taken over by off-comers with little knowledge of the district and none of the local people. There is a famous story of a party of students who came to the Traveller's Rest at Ulpha and found an apparently uneducated

Wanthwaite Quarries, Helvellyn

landlord speaking an uncouth Cumbrian dialect. To pull his leg they sent him a letter in Latin asking for their bill, and were surprised to get it in Greek with a note pointing out the mistakes in their own Latin. Today the surprise would be to find a landlord who could speak the dialect.

Yet there still remain inns like the Woolpack at Eskdale which, in spite of all the comforts they can offer to the visitor, have not broken with the local community from which they sprang. In some of them the shepherds' meet is held once a year, and the dialect clicks across the tables in the bar-parlour and wrestling trophies hang beside the dart-board. Others – the Wasdale Head and the old Dungeon Ghyll in particular – have become the unofficial base of the rock-climbers, where you risk breaking your neck from falling over the ropes and boots which lie about the entrance.

P.L.

Country Houses

There are, of course, castles and pele towers in the Lakes which have become the dwellings of the wealthy, and there are old fortified farmhouses which have gone on being farmhouses and refused to become mansions. But the great house of Trollope's England and the stately home of ours is almost entirely missing from the dales. Instead we get those nineteenth-century country houses which were built for rich cotton merchants and the like to retire in. The style came from that of the more grandiose Victorian villa, and retains a likeness to it in the many gables, the steep-pitched roofs and the bay or turret windows. Brantwood – which Ruskin brought without bothering to come up to see it – moves towards the historical pageant with hints of a Highland fortress, while at Randy Pike near Hawkshead, once owned by a friend of mine, the style is so obstinately whimsical that a guest used to have to walk along a corridor, down the stairs, across the floor of the house, upstairs again and along another corridor to get to the bathroom.

Yet for all their period eccentricities such houses have grown into the scene because they have been given a skin-graft of native stone. Rock-like and lichened in walls and roof, and with their woodwork painted dark green – though, today, a dark red and a criminal metallic blue are often to be seen – they almost disapper behind the yews and firs and enormous haystacks of rhododendrons.

P.L.

Lowther Castle – and Lordy

Lordy, or Hugh Lowther, the fifth Earl of Lonsdale, kept up a fantastic scale of living. At his peak, his income was said to total almost £4,000 a week, which he spent with vigour.

Lowther Castle, the work of Robert Smirke, has been a roofless shell since 1956, like an enormous box-barracks for toy soldiers left out on the carpet after the children have gone to bed. It is set in miles of parkland, with huge, open swards and carefully sited trees, and commands the middle Eden over to Cross Fell. Even today it still calls all eyes to it by the sheer scale and impudence of its rhetoric.

But a Cumbrian brought up as I was during the Depression of the 'twenties, cannot but look somewhat ironically on that hollow façade with its back to the mines that made the money to build it. The Lowthers, of course, were well-established on the Cumberland–Westmorland border before the Norman Conquest, and for centuries played an important part in the politics of the North-west without, however, attaining the front rank in either power or wealth. In 1696 Sir John Lowther was made a viscount, but it was not until the middle of the eighteenth century that the family's fortunes began their spectacular upthrust. That was the time when Sir James Lowther of Whitehaven began to realize, more clearly than his predecessors, the vast potentialities of the local coal and iron. It was he who planned Whitehaven New Town, built his house at the Flatt (rebuilt by the next baronet as Whitehaven Castle) and then died, in 1755, one of the richest men in the country. His wealth went to another Sir James Lowther, the fifth Baronet and later first Earl of Lonsdale. This 'little contemptible Tyrant of the north', as his Whig opponents called him, had his henchmen all over the county and nine Members of Parliament in his pocket ('Lord Lonsdale's Nine-pins'), any one of whom might be ordered to apply for the Chiltern Hundreds if he did not vote as he was told. He had no pretensions to aristocratic grandeur, but he bought estate after estate until he made iron-ore mining in the old county of Cumberland practically a Lowther monopoly. Eventually he became the bugbear of local legend, was reputed to have the evil eye, drove through his villages at headlong speed and kept the embalmed body of his mistress in a glass-covered coffin.

When he died in 1802 the earldom died with him but was recreated in 1808, and it was the new earl who built the present Lowther Castle – a romantic folly which took itself far too seriously – and made handsome amends to Wordsworth for the first earl's miserly treatment of the poet's father. In spite of its blown-up magnificence, Lowther Castle was never really a home. The nineteenth-century Lowthers lived most of the year in London or the Midlands, fanatically devoted to hunting. 'William the Good', the first earl of the second creation, was, in fact, one of the pioneers of modern fox-hunting, and if Cumbria's reputation is to be associated with that miserable sport, we ought more properly to sing 'D'ye ken Lord Lonsdale' than 'D'ye ken John Peel'. Then, in the early twentieth century there emerged a new kind of Lord Lonsdale: Hugh

Lowther, the Yellow Earl, who survived several Victorian scandals, knocked out John L. Sullivan (at least, by his own account) and became Britain's ambassador of sport and perhaps the best-known English peer in the world. In Lordy's time entertaining at Lowther was about the chief source of employment between Penrith and Shap. He had his regiment of yellow-liveried servants, who observed among themselves precedence and protocol as strict as that of any eighteenth-century German court. He had his fleet of yellow motor-cars and his pack of yellow dogs. He flattened twenty farms to make his park the largest in England, and when the Kaiser stayed at Lowther in 1895 hundreds of rabbits were let loose in a nearby fir-wood so that the imperial guest could have an easy shot. Finally, in his old age, with cigar in mouth and gardenia in buttonhole, he became a kind of Coniston Old Man of Lakeland sports, patron of hunting, hound-trailing, wrestling and fell-running, whose annual visits to Grasmere were welcomed like those of royalty. And outside Cumbria scarcely one in a hundred of those who were familiar with his name and appearance connected him with the collieries of Whitehaven or the iron-ore mines of Millom.

G.L.

The Felling of the Forests

By the time the Ice Age had entirely given way to the present temperate climate, the climax vegetation of the dales was a thick oak scrub, mixed with chestnuts and some other deciduous trees.

The first men in the Lakes lived above the tree-line on what are now bleak moors. But as the hunter gave way to the agriculturist, and as flint scrapers gave way to axes which would cut wood, men began to fell the trees.

No doubt the process was very slow. Medieval Cumberland still had three great forests – Inglewood, Allerdale and Copeland – and, though the term forest meant not necessarily woodland but land enclosed for the protection of game, Inglewood, at least, was well wooded and famous for its timber. In the Lakes proper, an early result of the felling of the woods was that the dale-bottoms became habitable and soon proved to be fertile. After all, thwaite, a clearing, is about the commonest of all elements in our place-names.

But the success of settlement in the dales led to further felling which brought about a further result. For the land lost its annual supply of leaf-mould, it lost protection from wind and frost, and, above all, it lost the reinforcement of tree-roots which had bound and knitted the soil together. The valley sides and the lower fell-slopes were exposed to sun, wind, frost, rain and the scouring of the sykes and becks. And then, as if to speed up this process of erosion, the dalesmen took up sheep-farming.

As far as the landscape is concerned, sheep-farming has been almost as destructive as the Ice Age. Sheep crop very closely, laying bare the surface to all the agents of erosion. And what is worse, they extract the minerals from the soil, transferring them into the wool instead of repaying them in the form of manure as the other animals do. The result of centuries of such impoverishment and erosion is that land which once could nourish oaks is now good for nothing but bracken.

P.L.

Forestry

The Forestry Commission strives now for a more natural look in its planting. Norman's criticism of the dead blackness of Whinlatter is being answered, for replanting has changed much of the forest's nature. The trees are more varied, with open spaces built in, especially along the becks. At Bassenthwaite, too, much has improved.

The Forestry Commission's main aim, of course, is not the conservation of the soil but the economic production of timber. Yet its effect on the soil – and indeed on the whole life and scenery of the Lakes – is likely to be great and has already caused much controversy.

First of all, the commission agreed not to buy land in the centre of the district, leaving free the main mountain block and the dales in which lie Derwentwater, Crummock, Ullswater, Grasmere and Rydal. Its older properties are in Ennerdale, around Whinlatter Pass, on the spurs of Skiddaw above Bassenthwaite, and in upper Eskdale around Hardknott. It has carried out planting in lower Eskdale, in Dunnerdale, in Yewdale, and all along the moors between the eastern side of Coniston Lake and the Rusland valley. It was, in fact, the planting in Dunnerdale and Eskdale which aroused the greatest opposition, especially from that fiery Friend of the Lake District, the late H.H. Symonds.

The chief objection was to the planting of conifers, not to hardwood or deciduous trees. The commissioners, therefore, agreed to plant hardwood whenever they can, but this is rarely possible on the land which they own. On the wetter moorland and fellsides the dark, unvarying Sitka spruce seems about the only tree which will grow profitably.

The earlier plantations did confirm the fears of the objectors, for the trees were planted regularly, in straight rows, so that it looked as if the mountain-slopes had been combed. The planters often left wide rides (intended, no doubt, as fire breaks) which climbed vertically, in a dead straight line, for hundreds of feet, as if a mad barber had run his clippers up the fellside. This patchy, angular, green-tartan effect became particularly obtrusive in the plantations on both sides of Bassenthwaite Lake.

Then, again, some of the spruce plantations, such as those around Whinlatter, had a dead blackness beneath their boughs which turned the stomach like a charnel-house – a blackness quite different from the cathedral gloom of the limestone yew-woods, which are equally dark but not dead. The trees, crammed together so that not a splinter of sunlight skewered through, seemed to be dying as they grew the lower boughs already brown and withered with a poisonous compost-heap of dead needles lying about the roots. There was no undergrowth, no bramble, no cherry or other berried tree, practically no bird life, and not a sound to be heard.

But the commissioners seem to have learnt a lot from these earlier mistakes, and much of their later planting has been planned with the skill of a landscape gardener. Instead of setting the trees in squares and rectangles, they let the line of planting follow the natural line of the contour. On the Hawk, for instance, a 600-foot hill in the Lickle valley above Appletreeworth Beck, the conifers surge up and break in a curving wave against the outcrop of the rock. The darker green of the trees has taken the place of the lighter green of turf, but the pattern of the fellside is otherwise unchanged.

Again, instead of planting acres upon acres of the same tree – like vast rolls of coconut-matting laid across the fells – they began mixing their species. They planted spruces and firs, with here and there some oak and birch. The differing blue-greens and grey-greens and yellow-greens give a pleasant variegated look to the fellside, especially when the trees are planted in irregularly shaped clumps with a border of oaks or birches along the edges. In mid-Duddon, along the mile or so below Troutal, the commissioners have planted the slopes as imaginatively as Capability Brown, setting mixed conifers and hardwood apparently at random along the outcrops of crag and scree, and making the river banks into a wild garden – a rockwood, in fact.

Above all, they are planting larch. I do not know what the commercial value of larch wood may be, but many new larch woods have sprung up, both on the land of the Forestry Commission and on private estates. Of course, you may call the larch a foreigner if you like. Wordsworth, in his *Description of the Scenery of the Lakes*,[1] scornfully attacked all who planted the tree, calling it 'less than any other pleasing', 'disagreeable' in spring and 'spiritless' in autumn:

A moment's thought will show that if ten thousand of this spiky

---

[1] First published in 1810 as an introduction to the Rev. Joseph Wilkinson's *Select Views in Cumberland, Westmorland, and Lancashire.*

tree … are stuck in at once upon the side of a hill, they can grow up into nothing but deformity.

But, surely, Wordsworth was wrong, and the larch, though not indigenous, has made itself thoroughly at home in the dales. Its April green is the quickest among the fells, stinging one into an awareness of spring as it gushes up the gills like a backwash of the beck. In winter its chalky-yellow or near-purple smudges a softness over the diamond-blue hardness of the rocks. And no other tree smells so strongly of Easter.

The real importance of afforestation is that it is an attempt to slow down the process of erosion and the improverishment of the soil, and also to keep the district economically alive instead of letting it become entirely dependent on the tourist.

P.L.

Industry in the Lakes: Slate

If you look in the villages of the district you will find that often they have grown up, not around farming or marketing, but around some local industry. Mining became the most important of these as early as the reign of the first Elizabeth, with centres at Keswick and Coniston, and though it shifted to the coast in the nineteenth century its place was taken by quarrying. Flakes of Langdale, Tilberthwaite and Kirkby Moor were hammered on to the roofs of hundreds of thousands of houses in the industrial north, and the demand gave a new prosperity to villages like Chapel Stile and Coniston. Many of these quarries are now closed down, though without anywhere creating those battlefield landscapes or rubble and ruin which are found in the old quarrying districts of Wales. Cumbrian slate is still in reasonable demand, however, not only as local building material, but also as a handsome stone-facing which can be used most effectively in modern architecture. Stone from Broughton Moor has been exported to Australia and some of it was used in the new Coventry Cathedral.

P.L.

Quarries

Small abandoned quarries abound in Lakeland and examination will often reveal where the stone was used – a road, a wall, a cottage, perhaps even a church nearby. At the century's turn, stonebreakers sat on sacks in the hollows knapping rock for roadmaking at 16 shillings or so for a seventy-hour week.

The quarries which provided the stone for Lakeland walls do not mar

Kirkstone green slate

the landscape in the least. From a distance they look like the scars on an old man's face; close at hand, they are as charming as any natural gill or grotto. I am thinking not of the large commercial quarries but of small fellside pits dug to give a farmer stone to build a byre or a wall. There are scores of them, all over the district, abandoned and mostly half-full of water. Sometimes, near the farms, they are used as shelter for a fowl-house or a dump of swedes. But sometimes they are on a steep slope, so that, when one side of the quarry is level with your feet, the other is high above you, the walls sloping up and round like the shovel which grocers once used for weighing out sugar. The rock is dark and thorn trees bend over it, making it darker still. It may be quite bare or it may be festooned like the Hanging Gardens of Babylon with spleenworts and lichen and hairy bittercress. If the quarry is open to the sun, there may be the white buttercup flowers of crowfoot floating on the water or even grass of Parnassus in the mud. If there is soil on the ledges, there may be the bush-like tutsan, or St John's wort, the fruit of which begins as a bright yellow bead and ripens to almost black. And even if there seems to be no soil at all, there will still be brambles, clinging on, black-green or red, throughout the winter.

P.L.

Kirkby Roundheads

The largest slate quarries in the district, indeed in the north of England, are in the Silurian rocks at Kirkby-in-Furness. The rock is very strong and durable, known to architects as Westmorland blue slate – though it comes, now, from Lancashire. Locally it is known as Kirkby Roundheads, which is the name inevitably given to all local cricket and football teams and the like. It is dark bluish-grey, rather a dull colour, and not, as you would think, a very exciting covering for houses. It makes you think of grimy, long streets in industrial towns. But when you have seen these slates, seasoned and purpled by aged, dripping with rain, or steaming and faintly lilac under the winter sun, you will agree that they are not without beauty.

As building material none of the Lake District slates can compare with sandstone or limestone for variety. Nevertheless they are more colourful than is often thought. When the slate has weathered it often shows veins and crusts of mineral, green or brown or red, so that a street of houses, generally thought of as dark blue or grey, is seen, when the stone is dry and the sun clear but not too strong, to be dusted over with reddish-gold like a tiny fungus, or like pollen on willow catkins.

C.W.

Mining in the Fells

Mining has a long history in the Lake District. The Celtic tribes dug for copper. The Romans knew of the presence of copper, lead, zinc, iron and silver. By the end of the sixteenth century German miners were well established at Keswick, and furnaces were smelting ore mostly from the mines of Newlands, but also from Caldbeck and Coniston. Elizabethan Keswick was a busy, cosmopolitan industrial town, noisy with quarrels in three languages and with brawls between Cumbrian and foreign workmen until the latter married Cumberland girls and became Cumbrians themselves.

The main ores of the district were copper, haematite, blende (producing zinc) and galena (lead) – while the Goldscope mine in Newlands has produced some gold. Lead alone has been of any importance in recent times, and there was some post-war development at the Greenside mine at Glenridding, though this was closed in 1961, after having been used during the previous year by the Atomic Energy Authority for experiments in the detection of underground explosions. Commercially the most important deposit still being worked in the inner lake area is not a metal ore but the diatomite in the bed of a former lake at Kentmere – a deposit composed of the remains of the minute water-plants called diatoms. Barytes or heavy spar (sulphate of barium) has also been obtained in recent years from a number of small mines, mostly in the Caldbeck Fells and at Force Crag at the head of Coledale near Braithwaite.

Before the invention of gunpowder, mining was a very difficult operation. The miners of those times – almost mythically called the Old Men – worked like explorers in the dark, cutting openings just big enough to get through, prospecting for themselves, and in some cases raising ore on their own account and paying only a 'tribute' to the landowner. Local folklore is full of stories of miners who found rich deposits of ore, revealed to them by the fairies or the devil. Sometimes they made secret little hoards in a cave or tunnel, saving up for their old age, and then perhaps died before they drew out the balance, leaving it for future generations to find.

P.L.

Bombshells and Cannon-balls

Even after the introduction of gunpowder, mining among the fells reminds you of the enterprises of the Merchant Adventurers. Methods were so crude that any mine was a gamble. One after another failed, changed hands, was let go derelict, then opened again. More recent miners have found valuable ores in the rubble left by the Old Men, and from time to time there is speculation about the practicability of reopening some of the mines.

Mining among the fells falls roughly into four districts – the Caldbeck district, the Keswick district (including mines in Borrowdale, Newlands, Thornthwaite above Bassenthwaite, and Threlkeld below Saddleback), the Helvellyn and Ullswater district, and the Coniston district.

The galena found in the district is usually rich in silver, yielding up to 25 ounces a ton when smelted. £4,000 of silver was extracted from lead in Cumberland and Westmorland in 1909.

The chief source of lead in the county has been not the fells but the district round Alston, in the east of the county, on the Northumberland border. These mines were certainly worked in the twelfth century and were known then as the Carlisle Silver Mines. They were so important that the miners were given special privileges (such as the right to cut as much wood as they liked for smelting), which they claimed with great tenacity.

Besides these fairly widely distributed ores, there is tungsten in the Caldbeck Fells, and the famous graphite or plumbago mine, near Seathwaite, in Borrowdale. This, before it was worked out, was one of the wonders visited by tourists (including Thomas Gray). The wad, or blacklead, is a black shining earth, found in sops or pipes of various sizes. A deposit found in 1803 yielded 31¾ tons, worth then about £100,000. It was used in the eighteenth century for casting 'bombshells, round-shot and cannon-balls', and was so valuable that guards were set round the mine, and the miners were stripped and searched when they left work. Later it was used for the lead pencils manufactured at Keswick.

Besides these ores in the fells proper, the surrounding lowlands offer gypsum, magnesium limestone, fireclay, shales and clay for brickmaking, and, of course, iron and coal.

Of the fell mines Coniston is probably the oldest, having been worked, it is thought, on and off for about two thousand years. In the middle of the last century it employed hundreds of men and boys, but then declined and was closed down before 1890. What remains of the building became a youth hostel. The choice was a happy one, for the hostel lies in a sort of combe or scoop between the Old Man and Wetherlam, looking down to the lake. Wise walkers will approach it over the shoulders of the fells from Dunnerdale or Langdale or Tilberthwaite, instead of making for the village and then having to face a 1,000-foot climb at the end of the day. The choice is happy, too, because the old mines of the Lake District have become romantic. Whatever dangers and handicaps the Old Man may have had to face, we now feel a great attraction to these little tunnels and caves, where the wounds are already healing and the bones knitting together. The old buildings, always of slate, have been sliding back to scree again, the underground springs have found new runnels in the empty levels, and lichen and gorse, or, lower down, blackberry and rowan, have been closing the mouths of the shafts.

C.W.

Doffed caps

When my father started work in the 1890s Odborough was in its first full urban prosperity, drawing wealth from one of the most wonderful deposits of haematite iron ever discovered. Its social hierarchy, however, was still largely rural. The town children doffed their caps to the squires from the country as they drove by in trap and gig. The shop assistants bowed to them, even when they did not pay their bills. The very bosses at the mines pretended to be country gentlemen and wore tweeds and judged at the agricultural shows. In such a society, as in that of Jane Austen's day, it would seem that tradesmen could find no honourable place.

P.P.

The Iron Trade

The name of Force Forge in the Rusland valley reminds us that man's mark on the area is not entirely agricultural, for these southern dales were one of the earliest centres of the iron trade. At first this was on a very small scale. The ore was smelted by charcoal and, since it seems to have been easier to take iron to the woods than charcoal to the mines, the first bloomeries sprang up along the shores of Coniston and in the valleys of the Duddon and the Crake. By the seventeenth century large furnaces were being built, together with small forges, and could be found at Coniston, at Cunsey Beck, close to Windermere, at Ulpha in Dunnerdale, at Hackett, near Colwith on the Brathay, at Burblethwaite on the Winster and at Low Wood and Backbarrow on the Leven. Yet, in spite of all this enterprise, methods of manufacture remained rather primitive and lagged behind those used in some other parts of England.

In 1711, however, a group of Cheshire ironmasters decided to take advantage of the Lake District's potentially large supply of charcoal by setting up a more modern furnace at Cunsey on the west shore of Windermere. Local industrialists responded with enormous spirit to this challenge from the off-comers, and four of them immediately founded the Backbarrow Company, where they were to introduce the most advanced smelting techniques of the time.[1] Two and possibly three of the four were Quakers, and their society gave them valuable links with

[1] See J.D. Marshall, *Furness and the Industrial Revolution* (Barrow-in-Furness, 1958).

other iron centres at Bristol, Warrington, Lancaster and Whitehaven, so that the Backbarrow furnace soon became one of the most successful and forward-looking in the north of England.

Similar furnaces were established at Nibthwaite and Penny Bridge on the Crake, at Leighton near Arnside, Newland near Ulverston, and Duddon Bridge. At Lindale a small foundry was set up by Isaac Wilkinson and his son, the great John Wilkinson, who also had a share in the Low Wood ironworks at Haverthwaite, which was later to be the site of a factory producing gunpowder for the local mines and quarries. Eventually, as the Industrial Revolution rolled on, coke replaced charcoal, and the eighteenth-century plants closed down – even Backbarrow, which, for a while at least, remained the oldest working ironworks in Europe.

G.L.

The Greatest Discovery

In Furness, many of the pits were working in the eighteenth century, supplying ore to the charcoal furnaces of Backbarrow and nearby valleys, though it was the opening of the Furness Railway in 1846 which really started the boom. To begin with the railway was as local as the Eskdale Ratty Railway. The first section ran merely from Dalton to Barrow, with links to Kirkby and Concle on the Walney Channel, but soon afterwards the small Roa Island was connected by causeway to 'the neighbouring island of Great Britain' so that the railway could reach a deep-water pier. In 1847 the line was extended to Broughton, and in 1854 to Ulverston, but it was not until 1857 that it was prolonged across the bay to meet the main Lancashire system at Carnforth. Before that time, almost the main purpose of the railway was to carry ore to the port of Barrow for export to South Wales and elsewhere, though there was also a passenger service, with connections by steamer, across the bay, bringing tourists from Fleetwood to spend the day at Furness Abbey. Even rolling-stock and locomotives had to be brought by sea – one of the latter, known to everyone as Copperknob, stood for many years just outside Barrow station, like an antique clock in a glass case.

Before the boom, mining was centred on Dalton and Lindal, and it was the coming of Henry William Schneider, an iron merchant and industrialist of Swiss descent, which changed this as it changed so much of the face of Furness. It is said[1] that Schneider was on a visit to the Lake District in 1839 when he was shown a small iron mine near Askam. The following year he took out a lease of the mining rights at Park, near the

---

[1] See J.D. Marshall, *Furness and the Industrial Revolution* (Barrow-in-Furness, 1958)

shores of the Duddon estuary, in the royalty of the Earl of Burlington. With three other partners, he founded the Furness Company and built a jetty at Barrow to ship the ore. For ten years they had next to no success at Askam, though they did fairly well from an older mine at Whitriggs near Lindal. Then in 1850, when hope had almost been given up, the company decided to prospect once more at a site which had already been tried and abandoned. And so, in October 1850, there was made the greatest discovery of haematite iron-ore then known to British mining history – a continuous mass, 200 yards by 300, of between 8 and 9 million tons of finest quality ore. A few years later even this was surpassed by the finds at Hodbarrow, but by that time the Furness annual output of ore was already greater than that of all West Cumberland, and Barrow was at the beginning of its long career in iron and steel.

The story of the rise, prosperity and decline of the Furness iron industry is full of over-life-size Victorian personalities, stiff, ruthless, yet, in their own way, benevolent and far-seeing. It is as if the statues had stepped down from their plinths in the Barrow streets and were striding about a still empty countryside, casting around them mining-shafts, quarries, blast furnaces, railway stations, workers' houses, schools, churches and even town halls.

G.L.

Hodbarrow Mines

At Millom, where the iron emerges on the coast, the landscape takes on a salty taste, and the limestone is yellowed and gritted with sand. The magnificent Hodbarrow mines were the foundation stone of the town in which I was born – though, oddly enough, that stone (i.e. limestone) does not show itself anywhere in the streets, for the houses are built almost entirely of slate. The mines lay a mile or so away on the promontory which acts as the southern kerbstone of Cumberland county. The first shaft was sunk at Towsey Hole, at the exact point where the rocks grapple with the tide. When I was a boy my dog chased a rabbit and fell down the shaft, to crawl out again, cut and bruised but otherwise unhurt. Nearby is a ruined windmill, used as an office in the early days of the mine, and not far away is the first lighthouse, built on the limestone pavement – as full of fossils as Cumberland cake is full of currants – which shelves down to what was then the shore.

But as more ore was detected, that shore was slowly pushed backwards. A sea-wall was built to keep out the high tide, and, later, when ore was discovered beneath the sea, another wall was thrown out in a great arc of a mile and a quarter stretching from Hodbarrow Point to Haverigg. Finally the older wall cracked and collapsed like the Great

Wall of China as the land caved in over the abandoned workings.

P.L.

Blast-Furnaces

The modern haematite pig-iron industry did not begin in Cumberland until the middle of the last century. In 1841 blast-furnaces were opened at Cleator Moor – a strange town, which sprang out of the bare rock into sudden prosperity and remained, chained to the rock like Andromeda, long after that prosperity had been blasted away. In the next decade furnaces were set up at Seaton, Harrington and Workington, and (in Furness) at Barrow. The trade expanded in the sixties and seventies, spreading to Distington and Maryport in West Cumberland, to Millom in the south, and to Ulverston and Askam in Furness.

Workington and Barrow have become large industrial towns, standing rather apart from the fells. Millom retained to the end the smaller scale of the nineteenth-century furnace, and stood within shouting distance of the western fells, the last conspicuous sign of a 2,000-year-old industry.

There could be no argument about its conspicuousness, at any rate. The works were sited on a peninsula which almost shuts up the mouth of the Duddon. At high tide they advanced into the middle of a sea-loch, and were visible from Scafell, Scafell Pike, Great End, Harter Fell in Eskdale, Crinkle Crags, Bowfell, Grey Friar, Dow Crag, Coniston Old Man, and from some points on Kirkstone. Seen from the hills between Broughton and Coniston, they made a fine, swinging climax to the estuary, trombones, tubas and euphoniums marching out at full blare. If the oakwoods are what the botanists and ecologists call the climax vegetation of the dales, then these ironworks were the climax industry of the coast.

But, as with the oakwoods, it is a climax which has been passed. For the method of producing steel from iron ore by the intermediate process of pig-iron was gradually being superseded, and the Millom ironworks were closed in October 1968, bringing heavy unemployment to a town which had relied on iron for a hundred years. The empty shell of the old furnaces and the unsmoking chimney-stacks had a pathetically archaic look about them. Small, isolated, blasting defiance at the fells, they belonged to the Heroic Age of Lake industry.

P.L.

A Crop That Exhausts

Norman was ahead of his time when he urged the preservation of industrial sites. Times have changed. Today throughout Britain just about anything with historical pretensions is smartened up, labelled and preserved.

I have often thought that the National Trust ought to preserve some typical examples of the landscape created and shaped by industry and then deserted: abandoned ironworks and slag-banks, old clay pits, old quarries, old lead workings, decayed ports and wharves, brick-fields, gravel-pits, broken-down factories and warehouses, derelict collieries, and worked-out iron-ore mines. It is not just that all such places have an obvious romantic charm, with their reminder of mortality and of the vanity of human wishes. It is rather that they give a glimpse beyond the scale of history; they set man in the greater perspective of biology and geology, of the prehistoric and post-historic processes of nature. Here, in the flashes among the slag-banks, or in the rubble-heaps of collieries, we can see nature fighting back, recolonizing the former enemy-occupied territory. It is not a ruin, but a renaissance.

And of all these types of industrial landscape, that of the iron-ore mines is by far the most agreeable both to the eye and to the nose. There is no dirt about iron ore. It comes to the surface in clean lumps, about the colour and size of a pickled cabbage. It has neither the deadness of slag nor the grime of coal. In many ways iron-mining is very like agriculture – a root crop, deeply dug, the harvest of which is stored like huge clamps of turnips or mangold wurzels. But it is a crop that exhausts. After the first gathering the land lies fallow for ever.

P.P.

Charcoal Burning

The reek of smoke from the charcoal burners' pitsteads once stole through many a Lakeland wood. Today sturdy trees grow where the burners toiled, and scarcely anyone remembers the skills of the trade.

In Low Furness the early blast-furnaces or forges depended on charcoal. So that in nearly all the little valleys running down to Morecambe Bay there grew up a colony of woodcutters and charcoal burners (Ashburner is a very common name in the area), together with small saw-mills, usually driven by water-power. And beside the saw-mills there sprang up bobbin-mills, worked by water to supply the cotton trade of Lancashire. As a child I found something strange in the idea of bobbin-mills, as if they might be run by gnomes or dwarfs, so that when I heard that there were bobbin-mills at Ulpha in Dunnerdale I was quite ready to believe my father when he assured me that there were treacle mines there too.

P.L.

Swills

The best of these extremely practical baskets were made out of hazel and oak. In the old days the swill-makers steamed them into shape; today the few that are made are usually whittled.

The swill is large and oval, shaped like a coracle, and made entirely by hand. There is an upper rim formed of the branch of a tree, about a thumb's thickness, and usually with the bark left on. The body of the basket is made of strips of wood, two inches wide at the centre, plaited in a pattern of elliptical curves. The whole is not nearly so heavy as might be expected, and gaps are left as handles at either end of the rim. It is, however, very strong. If you threw it out of a second-floor window the road would more likely be damaged than the swill. You can lift heavy weights in it – potatoes, logs, coal – and the farmers use it to carry turnips to the sheep in winter. Their wives use it for washing, and there can be no more serviceable clothes-basket than a swill, for whichever way you put it down it swings on its round bottom and rights itself like a loaded chessman. It stands up to wet and wear and has the beauty of simple shape which you find in toadstools and stones.

C.W.

Stone Circles and Crosses

The Megalith Builders

For me, only one sign is written clearly on the landscape of early times –
that of the great stone circles.

The people who built them came from France and Spain, arriving in
our district some time between 1800 and 1500 BC. They came by sea,
spreading along the south-west coast of Cumberland, and along the
River Derwent to Keswick and the Eden valley. In the North-west there
are none of the more magnificent remains, like those at Stonehenge, but
there are many smaller examples, and nowhere are they so strange and
compelling to the imagination as on the moors or the Cumbrian coast.
The three largest are those at Little Salkeld (Long Meg and her
daughters), at Castlerigg near Keswick, and at Swinside near
Broughton-in-Furness. There are also smaller circles in various states of
preservation, as well as fragments of circles, single monoliths and cairns.
Some of them are inaccessible and hard to find; others – like that on
Cold Fell between Ennerdale and Calder Bridge – lie at the side of a
road. They should not all be classified together, because they were built
at different times, by different peoples, and served different purposes.
Most of the smaller circles enclose burials and this may be true of the
larger ones also, though it is hard not to believe that these were
gathering-places of some sort.

Of the circles which remain more or less intact some of the stones
have toppled over and some have been removed by farmers. The rest
must look much as they did to the people who put them up. Long Meg
is a fine example of a circle with a gateway and an external menhir.
Castlerigg is not quite so large, but has a kind of internal chamber
which, however, may not have been part of the original construction.
Swinside is smaller still, and the stones, instead of being spread out,
must have been set so close to one another that they touched and made
a stone fence.

Of these three circles, Castlerigg has the most magnificent site. It
stands on a little knoll with the dip of a valley on nearly every side and,

beyond the dip, a circular rim of mountains. Standing at the gateway and looking across the circle, you see the shallow valley of Naddle Beck, very green among the rougher fellsides. Parallel is the larger St John's-in-the-Vale, seen through a gap in the low Naddle Fell, and beyond it, the Helvellyn range. To your right, across the valley where Derwentwater lies (unseen from here) are the fells of Buttermere and Newlands, and behind you, nearer and more solid, Skiddaw and Saddleback. Its more immediate surroundings are much tamer – a neat field with a road on two sides of it and a couple of stiles. Passers-by get out of their cars, climb over the stiles, photograph the circle and drop sweet-papers in the holy-of-holies.

Swinside, however, still remains comparatively remote and unvisited, though it can be glimpsed at a distance from the road over Bootle Fell – seeming embedded in its cathedral close of munched and manured green. It is even possible to force a car along the road from Broadgate at the risk of breaking the axle. But for the most part the circle is as hard to reach as it was in Wordsworth's time.

P.L.

A Visit to Swinside

When he was fourteen or fifteen, Norman set off for the moors and explored one of Lakeland's eeriest stone circles.

One afternoon in November or December I set off from home not knowing where I was going, and went along the road out of the town, past the football field, towards the Green and Broughton-in-Furness. It had snowed during the week, and there were whips and slashes of snow on the lower hills, but the clouds were too low for me to see if the high fells were more thickly covered. By the time I had reached the Green it had become apparent that the place I was going to was Swinside. I passed through the village and up the hill by Thwaites church. There was little traffic in those days, and I walked along a grey empty road under a grey and darkening sky.

I turned off the main road and along the track which led to the circle and soon I was out on the open moor. There was snow everywhere, flat and desolate, with tussocks of grass pushing through like hairy warts. The clouds were not far above me, thick and yellow-brown, rubbing on the roof of White Combe. The snow was yellow-brown, too, and you could scarcely tell where snow ended and cloud began. There were shadowy mists and that kind of silence which makes you feel that the air is a solid block. I was thoroughly scared but was determined to go on until I could see the stones. They stand on a little plateau with the smooth fells of the Black Combe range surrounding them on three sides like an ancient earthwork. On the fourth side the land slopes along the line of the beck towards the Duddon estuary which, however, is not visible from the circle. It is dreary, slovenly country, with not much rock on the surface and the grass sour with bog. And there, at last, I saw the stones, black, huddled and hooded, with the snow mounded against them on the one side. There was no comfort in them, no hint of anything to do with humanity at all. They were as frightening as the moor, yet they were not just a part of it. They were separate, persisting through the centuries in a dumb, motionless struggle. They were in opposition to the moor, struggling against it, just as I was – but they were not on my side. I turned and went as fast as I could down the snowy track to the main road, and walked home towards the friendly glare of the furnaces purring through the mist.

P.L.

Long Meg

Long Meg and her Daughters is another of the more remarkable places of worship in the county, if, indeed, it *was* a place of worship. Long Meg is the largest of the three major stone circles of Cumberland, though its setting is one of less grandeur than either Castlerigg or Swinside, while the cart track lying across it seems to reduce it in size and mystery. To me, the most mysterious thing about it is the fact that – apart from Long Meg herself, a toothless hag of red sandstone – the stones are all of the volcanic rock of the fells, though they stand on sandstone ground with large outcrops of limestone on either side. Probably the explanation is merely that it was easier for the Neolithic people to collect and transport the glacial erratic boulders of the volcanics than to hew or dig out rocks of sandstone or limestone, even though these were nearer at hand. But may it not perhaps have been that the volcanic rocks seemed a more appropriate building material for the circle simply because they were part of the stuff of the hills?

Long Meg, Castlerigg and Swinside – which Wordsworth, somewhat fancifully, called

> ...some famed temple where of yore
> The Druids worshipped –

are all that now remains of what was once a large number of stone circles.

G.L.

Vanishing Circles

The destruction which has gone on among these monuments is almost beyond belief. As well as Swinside, there were at least five other circles in South Cumberland – at Annaside, Gutterby, Kirkstones (two) and Standing Stones, Kirksanton. Scarcely anything remains of any of these. Other circles have been cleared out of the way by farmers, or the stones have been broken up for making walls and fences. Vanishing circles have been recorded also at four or five places in the north of Cumbria, and one or two near Keswick in addition to that at Castlerigg. One called the Grey Yards on King Harry Fell not far from Carlisle must have been next to the largest in the country. All these seem to have been destroyed in the last two centuries and there may have been others of which we have no record.

P.L.

Crosses

The English introduced a type of monument which is typical of the lowlands of the dale counties though it is not confined to them. This is the sculptured stone, usually a cross, which was set up at market-places, in the churchyards or beside graves. There are some fragments of Celtic carving which may be pre-Saxon, but the finest work came in with the English and can be seen in the great cross at Bewcastle near the Border. Bewcastle is many miles away from the Lakes but there is a smaller cross at Irton church, just below the Eskdale and Wasdale fells. This is a most attractive work, carved with scrolls of fruit, leaves and flowers and with panels of a geometric pattern. It still has its cross-head, with the arms free (i.e. not enclosed by a wheel), while the 'arm-pits' are cut in a curve which gives grace and movement. It stands in a churchyard, among a group of church, school and one or two other buildings, islanded in fields and seemingly far from any possible churchgoers. Yet a vicar told me that his congregation contained more Bachelors of Science than perhaps that of any other in England – because of the nearness of the Sellafield nuclear plant, of course.

There are several of these Anglian crosses, and more made by the Cumbrians themselves under English instruction. They can be found, of one sort and another, scattered around the county – at Beckermet, St Bees, Dearham, Aspatria and elsewhere. And there are many fragments in other places – broken bits of shafts built into church walls, fragments of different styles and periods heaped together, wheel-heads set beside shafts to which they do not belong. In many places, too, there is a tradition of a cross which has now entirely disappeared. For the country people seem to have treated the crosses as they treated the megaliths – not even the Christian symbol could save them.

P.L.

The Norse Crosses

The Cumbrian cross gradually gave way to a type characteristic of the race which was to come next to the dales – i.e. the Norsemen. There are a good many crosses which show Norse, or Celtic-Norse influence, including the Giant's Grave at Penrith, which has two hog-backs (curved grave-slabs lying not flat but on their sides) and two pillars. But by far the finest as well as the most famous of the Norse sculptures are those at Gosforth.

The Gosforth group consists of the remains of two hog-backs and three crosses, all of about the same period and possibly by the same hand. The standing cross in the churchyard is a most remarkable work. One's first impression is that it is so slender that it might easily snap in two. The lower part of the shaft is round, like a tree-trunk, and undecorated, and then, about four feet from the ground, it breaks out into a pattern, grows narrower, and is cut into four faces. Above, it tapers to a smallish wheel-head cross at the top. It has little of the serenity of the Irton cross, but its detailed carvings tell a complex story. On the east side is a crucifixion – a rather stiff warrior-like Christ watched by a soldier and Mary Magdalene. Above this is a dragon, its body knotted like a hank of knitting wool with a head at either end, while a man stands beside the lower of the two heads, forcing the mouth open with his foot. This, we are told, illustrates the old Norse story of Vidar the Silent, who was to avenge the death of Odin by opening the jaws of the dragon wolf.

Here and elsewhere on this cross Christian and pagan imagery are presented side by side. The stag chased by dogs or wolves is a conventional symbol for Christ, but other figures seem to illustrate stories from the Edda. Such sculptures with their blending of Christian and pagan symbols must have belonged to a time when the Norsemen were converted to Christianity but had not yet forgotten their old mythology and the stories told by the Skalds. It is very likely that they half-believed both Christian and pagan myths simultaneously. Certainly the dragon which is slain by St Michael on the dragon lintel at St Bees looks more as if he comes from the Edda than from the Book of Revelation.

P.L.

Nobbut God

The Celtic Past

As you look out from the North Head at St Bees you look right into the Celtic past of the county – the Isle of Man, the Mull of Galloway, the Isle of Whithorn, all of which, like Iona and Northumberland's Holy Island and the Farnes and St Patrick's Chapel at Heysham Head, were centres and bridge-heads of the Celtic Church. It seems strange to us that the Faith should have taken root and flourished on such far-away, inaccessible promontories and archipelagoes like some maritime plant washed in by the tide. It seems less strange, however, when you realize how the sea, which now divides island from island, was once the easiest means of communication. It is likely that St Bees was yet another of these holy headlands, though the only evidence lies in the legend of St Bega, a princess who fled from Ireland to avoid having to marry a heathen Viking and was shipwrecked on the coast near St Bees. According to one version, she was granted by the Lord of Egremont as much land as was covered by snow on Midsummer Day, whereupon she founded a nunnery on the acres sanctified by the Cumbrian weather. According to another version, she lived at St Bees as an anchorite for some years, then fled to St Aidan of Lindisfarne, who gave her permission to establish a nunnery at West Hartlepool.

G.L.

The Monasteries

In the years which preceded the Norman Conquest ecclesiastical affairs were very confused in the North-west. People were rarely sure to what bishop they owed allegiance, and even after Henry I had created the new bishopric of Carlisle, the diocese still remained disunited and poorly organized. The Church, in fact, carried out its spiritual and civilizing work chiefly through the monasteries, of which there were eight or nine larger houses, mostly founded by Norman barons. The Augustinians (Austin canons or black friars) set up priories at Carlisle,

Lanercost and Cartmel; the Premonstratensians, at Shap; the Benedictines, at St Bees and Wetheral, both of these being cells of St Mary's, York. The Cistercians established an abbey at Holme Cultram, and the Cistercian rule was also observed at Furness and its daughter house of Calder, though these two were founded, in the first place, by the Benedictines. In addition there were a number of smaller houses: a priory of Augustinian canons, originally founded as a hospital, at Conishead, near Ulverston; settlements of friars at Carlisle, Penrith and Appleby; and hospitals at Bardsea and elsewhere.

There were also two houses of Benedictine nuns – at Armathwaite, in the north of the county, and at Seaton, near Bootle. The Border, towards the end of the Middle Ages, was not the safest place for communities of virgins, and Armathwaite seems frequently to have been plundered, while at Seaton, though they escaped the raiders, the nuns were wretchedly poor. The annual income per head at Armathwaite has been estimated at about £2 14s. compared with over £24 per head for the monks of Furness,[1] and Seaton was almost certainly worse off than Armathwaite, for they had few endowments and could expect little help from the barren moorlands around Black Combe. Seaton, one suspects, was maintained less for the glory of God than as a home where minor landowners could farm out their unmarriageable daughters on payment of a small dowry.

Of the monasteries to the north and east of the area, Carlisle (or what was left of the church by the Reformers and Roundheads) is now the cathedral, Lanercost and Holme Cultram (the village is known as Abbeytown) have survived, in part, as parish churches, while Shap – the white limestone abbey by the banks of the River Lowther – is entirely in ruins.

P.L.

Cartmel Priory

Cartmel was by no means the largest of the Lake District monasteries, but its church is undoubtedly our finest medieval building. It lies in a shallow dint of a valley that, instead of cutting back among the mountains, seems to push itself out as a peninsula between the estuaries of the Kent and the Leven. Cartmel was really the priory of the sands rather than of the hills, and many of the parishioners, who had their own chapel of St Michael within the abbey church building, were fishermen and cocklers from Flookburgh and Allithwaite. This peninsula, jutting out into Morecambe Bay, was the obvious halting-place on the cross-bay journey where travellers could wait,

[1] See C.M.L. Bouch and G.P. Jones, *The Lake Counties: 1500-1830.*

The priory village of Cartmel

during the hours of high tide, either at the village inns or in the priory itself. There is still an old mile-stone (or, rather, guide-stone) in the village which gives the distance to Lancaster and Ulverston by the over-sands route. In fact, the prior and canons of Cartmel were responsible for maintaining a guide for the Kent estuary, just as the monks of Conishead looked after the Leven. According to tradition Mass was said for travellers on Chapel Island about a mile from the shore. This was the spot where Wordsworth heard the news of the death of Robespierre (*The Prelude*, Book X).

The village of Cartmel no doubt owes its existence (and, today, a good deal of its livelihood) to the priory, and, in return, the priory owes its present existence to the villagers, but for whom it would have been let go to ruin at the Dissolution. For the Cartmel people claimed the chapel of St Michael, in the south-east aisle of the choir – now called the town choir – and were allowed to continue worshipping there, while the chancel had its roof ripped off and was left to rot in the rain. Between 1618 and 1620, the chancel was re-roofed, walls and windows were repaired, and a new carved screen and canopies were added to the fifteenth-century canons' stalls which had somehow survived beneath the rubble and rough weather of eight years.

This church compels our wonder less by the details of craftsmanship (much of the nave, in fact, is rather crudely built, like a barn, of undressed stone) than by its organic wholeness. I once began a poem about it:

God's box of bricks …

That was all I managed to write but it was all I needed. For seen from the ground, the church is a huge child's castle of cubes tipped half-over so that the under-half is hidden inside. The old late-thirteenth-century tower is a cube, hardly higher than the roofs of choir and transepts. And the fifteenth-century tower (added about the same time as the Perpendicular east window) is another cube, half the size of the old one, and set diagonally inside it. The odd, one-box-inside-the-other effect of this double tower was not likely to start a new architectural fashion, but it gives to the building an individuality as strong as the local dialect; so that the whole church is like an enormous houseleek of gables, windows, battlements, buttresses, angles and wall-ends.

P.L.

St Bees

The old Benedictine priory of St Bees was founded in the reign of Henry

I on what may have been the site of St Bega's hermitage or nunnery, and, as with Holme Cultram, most of it was destroyed at the Reformation. What is left – i.e. the abbey church except for the choir, which was blocked off and allowed to go to ruin – has now become the parish church to the village.

St Bees, unlike Cartmel, is not a tourist attraction – parties do not come there by coach for the Sunday morning service. Yet it is one of the most interesting churches in Cumbria, with a particularly fine west end, made up of a Norman doorway, three Early English lights, and a single gable window above. The stone itself is exceptionally beautiful – a deep, red sandstone, red as cochineal. It is soft, too, so that the angular decorations of the doorway are being rubbed away as the face of the stone is recarved by the weather into the smooth organic shapes of bones and shells. It looks so soft that you feel you could mould and shape it with your fingers. The rain soaks into it, and in wet weather it grows as brown as coffee.

Edmund Grindall, who succeeded Matthew Parker in 1575 as Archbishop of Canterbury, was born somewhere in the district (possibly at Hensingham) and almost certainly attended the priory school, which, of course, was closed after the Dissolution. Realizing how much it would be missed, he persuaded Queen Elizabeth to grant Letters Patent to found a free grammar school at St Bees. It was one of the last acts of his life, and he did not live to see the setting up of the school.

The quadrangle, with one Elizabethan wing, faces the twisting main road and is rather pinched in appearance, but the school spreads sideways, as if it were advertising itself to the railway line. Most of the buildings are of the same sandstone as the priory, dug from the huge blackberry-coloured quarries near the village, but the memorial hall, above the playing field, is of wood and glass, with Josephine de Vasconcellos's *Hand of God* in Honister slate standing close beside it. Generations of parsons' sons and the sons of professional men have been educated at St Bees, and, though it draws many of its pupils from a wider area, it remains essentially the public school of Cumberland.

P.L.

Furness Abbey

Furness Abbey exists almost as if in another time-warp, in a beautiful, isolated valley so secluded that the centre of Barrow, a mere one-and-a-half miles away, might not be there. English Heritage look after the abbey, and much of the moss and mould have now been cleared from the stonework.

The monks of the North-west chose to build nearly all their larger houses on sandstone – Cartmel and Shap being the two notable exceptions – and Furness Abbey is on one of the very few outcrops of this rock to be found in North Lonsdale.

The soil of the Vale of the Deadly Nightshade is dark and rich; there are escarpments of red rock, and the trees hang down the slopes, fat and heavy. After the cheerful limestone of the Dalton district, the dark red walls seem sullen and introspective, greened over with moss and mould.

When the abbey was founded in 1127, through the gift of Stephen, afterwards King of England, Furness was a wild, isolated part of the country, inhabited by a rough people, speaking a dialect still half-Norse. But the abbey prospered, and at one time its possessions were almost as extensive as the Isle of Man. It owned farms and woodland, with their wool-trade and hunting rights, together with fishing rights in the Morecambe Bay estuaries and on Windermere and Coniston Water. It owned mills, salt-pans, and numerous small iron-ore mines, and the monks ran a considerable export and smuggling trade from Piel harbour. It was on Piel that the half-witted Lambert Simnel landed in 1487, with a large body of Irish and Flemish soldiers, to claim the throne of Henry VII. The Abbot of Furness kept aloof from this rising, but in 1536 the monks had a certain amount of rather ambiguous dealings with the leaders of the Pilgrimage of Grace – enough, at any rate, to give the king's commissioners an excuse for dissolving the community and pulling down the buildings.

Had Barrow-in-Furness then been in existence, even as a sizeable village, the church might have been spared as were the churches at St Bees and Cartmel. But it was judged that the parish church of Dalton was all that was needed to serve the few people on this tip of the peninsula, and the abbey was tumbled into ruin.

Furness is a text-book abbey, a large-scale model for the student, almost complete in the details of its foundation plan – church, chapterhouse, cloisters, dormitories, infirmary, kitchen, abbot's lodging and even the drainage and sewage system. Its grandeur does not depend on the romantic associations of change and decay. It is massive, bare and austere, with a long nave, and with the chancel arch still intact, high and poised. The sedilia in the chancel wall have an elaborately carved stone canopy, and the chapter house, too, was fairly richly ornamented. The bases of the six pillars still stand there, after the manner of classic ruins, and, though the roof is entirely gone, you can see by looking at the roof of the infirmary chapel how beautiful it must have been, ribbed and curving like bats' wings. Apart from these, and the pillars and arches of the cloisters, there is little decoration. Most of the stone is as plain as when it was quarried. Yet nothing is lacking, for this abbey does not need ornament, just as it does not need legends or ghosts or the ivy and trailing ferns which have been torn away. It was never a mere assemblage of artistic felicities. Its greatness lay in the way every stone was dedicated and adapted to the purpose for which it was intended. It was, in fact, as functional in design as a blast furnace.

P.L.

Calder Abbey

Calder Abbey was founded in 1134 by a colony of monks and lay-brothers from Furness, who, however, fled before the coming of William FitzDuncan and the Scots, leaving their wooden church to be burnt. (They then went on to Bylands in Yorkshire.) Later the Abbot of Furness sent out another batch of monks, and the building of the abbey proceeded until the fourteenth century with, apparently, little interruption from Scottish raiders. The local tradition saying that the abbey was partially destroyed in the Scottish raid of 1322 has not been confirmed by archaeological examination of the ruins. Indeed, the worst destruction seems to have come from post-Dissolution owners, one of whom drove a road through the chancel, while another built cow-sheds in the gatehouse and the south transepts. When Thomas Rymer bought the estate in the late nineteenth century, loads of stones from the abbey were being carted away for building walls, and it was only the prompt action of the new owner which saved the ruins from almost total obliteration.

P.L.

Holme Cultram Abbey

One can feel the centuries in this abbey. It is set in the fen country of north Cumbria where the silt lies deep. The ancient meaning of the abbey's name was a cultivated strip of land.

The old capital of Moricambe Bay was the village now called Abbeytown, once the site of Holme Cultram Abbey, the wealthiest of Cumberland's monastic houses. All that remains of it today is part of the nave of the abbey church, now used as the parish church of the village, and at first sight it looks rather disappointing. Indeed, the first time I saw it I did not bother to go inside. The north and south walls are of the eighteenth century, plain as a nonconformist chapel, with two rows of round-headed windows far too small for the size of the wall. The west doorway is enclosed by a sixteenth-century porch, which, with the odd-looking gable-end and bellcote above, makes the whole west end seem cluttered. It is not until you go into the porch that you see the point of it, for it shelters a magnificent Norman doorway, well worth travelling miles to see. The light from the several windows falls full on the columns of the door and on the tombstones, including one to the Earl of Carrick, father of Robert Bruce.

To go through that door is to have a strange experience. You feel that you are in a ruin, magnificently preserved and roofed over from the rain, but still a ruin. You are, in fact, in the centre of the abbey church, with the two wall arcades of red sandstone (not visible from the exterior) striding along on either side. In between the pillars, and in a kind of clerestory above the arcade, are the eighteenth-century walls, plastered and cream-washed, and pierced by the round-headed windows which now look not a bit too small. The line between medieval and comparatively modern is sharp; the effect incongruous but not unpleasing. Whereas the abbey churches at Carlisle, Lanercost and St Bees have been altered and adapted with the years, Abbeytown seems, like Calder, to have remained in the Middle Ages, though protected from the weather of time by an eighteenth-century shell.

Holme Cultram was a Scottish abbey to begin with, founded in 1150 at the time when Cumberland was ceded to Scotland by King Stephen. Chroniclers say that the founder was Prince Henry, son of David, King of Scotland, but the English Alan, son of Waldeve, Lord of Allerdale, probably had quite as much to do with it. It was, at first, a daughter-house of the Cistercian monastery of Melrose, and the great medieval wizard, Michael Scott, buried at Melrose, is rumoured to have been at one time a monk there.

G.L.

Carlisle Cathedral

The dazzling east window, inspired, as Norman says, by the great west window of York, appropriately has been restored by the York Glaziers' Trust. Restored, too, is the cathedral fratry.

To say that for an Anglican the cathedral of his diocese is his spiritual home probably sounds a bit too pious. Better say that he goes there like a child visiting the house of a well-to-do grandmother, feeling that he has his own small claim to the pictures and the china and even to the old-fashioned stuffiness of the place. That is how I feel about Carlisle Cathedral. So I will leave to others the job of recording and assessing the architecture, and will merely try to sketch down impressions gathered from a good many poppings-in, kneelings-down and walkings-round.

To begin with, Carlisle is one of our smaller cathedrals as it now stands. Once it was much larger. The original Norman nave alone was 140 feet in length, in eight bays, six of which were pulled down during the Siege of Carlisle (1644-5), the stones going to repair the defences of the city. The arches of the two remaining bays are buckled and bent, since there seems to have been some subsidence soon after building began, but they still give an idea of the dark, heavy, repetitive strength of the old nave – short, elephant-legs of pillars carrying a horizontal band of plain wall, with triforium arches and clerestory above.

This part of the nave is almost completely blocked off from the choir by the rood screen, and stands, now, as a kind of entrance hall, housing the Chapel of the King's Own Royal Border Regiment, which had its headquarters in the castle – after the well-known practice of honouring the men of war in the temples of the Prince of Peace. When you pass through the screen you pass into another age. The choir aisles still belong, in part, to the earlier time, and are dark, cloistral, and at a lower level than the main choir. And, on the back of the choir stalls in the north aisle you can see a series of monastic paintings which illustrate, with the aid of rough rhymes, incidents from the lives of St Anthony of the Desert, St Augustine of Hippo and Northumbria's own St Cuthbert – an extremely interesting example of a medieval strip-cartoon, though Professor Pevsner[1] casually dismisses them as all of c.1500 and all bad.

All this belongs to the past. But when you walk up the steps into the choir you see at once that Carlisle Cathedral is a living church which many people in the city regard as their parish church.

First of all you notice the colour. If it is morning, the sun may be pouring through the east window, a magnificent Decorated work, inspired by the great west window of York. The glass – some medieval in the upper tracery but Victorian below – has much blue in it, and there is a sky-blue roof with gold stars. Gold appears, also, on the reredos and canopy of the altar, set against the white stone of the pulpit, the khaki stone of the floor, and the lovely pink sandstone of the arcades. It is a swirl of colours with cross-beams of sunlight touching up the blue and the gold.

The eye is dazzled, almost hurt. But if you turn your back on the east, you will face the soothing shadows of the choir stalls – a doll's-house gothic cathedral of soaring turrets, pinnacles, gables, steeples and crockets, all carved in the fifteenth century seemingly out of solid black liquorice. And, underneath, if you go along turning up the seats of the misericords, you will find the usual medieval wood-carver's menagerie of angels, men and monstrosities, some devout, some comic, and all as lively as Charlie Brown.

G.L.

The Dale Churches

Dale churches, compared with their parish counterparts, are usually

[1] In *The Buildings of England: Cumberland and Westmorland* (Penguin Books, 1967).

Church at Hall Waberthwaite

smaller, plainer, sometimes rather mean in furniture and trappings, but often with a gruff bareness that knocks at the heart like poverty. Most of them have the look of a barn, with no decoration at all on the outside except, perhaps, for a little freestone tracery in the windows. Many have served a community of the same dozen or score of families for generation after generation, perhaps under the care of a parson who was himself part-time spinner and weaver and part-time farmer, if not, sometimes, almost part-time beggar.

Four such churches come into my mind, in widely separated parts, all of which have the reek of antiquity in their bones. There is St Anthony, Cartmel Fell, in the valley of the Winster, so low that it seems almost entrenched in its own graveyard. Inside, the smell and aura of the past is so strong that it might have been canned like fruit. There are two beautifully carved pews, a three-decker pulpit, and some fifteenth-century glass depicting, among other things, St Anthony and his pig. Cartmel Fell is now much visited, and so, too, is the old church at Martindale, on the east side of Ullswater, though it has to be approached by a switchback of a road from Howtown. For ordinary parochial purposes this church has been superseded by the larger, nineteenth-century building on the hill, but it is neat and cared-for and gives a good idea of what the dale churches must have been like in the century or so after the Reformation. It stands at the entrance to Bannerdale which – together with the parallel Boredale – is about the most deserted hidden-away valley still left in the Lakes.

Mungrisdale, a church very similar in outward appearance, still serves its parish, and lies only two miles north of the main Keswick–Penrith road, close to Souther Fell, the scene of the phantom procession which seemed to foretell the Rebellion of the '45. It contains a wall-tablet to the memory of Raisley Calvert, father of the young man of the same name who was nursed by Wordsworth, and left the poet the small legacy which helped him to set up house with Dorothy at Grasmere.

My fourth church is the least visited of them all – at Hall Waberthwaite, about a mile off the Whitehaven–Millom road, north of Bootle. This hamlet of a few farms and cottages – the hall itself has fallen down – stands where the rough road peters out on the banks of the River Esk near a ford leading to the steep wood-slopes of Muncaster. At this point the Esk scarcely knows whether it is still a river or already an inlet of the sea. The estuary is no wider than a decent-sized pond, and you cannot get even the most distant glimpse of the sea, but the marshes smell of salt, while sea asters and sea lavender bloom in mourning colours in the mud, and the high tide fills the gullies to the brim. Like so many of the dale churches this is a plain rectangle in form. There are rough, old-fashioned box-pews, but it has little of the consciously archaic about it. You feel that it has not yet accustomed itself to receiving extra-parochial visitors. Its antiquity is irrelevant and it goes on with its job with the persistence of a farmer who still uses the horse-plough to turn a field which the tractors cannot tackle. In spring the crocuses are so thick in the graveyard that you cannot walk along the path without treading on them. (The sandy soil of this part of the coastal strip seems particularly favourable to crocuses, and also to primroses which mass on the slopes of the railway cuttings in acres at a time.)

This air of belonging to no particular age or time is characteristic, too, of the chapels of the high dales. Some of them, in fact, are not particularly old, and many have been ruthlessly restored or rebuilt. Some are rough-cast and perhaps whitewashed; while in others the slate is left uncovered as in a byre. The most famous are probably those at Buttermere – so perfect that it might have been built for a film set – at Mardale and at Wasdale. The old church at Mardale, of course, is now under the waters of Haweswater reservoir, but that at Wasdale Head still stands, surrounded by the graves of fallen climbers.

P.L.

Strands: A Mid-dale Church

The church at Strands or Nether Wasdale is less celebrated than that at Wasdale Head, lacking the romantic appeal of the climbers' graves, but it is a far more interesting building. Inside, it is quite surprisingly light for a dale church. There is a most agreeable wooden arcade to the north aisle, added in the 1830s, and a wagon roof with plaster bosses. The tables of the Creed, Lord's Prayer and Ten Commandments, on either side of the little east window, date from the same time, and even the mid-Victorian wall-memorials, mostly of owners of Wasdale Hall and their families, show a surprisingly sober taste.

There is some older wall-writing, too, discovered in 1958, after having been under the plaster for many years; there is some medieval woodwork, rather injudiciously varnished, which came originally from York Minster; and there are also some amusing cherubs at the head of the pillars. And the Royal Arms of George III glares down from the west end on what in his day was still the high-and-dry Church that shut eyes and ears against Methodism, radicalism, the Industrial Revolution and the poetry of William Wordsworth.

G.L.

The Parish Churches

In Cumbria there is no local tradition in church architecture such as we find in the Cotswolds or East Anglia. For one thing, the dales were mostly too poor. For another, the slate was not a good material, or not, at least, for building in the styles of the medieval gothic. Moreover, partly because of the poverty and partly because of the slate, churches fell into disrepair and had to be rebuilt, or they proved to be too small and had to be enlarged. So that while we have many dale churches of twelfth- or thirteenth-century foundation, only a few of them remain in anything like their original state.

The finest of our largest churches stand outside the dales. It is not my aim to give a list of all those which are worth a visit, but out of some thirty years' persistent, desultory and unsystematic stopping and popping in, certain buildings stay in the memory. On the edge of the area, the Eden valley holds the churches of Appleby and Kirkby Stephen, while the Lune holds Sedbergh and Kirkby Lonsdale. At Sedbergh the children still tie up the churchyard gate during weddings and will not let the bride and bridegroom come through until they have paid a ransom in scattered coins. Nearer the Lakes, but again not really in the dales, is Greystoke, between Keswick and Penrith, a collegiate church, and one of the most attractive in the diocese, which owes much to the benefactions of the Huddlestons – a branch of the family which produced the author of *Naught for Your Comfort*, the Rt. Rev. Trevor Huddleston. The same family gave to Holy Trinity, Millom, a fourteenth-century chapel (really, a south aisle to the nave) which is one of the most serenely beautiful inventions of man to be found in these parts. A particular curve is repeated and varied, as if musically, in the tracery of the windows, one of which, 'the fish window', a gothic arch reflected upside-down beneath itself, is une-qualled of its kind in England.

I let my memory move across the Duddon into the district once in the care of the monks of Furness, where the church at Urswick, founded before the abbey, still stands beside a tarn which has always been called bottomless. Some of the Saxon work still remains, but it is not that which I remember, but the fancies of an early nineteenth-century wood-carver, who has decorated the choir stalls and the organ with all manner of musical instruments – viols, pipes and drums, even a barrel-organ with its monkey. Not far away, at Aldingham, is the church which became specially associated with the Durham miners from their convalescent home at Conishead Priory. Aldingham has a leper's squint – and, indeed, the whole church has something of a squint, since of the two arcades which run down the nave, one is of round arches, the other of pointed. It stands right on the kerb of Morecambe Bay, with a wreckage of cobbles around it and the spring tides battering at the churchyard wall.

                                                                    P.L.

Kendal

The parish church, which is next door to Abbot Hall art gallery, is enormous, the kind that the Victorians used to call a sacred edifice. It is completely rectangular and so wide that inside it looks almost square. No part of the church, except the nineteenth-century porch, protrudes from the rectangle, the chancel being merely the eastern end of the central aisle. Even the tower is built over its western end. Much of the building was restored in the nineteenth century, but such matters can be left to architects and church historians. What immediately strikes you on entering at the west end of the southern aisle is that you have come into a vast, forest-like landscape of verticals and spaces. The church has five aisles, which means that it has four arcades and four rows of pillars, the appearance and spacing of which change at every step you take. The whole is so large that the outer corners seem not only to be out of earshot of the pulpit but almost out of memory of the congregation. You go into the south-west corner, for instance, as if you were going into another building, another part of the forest. An imposing church, certainly, but a solemn-faced church, and one, I feel, that must look half-empty even when it is full.

G.L.

Half-way to Heaven

The parish church perches like a glacial erratic boulder on its own hill high above the roofs of the village. In Hawkshead the dead don't wait for Judgement Day but go half-way to heaven as soon as they are buried. The building, dating from the fifteenth and sixteenth centuries, is as typical a piece of local stonework as any wall or stile, though it is coated with plaster and at one time was whitewashed. It is also a kind of art gallery in itself, for it retains the old wall texts and geometrical decorations, mostly painted in the seventeenth and early eighteenth centuries, which used to be very common in this part of the Lakes. One of the texts, painted in 1711 by William Mackreth of Hawkshead, is sometimes pointed out as an example of the Westmorland dialect in church:

> In the beginning was
> the Word, and the Word
> was with God, and t'Word
> was God. John. j.j.

Personally, I think the painter merely ran short of space.

G.L.

Entertaining Tombstones

When you approach Burgh-by-Sands from Kirkandrews you wonder where the sands are, for the village has a rich, red, snugly inland look. It takes its name from the *burgh* or fort on Hadrian's Wall, on the site of which it stands. Indeed, stones from the wall went to the building of the church, which, appropriately, possesses one of the finest of all the fortified towers in the county. As with its neighbour at Newton Arlosh, there is no doorway on the outside, while the door on the inside still has its massive iron gate, with slits above it so that the defenders could shoot into the nave if the raiders broke into the church.

Yet the outside is even more interesting, for the graveyard holds the most entertaining collection of tombstones I have seen anywhere in the county. They belong largely to the nineteenth century – Regency and mid-Victorian. The earlier ones, of around 1810, are restrained and even elegant, in so far as carving in this crumbly sandstone ever can be elegant. The decoration is mostly of the kind you see engraved in the books of that time – excellent lettering, set in raised ovals, with trails of formal leaves. The Victorian stones are heavier, often sentimental, always didactic – the huge draped urn, books piled one on another, all labelled 'The Bible', heavy laurel wreaths and a formal tudor rose. The same ideas and motifs are repeated over and over again, combined in different ways, making one wonder if there can have been a family of local stone-masons who worked in the district, perhaps through several generations, changing slowly with the times. But whether or not this is the case, Burgh churchyard remains a remarkable display of the pop art of the past.

G.L.

Tottlebank: A Baptist Church

The Baptist church at Tottlebank, near Penny Bridge in the Crake valley, belongs to the seventeenth century, and is, in fact, one of the oldest of that denomination in the north of England. It stands a hundred yards or so from the road, looking indistinguishable, at that distance, from a farm. Its first minister was Gabriel Camelford, who had been the presbyterian vicar of Staveley during the Commonwealth. On his ejection by the Act of Uniformity in 1662 he allied himself with the Anabaptists and went to Tottlebank, making it a centre for the Puritan sympathizers of Low Furness, including the important Sawrey family of Broughton Towers, who almost alone among the local gentry, had supported Cromwell during the Civil War.

P.L.

Wesley Visits West Cumberland

John Wesley, impetuous and imperious, visited West Cumberland in 1759 and quickly got into trouble with the tides.

Wesley had been preaching at Liverpool and Bolton, and when he arrived at Lancaster in the evening of Friday 11 May, he was told that it was too late to cross the sands. But Wesley could not bear to stand about doing nothing, so, ignoring advice, he started at once across the Kent, or as he calls them, the 'Seven-mile' sands, and arrived at 'Fluckborough' about sunset. Here he spent the night, departing the next morning so early that he had crossed both Ulverston and Duddon sands and reached Bootle, eight miles north of Millom, by eight o'clock. But now the tides began to trip him up.

'Here', he writes, 'we were informed, that we could not pass at Ravenglass before one or two o'clock – where as, had we gone on (as we afterwards found) we might have passed immediately. After we were directed to a ford near Manchester [Muncaster] Hall, which they said we might cross at noon. When we came thither, they told us we could not cross; so we sat till about one: we then found we could have crossed at noon.'[1] In spite of all these hindrances, he managed to reach Whitehaven before night, but was determined never to use the sands again. It was, he agreed, some ten miles shorter than the overland route by Kendal and Keswick, but if you got out of step with the tides, you had to face continual delays; 'especially', he adds, 'as you have all the way to do with a generation of liars, who detain strangers as long as they can, either for their own gain or their neighbours'.

In many ways Wesley was a prophetic figure, looking forward to the nineteenth century and the great romantics, but in his attitude to the countryside he still belongs to the age of Defoe. As he waited, impatient as a horse in cold weather, beside the tidal Esk, or at Ravenglass, with its small smugglers' street and dune-locked harbour, he had no eyes whatever for the land. All the magnificence of the western dales was standing round about – Bowfell looking down Eskdale, Gable looking down Wasdale, Scafell between the two of them, and the Isle of Man across the water – but his thoughts were only for the souls he had to save at Whitehaven. When, two or three days later, he went to the Lorton Valley near Cockermouth, he comments that many of the people who came to hear him 'found God to be a God both of the hills and valleys, and no where more present than in the mountains of Cumberland'. It is a remark that might have been made some forty or fifty years later by another man from that same town, but how different, then, would have been its implication. To Wordsworth the fell country was the one place above all others in which to seek for God; to Wesley it was the last place where you would expect to find him, so that the witness of Lorton was a much more than ordinary sign of his mercy.

L.

---

[1] John Wesley, *Journal*.

The Quakers

Another religious body has contributed to the Lake scene buildings which rival the dale churches in their bare severity. The Quakers, indeed, have played an important part in the development of Cumbria – especially in the industrial towns outside the mining area. According to Burn and Nicolson, they first appeared in the district at Kirkby Stephen, where the vicar, Francis Higginson, incited the magistrates against them in the time of Oliver Cromwell.

It seems extremely unlikely that these Solomon-Eagle-like revivalists were indeed followers of George Fox, but the incident shows that the people of the Westmorland–Yorkshire Pennines were ready to listen to the unorthodox preacher. So that when Fox came to Sedbergh in 1652, passing on to Firbank where he preached a famous sermon on the stone outside the chapel, his words fell on fruitful ground. Some of his best-known followers came from the land between the Lune and the Kent, including Francis Howgill and Edward Burrough, the 'Son of Thunder and Consolation'. The following year Fox came to Cumberland. He went first to Bootle, on the coast, where he was set on by a band of toughs, and moved on through Cockermouth and Caldbeck to Carlisle, where, as he tells in his *Journal*, he was imprisoned 'in the dungeon among the moss-troopers, thieves and murderers'.

He goes on: 'A filthy, nasty place it was, where men and women were put together in a very uncivil manner, and never a house of office to it; and the prisoners so lousy that one woman was almost eaten to death by lice. Yet, bad as the place was, the prisoners were all made very loving and subject to me; and some of them were convinced of the truth, as the publicans and harlots were of old.'

About 120 years later, in 1772, an American Quaker, John Woolman, feeling 'a religious concern to visit Friends in the northern parts of England', made a kind of pilgrimage in the steps of George Fox. He visited Kendal, Preston Patrick and York (where he died of the smallpox), writing on the way a journal which has taken its place among the literary heritage of the American people. Woolman must have looked even odder than his forerunner of the leather breeches, for he went about entirely in undyed cloth, refusing to have anything to do with the vegetable dyes which were produced by slave labour.

Yet Woolman did not visit Swarthmoor near Ulverston, which has perhaps stronger ties with Fox than any other spot in the Lakes. For at Swarthmoor Hall he was sheltered by Judge Fell, whose widow, Margaret Fell, he later married. Near Swarthmoor there is a seventeenth-century Quaker meeting-house of grave, grey beauty, outside and inside, and with its own small burial ground. Fox's widow (who has been called the Mother of Quakerism) was not buried here, however, but a few miles away in the Friends' burial ground at Sunbrick on Birkrigg Common.

P.L.

Villages and Towns

Dale Villages

To a visitor from the south of England the dale villages often do not look like villages at all. They are more like a pre-industrial ribbon development – small terraces and single cottages strung out along the side of the road. There is no village green with church and pub and manor house standing round. The church is sometimes half a mile or more away and the vicarage even further. The reason is partly that the narrowness of the dale gives no room for the village to spread width-ways, and partly that the district is comparatively free from the feudalism which has dominated village life in many other parts of the country. Not only in the dales, but along the coast, and in many parts of the surrounding lowlands there is little sign of the power of the hereditary landowner. Appleby has developed under the benevolent shadow of Lady Anne Clifford's castle; Cark and Cartmel owe much to Holker Hall; and Askham is almost an extra-mural extension to Lowther Castle, even though the castle itself is now only a remnant of mock-gothic stage-scenery. But these are exceptions.

Of course, in the centre of the tourist area, no village is left alone. Watendlath, once almost proverbial for its inaccessibility, is now associated with one of Hugh Walpole's more preposterous heroines, so that the narrow road from Derwentwater is sometimes clogged with cars. But there are many others, in the less advertised areas, which are quite left off the visiting lists: Great Urswick and Scales in Low Furness; Hesket Newmarket and Uldale, back of Skiddaw; Sandwith, Haile and Beckermet near the coast. None of these – except perhaps those behind Siddaw – has the far-away, three generations-behind look of the picture-calendar village.

P.L.

Lower Kentdale

The more rural villages of Lower Kentdale lie away from the main roads:

Brigsteer and Levens in the north, overlooking the Gilpin levels; Yealand Redmayne, Yealand Conyers and Warton in the south, among the hills; Holme right in the middle. I find it hard to think of one apart from the others. They are all built predominantly of limestone, though often rough-cast and lime-washed. They are full of nooks and angles, of big round chimneys and heavy porches. There are gardens sheltered by fat walls, often piled high with water-worn sculptures, miniature Henry Moores and Barbara Hepworths prised away from the limestone clints on the fellside. (Hundreds of tons of such weathered stone have been carted off to make rock-gardens in the Lancashire holiday towns.) The walls are matted over with white and purple rock, with ivy and ivy-leaved toadflax, and often there are clipped yews (copied from Levens Hall) in front of the houses and sprawling orchards at the back. Limestone is one of the more workable materials, so that the local builders have been able to tackle structures that would have been risky in slate. Levens, for instance, has one of those little white church spires that gleam like a pillar of salt in the evening light. (There is another at Field Broughton, near Cartmel, and one at Bardsea, near Ulverston.)

Warton village in the southern part of Greater Lakeland is now being much built-about and suburbanized. It is the ancestral home of the Washington family, and their coat-of-arms, three mullets and two bars, which became the pattern of the Stars and Stripes, can still be seen, in the wall of the tower of the surprisingly large parish church. Formerly the arms were in the outward wall, but they suffered so much from the off-bay weather, that, a few years ago, they were literally pushed through the wall to the inside, where they are now rather faintly visible in the choir vestry.

G.L.

Villages in Pairs

In Westmorland they were fond of calling pairs of villages by the same name – Great Asby and Little Asby; Kings Meaburn and Maulds Meaburn, Crosby Ravensworth and Crosby Garrett. But of all the greats, Great Ormside is surely the littlest! The church gates are opposite the farm gates, but the church itself stands high above on Orm's hill. The tower, of the thirteenth century, massive as a quarry wall, doorless and almost windowless, was surely intended for defence against the Scots, like that at St Cuthbert's, Great Salkeld, lower down the valley. It looks even more like a fortress when you catch sight of the Eden flowing as if in a moat at the foot of the hill. Inside, the nave has an arcade carried on characteristic, short, bulky, Norman pillars. The chancel, partly rebuilt in the seventeenth century, has a fine example of a leper's squint and is, on the whole, not unpleasing, though, when I saw it, the walls were

Hesket Newmarket

coloured in a rather repellent shade of yellow.

G.L.

Cartmel: A Mark in the Register

Cartmel village is leisurely, ecclesiastic and not obviously on the road to anywhere. A tradesman, delivering in the district, is said to have passed within a hundred yards of the village once a week for years without discovering that it was there. Today, however, it gets many visitors, and is crowded every Whit Saturday and Monday for the annual race-meeting. The River Eea moons through it, between walls and behind bridges. There is a tiny town square with shops, houses, inns and the old priory gatehouse, all cramped together, yet so disposed and ordered, that they might be a stage-set for an Edwardian musical comedy. The village is conscious of its beauty, yet without coyness or undue pride. The houses are there to be lived in rather than to be looked at. There are cats on the steps and apple trees bulging up like captive balloons behind the limestone walls.

In the winter, it is a grey village; in spring, it is starch-white against the burst and spikiness of back-garden green. But in autumn, limestone and leaves alike are mulled over with yellows and browns, and the village becomes a harvest-festival jumble of roofs, trees, gables and virginia creeper. Wordsworth's old teacher, William Taylor of Hawkshead Grammar School (the Matthew of the Matthew poems), is buried in the churchyard, and the lines from Gray, mentioned in *The Prelude*,[1] can still be read on his tombstone. My own great-grandfather farmed at Hard Crag, just outside the village, and my grandfather was married to my grandmother in the priory, where my grandmother who could not write, put her mark in the register.

P.L.

*

I have a right to be proud of Cartmel as the home of my ancestors. Family pride apart, it is still a place of great presence. Often it is classed with Hawkshead in the beautiful villages category and it has something of the same look of rough, rural antiquity, though it would be sheer impertinence to call it 'quaint'. I would not even call it pretty. And though it has often won prizes as one of the best-kept villages in the country, it has done so by being neat and tidy, not by tarting itself up with window boxes or little trees in tubs.

What is unexpected is that, though it is at the hub of a valley of

[1] *The Prelude* (1860), Book X; lines 531–52.

glittering white limestone, that stone is scarcely to be seen in the centre of the village. The two honest-faced inns and the Priory Hotel in the little square are rough-cast and painted; the pillared and porched shops and the priory gatehouse are built of mixed stone, much of it red and brown and slaty rubble. But if you go to the bridge over the Eea, and look upstream, you can see limestone walls holding back the water and limestone steps going down to it. There is a legend saying that the Austin canons who founded Cartmel Priory heard a voice telling them to search for a spit of land between two streams which flowed in opposite directions. But unless they came when the Eea was in spate, they must have found it hard to decide which way it *was* flowing. For in ordinary weather the water lies as still as in a canal, though much clearer, so that in winter you can see bright green weeds fanning out like sea-anemones on the river-floor, while in early summer the surface is half-hidden with white water-buttercup and speckled with dropped apple-blossom.

G.L.

Grange-over-Sands: Batty Charm

Grange-over-Sands is something of an oddity. It was meant to be a rather sedate, old-lady like, Victorian watering place, but being built of the chubby, almost frivolous limestone from local quarries, it cannot have looked very sedate even at the start. It has an artificial lake of almost excruciating prettiness, with islands, weeping willows, twining paths and a whole wildfowl trust of tame ducks, though I cannot understand why anyone should want to look at 200 yards of ornamental plumbing when there are the twenty miles of Morecambe Bay on the other side of the railway. In summer Grange seems to be the place where campers and caravanners come when it is wet. In late autumn and in winter, on the other hand, it has a rather batty, self-indulgent charm, when the boarding houses are closed, the bathing pool is drained empty, the trees are withered to sodden yellows and browns and the incorrigible local stone pushes up its nose from every wall and rockery.

G.L.

Ravenglass

The Esk and the Irt rivers flow roughly parallel down Eskdale and Wasdale, about five or six miles apart, but when they come within a mile of the sea, each is diverted by the coastal ridge, the Esk flowing north and the Irt flowing south, until they meet and force their way into the sea immediately opposite the little in-between River Mite. It is here, on this trident of estuaries, that you find Ravenglass, a port at the time of the Romans, but now known to visitors chiefly as the station for the Eskdale Railway. The Romans made it their supply base for Hardknott Fort in Eskdale. In the eighteenth century, when ships from the West Indies could unload spirits, free of duty, at the Isle of Man, Ravenglass was famous as a smuggling port, the contraband being taken by pack-horse over Sty Head and Hardknott. According to tradition Whitbeck church was one of the places where the liquor was hidden, and the same is also said of Seaton Hall, near Bootle, a farmhouse built on the site of the Benedictine Priory of St Mary of Lekeley, the only nunnery in South Cumberland. The smuggling was suppressed by customs officers with the aid of the military, but, even as late as the middle of the last century, small ships still came into Ravenglass bringing supplies for the local farms.

Today Ravenglass is more of a yachting centre, yet the visitors who wander down to the waterside while waiting for the Ratty railway are sometimes disappointed. One can see why. For Ravenglass stubbornly refuses to look like a conventional seaside village. There is no harbour, no quay; there are no men in jerseys; nothing that you can be photographed standing up against. The houses on one side of the main street turn their backs on the sea, and bolster up their backyard doors and gardens with cement and sandbags to keep the tide out. For 2,000 years this settlement has been where it is because it is sheltered from the sea, and it is not going to change its habits now.

Ravenglass is still the most captivating village on the Lake coast. It is built of the Eskdale granite for one thing, and the houses are all either sparkling grey or rhododendron pink, often timbered and shuttered and gabled in a style which seems to have been caught like a rash from Muncaster Castle – the parish church is, in fact, three miles away, in the castle grounds. Above all, it is likeable for its snugness – its way of positioning itself on the old country principle that you can enjoy the view outside, but, inside, you want comfort. And, for its comfort, Ravenglass depends mainly on those two long spits of dune-land that delay the Esk and the Irt from reaching the sea.

G.L.

Seascale

Seascale is the first spot along the coast where the sandstone really shows itself. The church, the large hotel and many of the station buildings are of sandstone, and when the tide is out the lower shore looks like an accident case, with dark red splinters and collar-bones of rock, oozy salt trickles and black congealed scabs of seaweed. At Seascale the coastal ridge lifts itself high above the shore. The hotel, the former girls' school, and the red-brick villas are perched unprotectedly on their sandy cliffs as if the sea they were looking at was the English Channel. Right up to the 1950s Seascale remained, in appearance, stuck in the Edwardian age, like a little brick model of the Folkestone of Arthur Kipps. But with sixty-mile-an-hour gales hosing the windows with salt spray, Seascale was a healthy place; with neither pier, nor dancehall, nor cinema, nor fairground, it was a respectable place; and, tucked away, miles from any bombable area, it seemed, in wartime, to be a safe place. So that, like the rest of this part of the coast, it swarmed with children, both in holidays and in term-time. The cliffs carried the once widely known Calder Girls' School, now closed, and a preparatory school for boys, and there was another preparatory school at Gosforth and, of course, the public school at St Bees. The once-forlorn beaches became brisk, invigorating and virginal, and the piping of the oyster-catchers took on a slightly middle-class accent.

The fifties, however, brought a change which the shopkeepers, if not the parents, regarded as a change for the better. The world's first atomic-power station was built just two miles away at Sellafield, and Seascale jumped forward a whole half-century in five years. A new, expensive housing estate mushroomed, between the old village and Gosforth, and nearly all the habitable cottages and country houses within nine or ten miles were bought up by the Sellafield scientists.

G.L.

Gosforth: A Fascinating Study

Gosforth is built mainly of dark red sandstone, and the square, phlegmatic houses along the main street have the look more of a mining-town terrace than of a typical dale village. In fact, it is far from typical. Historically, it belongs with the roots of Cumberland, for the church precincts contain some of our most important Norse antiquities: two hog-backs and three crosses, of which the standing cross in the churchyard is the finest of its kind in England.

In spite of all its early associations, Gosforth more recently was jerked into the twentieth century and is now the home of many of the scientists who work at Sellafield. The early effects of this impact of new upon old, of a technical-minded, urban-educated, off-comer group on a static, partly ingrown, rural community was the subject of a fascinating study made by W.M. Williams.[1] His book contained much detailed observation of the church-going, drinking and sexual habits of the villagers, their taste in furniture, their attitude to contraception and the like. Its most interesting pages, however, dealt with the social hierarchy

---

[1] *The Sociology of an English Village – Gosforth*, International Library of Sociology and Social Reconstruction (Routledge and Kegan Paul, 1956).

Windebrow above Keswick

which then prevailed and with the way the new suburban scale of social status, based largely on money, was clashing with the old rural scale, based partly on family, but partly also on a man's personal standing in the community, a thing to be gained neither easily nor quickly. 'They've got to summer you and winter you and summer you and winter you, afore you mak friends in Gosforth,' runs a local saying, and some say you must live in the parish for twenty years before you are accepted. Thus, a well-to-do off-comer was rated lower in the social scale than an impoverished member of one of the old county families who lived in a small cottage and did most of the housework himself. On the other hand, when a local farmer's widow bid up to a high price for a house, the revelation of her wealth caused surprise but did not raise her social status. Needless to say, when the study appeared in print it caused some annoyance among the local people who had not expected their back-kitchens to be thrown open to the public in this way. But for those who want to know what life in the Lake District is really like, this is a valuable and highly entertaining book.

G.L.

Allonby and Silloth

Allonby is a village assembled round a green with a beck flowing through it – rather like one of the Pennine villages with the sea in the place of the fells. About the beginning of the nineteenth century it became quite a popular little resort for sea-bathing – then, of course, a matter of medicine rather than pleasure – and it seems to have made just the faintest attempt at a seaside elegance. Today this has all given way to cafés and souvenir shops and the battering of the Solway weather.

Silloth, on the other hand, has clung on to its elegance and is by far the best-looking seaside resort along the whole length of Greater Lakeland. The town was laid out in the mid-nineteenth century and stands well back from the shore, with the main promenade, as it were, opening on to a perpetual full tide of grass like the Stray at Harrogate. But the houses are prettier than those at Harrogate, as if the men who built them might once have spent a weekend at Brighton. The square terraces behind the promenade are spread wide and dour as the streets of Kirkcudbright, Silloth's sister town across the Firth, while the parish church seems to have been dumped down like one of those cardboard churches left on shop counters to collect money for missions.

When Silloth first began to be developed, following the opening in 1856 of the railway from Carlisle, it was planned as a port rather than a seaside resort. There were, at one time, regular passenger services to Liverpool, Dublin and the Isle of Man, and even today the harbour is used by cargo ships. Visitors see very little of the shipping, but the seafront still has a serious look about it, dominated, as it is, by the huge flour mills. It is not until you pass beyond the Green towards the road to Skinburness that frivolity breaks through in an anthology of about every kind of bungalow and villa that can decorate or disfigure a coastline.

G.L.

Keswick: Beauty, Horror and Immensity United

Keswick is a vigorous tourist town today, but its roots trail back centuries to wool-marketing and mining.

Keswick is the least Cumbrian town in Cumberland.

Its site is superb. It stands on a slope only a few hundred yards above the foot of Derwentwater. Southward, you look down the length of the lake into the wedge of Borrowdale, and beyond to the volcanic peaks of the Wasdale fells; northward, you are practically knocking your nose on the bottom steps of Skiddaw. It is a shop-window display, two of Cumbria's most characteristic types of landscape made accessible to the laziest passer-by.

It is this very accessibility which has ruined Keswick. As early as 1755, Dr John Dalton 'enumerated the beauties of the Vale of Keswick' in a poem 'addressed to two young ladies after their return from viewing the mines near Whitehaven'. In 1767, Dr John Brown explained 'that the full perfection of Keswick, consists of three circumstances, *beauty*, *horror*, and *immensity* united', to depict which 'would require the united powers of Claude, Salvator, and Poussin'.[1]

Thomas Gray, who came to the Lakes two years later, was similarly intimidated by the 'impending crags', and hurried past without speaking in case his voice should dislodge the stones and bring down an avalanche. Soon the district became the resort of tourists less timid than Gray and less aesthetically-minded than Brown, and, by the end of the century, Derwentwater was claiming to be the Jewel of the Lakes, though some visitors, disappointed with the weather, called it the Devil's Chamber-pot. And before long Keswick began to acquire yet another kind of fame. In 1799 Wordsworth and his sister had settled at Grasmere, and soon first Coleridge and then Southey came to Keswick. Coleridge drifted away to Hampstead, but Southey stayed at Greta Hall for the rest of his life. The name of Robert Southey means very little today. Even his one surely lasting contribution to English literature, the story of the Three Bears, is not usually associated with him at all. But in the early nineteenth century, in spite of Byron's ridicule, he was one of the lions, and helped to make Keswick into a place of literary pilgrimage,

[1] John Brown, *Description of the Lake and Vale of Keswick* (Newcastle, 1767).

perhaps even before Wordsworth did the same for Grasmere. In fact, throughout the nineteenth century the Lake Poets acted as highly effective unpaid publicity agents for the entire district.

It was this growing fame which changed Keswick. From being a small market-town it turned into what is essentially an industrial town in an industrial society – a town given over to the manufacture of holidays. There is nothing in this to be ashamed of, and Keswick, like Blackpool, plays an important part in the economy of the north of England. In the dusk of the summer evenings, after business hours, the streets are crammed with sightseers, inspecting old prints, new photographs, local watercolours, local weaving, local pottery, local woodcraft, local jewellery, local toffee and all the hideous gimcrackery that people take home to ease their conscience with those they have left behind. For just as the new housing estates of one industrial town are almost indistinguishable from those of another, so the shopping-streets of the country towns are becoming all very much the same, with their repetitive art-and-craftiness, their eager eye on the visiting tourist.

Obviously Keswick is not the only town in the district which has changed in this way. So, also, have Bowness-on-Windermere, Ambleside and Grasmere. What I have said about Keswick is, in fact, not so much a criticism of that town as a warning to all the others. At one time, when most people came to the Lakes by train, it could be said that the tourist towns – Keswick and Bowness, in particular – acted as collecting grounds for the visitors, where they were comfortably herded together like sheep in a fellside intake. The dales and dale villages, then, were left to the walkers. The danger today is that the smaller villages, too, have been losing their identity; that in trying to escape from the standardization of the cities men have been imposing merely another kind of standardization on the country.

Long before Keswick became a tourist town, it was a wool-market and a centre for the early mining trade. The copper mines hereabouts may have been worked even as long ago as the fourteenth century, and, by the end of the fifteenth, they were leased out to a colony of Dutch and German miners who ran them until the time of Queen Elizabeth. The mines where they worked were scattered across several of the nearby valleys – Borrowdale, Newlands, Threlkeld and Thornthwaite above Bassenthwaite – and produced not only copper, but lead, silver, zinc, and haematite iron, while Goldscope in the Vale of Newlands gave some gold as well as silver. Mining of copper died out, to all intents, during the Civil War of the seventeenth century, and most of the other mines lingered only half-heartedly or dwindled away, the one notable exception being the working of graphite or plumbago or black lead (locally known as wad) near Seathwaite in Borrowdale. This continued with great success well into the nineteenth century and was the foundation of Keswick's pencil-making industry of today.

Historically, then, Keswick is as Cumbrian as the rest of the county, for, like the west coast, it springs out of the mines, out of the rock. By the middle of the nineteenth century, however, Keswick was no longer a mining town and had become, instead, the main junction for the Lakes, and, above all, the pay-box for Borrowdale.   G.L.

*

The older working-town Keswick has been disappearing beneath the over-night luggage of the new tourism. Shopkeepers, café proprietors and hoteliers own the main streets now. Admittedly they have not done their worst, though some excessively ugly shop-fronts have been introduced, and there have been attempts, here and there, to jazz up the town as if it were the promenade at Morecambe. I once complained that there was a blur of damp good taste over Keswick, but this is being blown away in the exuberance of the new campers, from the North-East and elsewhere who know their pop better than their Wordsworth. Yet, in the shop below the Royal Oak you can find a set of stained-glass windows, each with an appropriate quotation dedicated to the Lake Poets, including – oddly enough – P.B. Shelley. Perhaps, if they had waited a year or two they could have filled in the final window without having to go out of the district.

It is easy to make fun of Keswick and a Cumbrian with any self-respect feels almost obliged to do so. But it is quite unfair. For what has happened to the town is not its own fault but the result of modern man's inability to enjoy himself without making a mess of the spot where he does so. The fate of Keswick was decided when the first eighteenth-century travellers crossed over Dunmail Raise in search of the Picturesque.

The town itself is not without beauty. Visitors of all kinds are accommodated and made to feel at home, from young men carrying guitars, to evangelical clergymen attending the annual convention in what – perhaps wrongly – has been called the largest marquee in the world. To live and die in Keswick would be a happy lot for any man, though happiest for those who lived there not less than seventy years ago.

P.L.

Coniston

Copper has been mined at Coniston on and off for about two thousand years, and as recently as the last century the mines employed 900 men and boys. At the time of the German miners, the copper ore was carted over Dunmail Raise to be smelted at Keswick, but later it was carried down the lake by boat to Nibthwaite, carted to Greenodd or Ulverston, and thence went by sea to Wales.

The mines are now closed and the mine buildings became one of Coniston's two youth hostels, while the rock still gives employment to local men at the famous Broughton Moor quarries. The main livelihood of the village probably comes from the visitors. There are few new houses, mostly tucked away, and a small council estate, not tucked away at all, but, at the same time no great eyesore. There is a modern comprehensive school, serving the youth of High Furness, cafés serving the same, and the Ruskin Museum with its set of musical rocks. Yet Coniston remains an honest slate village, plain but not fussy.

P.L.

Millom

It has pleased some people to sneer at Millom. When the Millom Council decided to subscribe to a tourist organization, a Barrow paper printed a comic cartoon about it, forgetting that the area served by the council includes the Scafells, the shore of Wastwater, Eskdale, Devoke Water, Ravenglass and Silecroft – places which, as tourist attractions, compare favourably with Barrow town hall. But Millom has one distinction not shared by any other of the industrial towns of the area. It is built of true Lake District slate. The Furness iron towns are built mostly of limestone: the west Cumbrian towns of sandstone. The iron-ore mines of Millom were sunk in the limestone, of course, but the town itself is built upon and out of the Coniston flags and grits which lie along the Cumberland side of the Duddon estuary. Small, drab, out-of-date you may call it if you want to, but it is as much a part of the Lake District as Hawkshead or the islands of Windermere.

G.L.

Aspatria

Keswick, Coniston, Millom – mining has playing an important part in their development, and so too with offbeat, fringe Aspatria where a whole saga of coal was once enacted.

Aspatria is a kind of frontier town. The pits have been closed for a long time, and the country is creeping up again. Farms back on to the main street, and a stranger who dropped in from a balloon would find it hard to tell if he were in a mining village or a country market town. This is the extreme northern tip of the industrial west where the regional dissimilarities of the Lakes clash close one against the other. The town has its roots in the coal seams, and the coal has put its mark on streets, houses, farms and church. But the old forest of Inglewood seems not entirely uprooted in the country round about, and the fells are not far away to the east nor the Solway to the west.

And Aspatria has its own special distinction, for it was the birthplace of Sheila Fell, daughter of a retired coal-miner, and an artist whose work has been placed by critics in the great English landscape tradition. Her pictures are sombre, brooding, often dark, with the human figures hardly to be differentiated from the soil and rock on which they work. No other Cumbrian-born painter has been so successful in interpreting the basic character of our landscape.

G.L.

The Wool Towns

The manufacture of woollen goods began in Kendal some six hundred years ago. John Kempe, of Flanders, came over to England in 1331 to introduce improved methods in weaving, though, in spite of Cornelius Nicholson,[1] there is no real proof that he settled in Kendal. Other Flemish weavers may have come to the town, however, for Kendal cloth was mentioned in enactments before the end of the fourteenth century, and in Tudor times the town was supplying London with much of its everyday wear – plain, hard-wearing stuff, rather coarse, and known as Kendal cottons.

Most of the wool was spun by the housewives in their own homes and woven by their husbands on cottage looms, after which it went to the town, to the fulling mill and the dyer. It was for its dyes, in particular, that Kendal was famous. Its spotted cottons – white spotted with red, green or blue – were worn by the English bowmen at Flodden Field. Better-known still was the Kendal Green of Falstaff's 'three misbegotten knaves'[2] – a colour obtained by dyeing the cloth first of all with the yellow of dyer's greenweed (*Genista tinctoria*) and then with a blue extracted from woad. The greenweed, rather like a dwarf broom, still grows in the district.

The trade began to expand in the reign of Edward IV, encouraged by the powerful Parr family of Kendal Castle, who gave to Henry VIII the wife who was to become his widow. By her time the trade had spread into the neighbouring towns and villages – up the Kent to Staveley, down the valley to Milnthorpe, over the low hills to Windermere, and along the Rothay and the Brathay into Grasmere and Langdale. It has been estimated that, in the fifteenth and early sixteenth centuries, there

[1] See: Cornelius Nicholson, *Annals of Kendal* (1861).
[2] *Henry IV*, Part 1, Act II, sc. iv.

Kendal

were at least eight walk-mills or fulling-mills in the parish of Grasmere alone.

Soon, however, the trade began to decline, and when the plague reached the district towards the end of the seventeenth century, it carried off many of the workers, especially the cottage weavers. Kendal cloth was now right out of fashion.

In the smaller towns and villages, the trade dwindled and dwindled until at last it disappeared almost entirely. These smaller towns fall into two groups – those built on the slate and those built on the limestone. And the slate villages include most of the best-known tourist centres on the southern side of the Lakes: Ambleside, Grasmere, Hawkshead and Skelwith Bridge. Now when the wool industry collapsed these spots were left almost derelict. The valleys – Langdale, especially – became what 300 hundred years later would have been called a distressed area. The population was far greater than the land could support, and there are signs of desperate attempts to plough barren patches of fellside for the sake of a handful of oats. Hawkshead still carried on its wool-market, but for the most part the towns tried to adapt themselves to the new conditions. Fulling mills were turned into tanneries, while bobbin-mills and saw-mills were set up in the old warehouses.

It was in this grim industrial perspective of prosperity, unemployment and reconstruction that the national park villages took shape. The old mills have closed down, and the buildings have disappeared or have been altered until they are no longer recognizable, but there is still the print of the practical about the houses and streets.

P.L.

Kendal

Kendal – it was originally Kirkby Kendal, so called to distinguish it from Kirkby Lonsdale and Kirkby Stephen – serves the area with shops and lawyers, holds biannually what it claims to be the oldest musical festival in England, and houses an adventurous art centre at Abbot Hall. Yet it is quite free of the over-bred refinement of the cathedral city or the self-conscious tweediness of the county town. Its long main street – now, part of it, strung on to the A6 – takes a rough individuality from its hilliness and from the fact that many of the buildings still show the slate they were first made of, but its artificial smile, of shop-fronts and offices is not very different from that of almost any mid-sized northcountry town, the town hall being a typical example of Municipal Comic.

The really important thing about Kendal – important not just for itself but for the whole of the southern Lake District – is that it is still alive in the present. It lies on the most popular approach route to the Lakes, only about seven miles from Windermere, so that there are plenty of antique shops, gift shops, cafés and hotels that cater for the tourist, though he is not allowed to feel that he owns the town.

P.L.

Kendal Adjusts

What interests me most about Kendal is not its early history but the way the town has adapted itself to the present day. Of course, the history is interesting enough. There are traces of a British settlement at Castle How, near the county hospital, while the Roman camp beside the river at Watercrook was both an important station on the system of supply roads between Chester and Hadrian's Wall and a link with the coast via Ambleside and Hardknott. In the late twelfth century, the barony of Kendal was created by Richard Coeur de Lion, who later divided this in three, giving the portion with the castle to Sir William Parr.

Kendal rose to be the main commercial centre of the Westmorland wool trade. Much of the cloth, woven on cottage looms, was brought into the town by pack-horse, and the streets and yards were bustling with stables and inns.

It was in the seventeenth century, when the Westmorland homespun went out of fashion and the trade declined in the villages, that Kendal began that course of adjustment which so rouses my admiration. First, it shipped its goods to the plantations of America, where the owners were not unduly fastidious about the kind of cloth worn by the negro slaves. Then it began a reciprocal import business, more particularly in tobacco and snuff, and still remains one of the main centres of snuff manufacturing. (You can see one of the snuff warehouses in Lowther Street, with a painted negro snuff-taker jutting out from the wall like a ship's figure-head.) Today there are light engineering industries and the important K-shoe factory. The town also houses the head offices of the Provincial Assurance Company.

Kendal looks like a market-town and, in fact, has a lively, Saturday market. It looks, also, like a tourist town, and many travellers stop there overnight on their way to Scotland or the Lakes. Yet for all this it is essentially an industrial town and one of the most remarkable in England. It is relatively small, with some 24,000 inhabitants, and, unlike similarly situated country towns such as Harrogate or Clitheroe or Hexham, it has no large area of population lying fairly close at hand. So Kendal has to rely on itself and on its immediate environment, and it is just this that has made it so self-sufficient, so self-contained and so proud of itself.

The town has brought work and independence to south Lakeland. Of course, there is always the danger that the town's comparative prosperity will turn the nearby villages into suburbs, but if there were two or three more Kendals scattered about the Lake District I should be much more optimistic about the future of the whole area.

A splendid act of local enterprise was the restoration of Abbot Hall, built in 1759 by Carr of York for yet another member of the Dallam Tower Wilsons, who, however, left it after ten years. The house was bought by the Kendal Corporation at the end of the last century but remained uninhabited and began to fall into serious disrepair. More recently, however, it has been most imaginatively renovated, and has become both an adventurous art gallery and a very lively local centre.

G.L.

Appleby-in-Westmorland

The first thing to be said about Appleby is that there is nothing at all ambiguous about it. It so obviously belongs just where it is: a sandstone town in sandstone country, built round a castle set on a hill in a crook of the river. There was a keep at Appleby as early as 1174, when it is said to have been besieged by William the Lion of Scotland. King John, in 1203, granted the estate to the family of Veteripont or Vipont, and by the late thirteenth century it had passed into the hands of the Cliffords, one of whom was the Shepherd Lord whose adventures were turned by Wordsworth into 'The Song at the Feast of Brougham Castle'. Then, in the seventeenth century, it came to the last of the Cliffords, the Lady Anne, who, in both stone and story, left more to be remembered by than any other woman of Westmorland.

Yet it was only after years of waiting and legal wrangling that Anne Clifford came to her own. Her father, the third Earl of Cumberland, who died when she was sixteen, had quarrelled with her mother, and, as an act of spite, disinherited his daughter. King James upheld the will, and it was not until the last of the male line of the Cliffords died, in 1643, that Lady Anne came into the Clifford estates. By this time she was fifty-three and was the Countess of Pembroke by her second marriage, having already been the Countess of Dorset by her first. She quarrelled with both husbands, and, having left the second one, travelled north in 1649 to her great inheritance. In Yorkshire she had two castles: Skipton, where she was born, and Bardon Tower in Wharfedale. In Westmorland, she owned castles at Appleby, which she chose for her main home, at Brougham near Penrith, at Brough-under-Stainmore, and at the remote Pendragon, in the valley of the upper Eden, which looks as if it cannot have been inhabited since the time of King Arthur let alone that of Lady Anne. All these she repaired or rebuilt and made each her place of residence from time to time, though Appleby and Skipton remained her favourites. She was almost equally conscientious about the rebuilding of churches. As well as restoring the parish church at

Skipton, she largely rebuilt the older of the two churches at Appleby, St Michael's, Bongate, and repaired the parish church, St Lawrence's, where she erected an alabaster memorial for her mother and prepared a sombre, much-escutcheoned tomb for herself. She repaired the church at Mallerstang, and completely rebuilt both the chapel at Brougham (it was altered and refurnished in the mid-nineteenth century by Lord Brougham) and the isolated church of St Ninian, known as Ninekirks, on the banks of the Eamont, which, I am told, remains almost exactly as the countess left it – perhaps the most interesting seventeenth-century church interior to be found in the north-western counties.

Lady Anne's biographers[1] tell how she regularly received the sacrament in all her churches, how she set up a pillar on the Brougham road at the point where she last saw her mother, and how she built and endowed St Anne's Hospital for the old women of Appleby. Piety, daughterly affection, charitableness – these are the virtues we are asked to admire. And, no doubt, they were admirable. Yet George Watson, one of the earlier, though not the earliest, of her biographers, adds ominously: 'It is somewhat singular that a woman so high-minded, religious, and discerning should have made two such unhappy marriages.' It does not seem so singular to me. For, even allowing for the fact that her two choices were pretty bad ones, she can never have been a comfortable woman to live with. She was thirteen when she watched the funeral of Queen Elizabeth, and she lived right through the reigns of James I and Charles I, and the Commonwealth, until well after the Restoration. By her second marriage she was related both to Sir Philip Sidney and to George Herbert, but poetry does not seem to have been one of her interests. In spite of her loyalty to the Church of England, there seems to have been something of the puritan about her, in temperament if not in politics. There is a seventeenth-century cross at the head of Boroughgate, just outside the walls of the castle, with the inscription. 'Retain your loyalty Preserve your rights.' Lady Anne would have approved, but the rights would most certainly been *her* rights.

When she looked down Boroughgate from the top of the castle hill, she could have seen a good deal of what we see today – the low, almost apologetic, almshouses with their equally demure courtyard, the sixteenth-century moot hall, parked, thoughtfully, at the side of the street and the rather sprawling church of St Lawrence. She would not, however, have seen the fine Georgian houses which have been built since her time, or the Gothic-revival, cloister-like screen which divides the churchyard from the street, or the little market-hall, or the agreeably Victorian Tufton Arms, named after one of the families connected with

---

[1] George Watson, *Anne Clifford* (Penrith 1901); George C. Williamson, *Lady Anne Clifford* (Kendal, 1922); C.M.L. Bouch, *The Lady Anne* (Penrith, 1954).

the Cliffords, where not even the garaged cars of the hotel residents can dispel the Dickensian charm of the old stable-yard. Boroughgate was originally laid out around the beginning of the twelfth century to be in the New Town of Appleby, the Old Town having been centred on Bongate, behind the castle and on the other side of the river. The street has grown and renewed itself, and signs of most of the intervening centuries can be seen somewhere along it. From the top, by the Preserve-your-Rights column, where the street is at its widest, bordered by grass and trees, it drops like a water-chute right into the narrower canal of the lower street, with the cloisters to stop it from sweeping into the church. Look up, from the eighteenth-century cross at the bottom of the hill, and you will see a totally different view – a steep-sided funnel lifted upwards to trees and the sky, and the castle seeming almost to be above that. Seen from either end, it is surely the most beautiful street in Greater Lakeland.

G.L.

Kirkby Lonsdale

Kirkby Lonsdale does not look like a town of the Lakes. The beautiful, yellowish limestone of which it is built reminds one of the Cotswold villages, though it is less rurally quaint and more urbanly elegant. In fact, there is scarcely a house in the main street or around the old Swine Market which is not a pleasure to look at – the stone crusted and dusted with orange or olive-green. Alleyways lead to courts and yards, and gaps between the buildings give views of Barbon Fell across the Lune. And the whole town is clean, uncluttered and well cared-for.

Yes it still has close connections with the Lakes. It is built of Kentdale limestone, and it owed its early growth to the wool trade centred on Kendal. I will say little here about the other attractions of the town – its church with the superb Norman nave (almost a little Durham) and good wood-carving; the far-stretched graveyard and vicarage green; the famous 'Ruskin' view, and the Devil's Bridge over the Lune.

G.L.

Bowness and Ambleside

It is a moot point nowadays whether Ambleside really has avoided being swamped.

The old wool town, or village, of Bowness has practically disappeared under a tidal wave of tourism. Yet it has its old church (with medieval glass in the windows taken from Cartmel Priory after the Dissolution), while something of the homespun dignity which the eighteenth-century visitors admired still hangs about the curve of the road up the hill to Windermere station, and, here and there, in the side streets, where Victorian boarding-houses rise up steep as spoil-heaps at a slate quarry.

Ambleside, on the other hand, though taking as much of the holiday surge as Bowness, has managed not to be swamped. For one thing, the landing-stage and the promenade under the tulip trees are at Waterhead, three-quarters of a mile from the centre of the town. For another, in spite of all the thousands of visitors in summer, Ambleside remains stubbornly local. Go there in winter and you'll find it getting on with its job of catering for the all-round-the-year population of the district. There is nothing picturesque about it – except for the old mill, now a studio, and the little house on a bridge which is surely the National Trust's dottiest property. Yet the four-storey slate terraces – superbly built or they would have fallen down under the vibration of modern heavy traffic – seem to me as essentially Cumbrian as any of the lichened fell-farms of Eskdale or Little Langdale.

G.L.

Grasmere

Grasmere is at the very hub of the dales, and the lake lies in such a dolly-tub of hills that you are puzzled as to how the water can leak out. The dream-like double valley of Near and Far Easedale – as perfect and unspotted as if it had been preserved under glass – is only an after-supper stroll from the hotels, with a waterfall so convenient for viewing that it might have been rigged up by the water board. Stone for stone, Grasmere has changed little since the last century. The church, more than any of the larger churches of the district, has the look of belonging to the fells, even of accepting the fells as part of the congregation. For when the building was enlarged, the north wall of the nave was modified into an arcade, to carry the roof

> ...upheld
> By naked rafters intricately crossed,

as Wordsworth accurately said. So that you sit in the pews with a fell wall at your side, not quite knowing whether you are indoors or out.

Yet, though the stones may be the same, Grasmere has changed so enormously that you can hardly call it a village any more. In winter it is an abandoned encampment of empty hotels; in summer, a fairground. For the part of it called Town End has become that most embarrassing of all tourist attractions, a literary shrine. Of course, Hawkshead has its connections with Wordsworth as well as Grasmere. He attended the grammar school there and lodged with Anne Tyson at her cottage at

Colthouse about a quarter of a mile from the village. The years at Hawkshead, in fact, when he boated and skated and robbed birds' nests and walked round Esthwaite Water nearly every morning before breakfast, are of far greater importance for the understanding of the poetry and the man than the time he spent at Grasmere. But at Hawkshead the memory of the poet has been ousted from popular favour by that of Beatrix Potter, so that it is Grasmere which has to take the full brunt of the part-bored, part-curious, part-sniggering pilgrims. To me, Wordsworth is one of the supremely original minds of all English poetry, and for many years I conscientiously refused to join the queue at Dove Cottage. But one day, when I was visiting the nearby Wordsworth library to examine its superb collection of manuscripts, one of the trustees took me into the cottage at lunchtime when it was closed and empty. The rooms are small and dark, opening so abruptly, one into the other, that there can have been little privacy, especially when the place was full of children. The garden at the back rears up, steep as a fellside, with one great rock from which you can gaze down on the upstairs windows. You can imagine a female relative in every room industriously copying out poems. It is not primarily of the poet that you think, though much of his best verse was put on paper at Dove Cottage, for his great days of experience and vision had come and gone before he ever went to Grasmere. It is the rest of the household who come to mind – Dorothy, his sister; Mary, his wife; Sara Hutchinson, his sister-in-law; the children; the visitors; Coleridge; De Quincey and later Hartley Coleridge who became tenants of the cottage after the Wordsworths had left. Dove Cottage was not the only house the family lived in. There was Allan Bank, where the chimneys smoked, and Grasmere Old Rectory, and Rydal Mount, where the children grew up and Dorothy declined into senility and the poet into his old age. But it is Dove Cottage which seems so closely packed with powerful personalities that you wonder it did not explode.

G.L.

Hawkshead

One of the main Wordsworth centres is Hawkshead, where the poet attended the grammar school and lodged during term time at Anne Tyson's cottage. This is the country of the first two books of *The Prelude* – the woods around Esthwaite Water, with Windermere on one side and Yewdale and Coniston on the other, and with the Old Man, Wetherlam and the Langdale Pikes staring down into the dale. I doubt if many people go to Hawkshead now with Wordsworth in mind, especially since it has been shown that Wordsworth's lodging was not in the village at all but about a quarter of a mile away at Colthouse. It was

Beatrix Potter who discovered the first evidence which led to the identification of the Colthouse cottage; yet Hawkshead still gets its visitors, hundreds and hundreds of them, for reasons which we must now face.

Hawkshead, then, is quaint, fascinating, picturesque, old-world. It deserves all those adjectives which I have tried to avoid, and, moreover, it deserves them in a deliberate and precise sense. If the word 'quaint' could have all its pseudo-quaintness washed off it to mean just quaint again, then that is what Hawkshead would be. But unfortunately it has had to suffer the same treatment as all the other quaint villages, to be photographed and watercoloured until its individual and delicious oddity has become that of a doll's village, an exhibit in a museum lacking only the fluorescent lighting and the glass barriers.

Yet it is hard to see what else could have happened, for its oddness is not the kind which could easily have been adapted to present-day life. It is so small, to begin with. It had to be preserved or else to be damaged beyond all knowing. Its origin, like that of Ambleside, was in the wool trade, but its beauty as it exists today seems quite unrelated to any practical way of living. It is the beauty not of purpose nor of design nor of art, but merely of accident – of narrow lanes and whitewashed walls, of cottages with stone staircases on the outside, of Flag Street and Pillar House and the Red Lion yard. You walk among the houses almost forgetting that they *are* houses, and seeing instead parallelograms of plaster, elephant legs of pillars, slated tunnels and angles and corners, with mauve and green shadows pinned against the whitewash. In this rather abstract way, Hawkshead manages to exist and to hang on to its beauty, but it has had to pay a great price.

P.L.

The Market Towns

The towns we have mentioned have mostly been those of the dales. There remain the market towns scattered all over the county, among the hills and in the lowlands. Their main characteristics are not dissimilar from the dale towns. They are built of the local stone (whatever it may be); they are solid, practical and never pretty or archaic. On the whole they have more in common with the small manufacturing towns you find in the Yorkshire Pennines than with the Tudor and splash towns of the Midlands and the South.

There is Appleby, once the capital of Westmorland; Brough, with its horse-fair; Kirkby Stephen; Ulverston; Whitehaven; Cockermouth, a quiet town, looking as if it were made of plastic, with the fells on one side and the iron and coal country on the other; Wigton, a comfortable red-tweed town; Brampton, on the Roman wall; and Penrith.

Yet each of these, and of others I have not mentioned, has its own personality, and it would be tempting, if there were space, to compare and contrast them. To consider, for instance, two which lie on opposite sides of the district: Penrith and Ulverston. Penrith is the chief of the sandstone towns – red, solid and comfortable, and it opens from lower Patterdale to the farming country around the Eden. Ulverston, on the other hand, is grey and white and lies between the Morecambe Bay valleys and the mining district of Furness. Both owe much to the eighteenth century – Penrith its church, its many nonconformist chapels and meeting houses, and the square houses behind them; Ulverston its more elegant streets on the outskirts, for Ulverston was the fashionable resort of North Lonsdale in the eighteenth-century, and the country gentry came to it for the theatre and dances. Moreover, each town is dominated by a small hill. At Penrith it is the Beacon. The houses are stepping up the side of it now, the dead are buried there among Van Gogh cypresses, but the Beacon still retains something of its old grimness, as when the boy Wordsworth saw the remains of the gibbet, where had hung in chains the body of Thomas Nicholson, executed at Carlisle for the murder of Thomas Parker, a butcher.[1] At Ulverston it is the Hoad, rather more detached than the Beacon but no more rugged. It looks across the salt marshes of the bay, and very rightly carries a monument shaped like a lighthouse. From the top of the lighthouse you look up to the Windermere fells, but outwards too, to the sea and Barrow shipyard and even to Blackpool Tower. As a lad I climbed the steps to fulfil a holiday task, which, so far as I can remember, was to see which way the wind was blowing.

Before the Victorian era these towns must have been isolated and even rather primitive. Roads were very bad, and communications lay through wild and marshy country. They were far from the metropolis, from a university, and from any fashionable centre like Bath or Scarborough, yet they managed to produce a reasonable number of remarkable people. William and Dorothy Wordsworth were born at Cockermouth; Thomas Tickell nearby at Bridekirk, whence he went to Egremont, where his father was rector, and to school at St Bees. John Dalton, the chemist, came from the same district, Eaglesfield near Cockermouth, and George Romney from Dalton-in-Furness. Apart from Romney, who is no great boast, the Lakes have been poor in painters, although they have attracted so many. 'Warwick' Smith, the friend of Francis Towne,[2] was born in Cumberland and left many topographical

[1] *The Prelude*, Book XII. See *Wordsworthshire*, by Eric Robertson, for the reasons why this incident should be associated with Penrith Beacon.

[2] Towne himself made some very remarkable drawings of the district, and so, of course, did Turner. Constable left some early watercolours of Langdale and Borrowdale, and Ruskin's work should not be forgotten. [See also the paintings of Sheila Fell, under Aspatria – I.H.]

drawings, and there have been crowds of sketches and watercolourists whose work hangs in every teashop in the district. But of our native artists, none, I think, catches the glint and glance of the air more truly than Beatrix Potter. Hartley Coleridge is our best poet since Wordsworth.

C.W.

Whitehaven

Whitehaven was founded not on iron but on coal. The true beginning of the town dates from 1630 when the lands of the old St Bees Priory passed into the possession of Sir Christopher Lowther. There is no river at Whitehaven; the harbour is open to the sea and depends entirely on the tides. So Sir Christopher built a pier in 1634, but died ten years later, leaving the estate to his son, John, who was then two years old. Whitehaven was still only a village of forty or fifty houses and had to wait until the boy grew up before it could itself begin to grow. Sir John first of all gained government confirmation of Whitehaven's right to hold a market. Then he set about buying more land, made a successful claim to the foreshore, acquired the mansion called the Flatt, and laid down the basic street-plan upon which the town still stands today. By the time he died, in 1705, Whitehaven had a population of over 2,000,[1] a large coal trade with Ireland and the beginnings of an export and import trade with America.

All this continued to expand under Sir John's heir, his second son, James (later Sir James) Lowther, locally known as Farthing Jemmy. By the mid-eighteenth century, the town had become one of the three or four most important ports in England and looked like developing into a great northcountry centre for trade with the New World. Men like Walter Lutwidge[2] sent out ship-loads of English goods to Virginia and imported rum and tobacco in return. The importing of tobacco, in fact, became for a time one of Whitehaven's principal trades and was the special concern of Wordsworth's uncle, Richard Wordsworth, Controller of Customs[3] in the town.

The tobacco trade dwindled, and was finally killed by the American War of Independence, but the coal trade continued to grow, so that when Farthing Jemmy died in 1755 he left his successor what amounted to a small but very powerful industrial monopoly. That successor was

---

[1] See Daniel Hay, *Whitehaven: A Short History* (Whitehaven, 1966).

[2] See Edward Hughes, *North Country Life in the Eighteenth Century*, Vol. II (Oxford, 1965).

[3] The same post was offered to the poet himself, in 1815, but he declined as it would have meant that he would have had to leave Rydal for Whitehaven. See Mary Moorman, *William Wordsworth: A Biography* (Oxford).

another James Lowther, later the first Lord Lonsdale, the Wicked Earl.
(In fact, Sir James did not originally intend that this other James should
be his heir, since in his will he bequeathed the Whitehaven estates and
coal mines to Sir William Lowther of Holker Hall near Cartmel, who
died before him, in 1753. If Sir William had lived longer, or had left a son,
the subsequent fortunes of Whitehaven might have been very different.)
By the time that the future first earl succeeded to the property the town
already claimed a pottery and a glassworks, a shipyard and all the
sail-making and rope-spinning and other trades that went with it. The
population was flourishing, but the town was so jammed in between the
sea and the three hills round the harbour that it could not easily spread.
Instead, the squares and open spaces between the streets of the original
seventeenth-century plan were filled up, and hundreds of families were
packed into narrow, airless courts cupboarded behind the wide and
imposing main streets. In recent times these courts were being pulled
down, you could see the thick walls of rubble or cobblestones, the
dungeon-like basements, the twisting stone steps that led to the upper
rooms. When you remember also, the starvation wages, the recurrent
epidemics and the appalling conditions in the mines, with their dangers
from fire-damp, explosion, fall of roof or inrush of water, you begin to fill
in a picture that is distressingly familiar. One other thing should be
remembered. Men and women did not flock into Whitehaven because
they wanted to live in degradation, but because the wages, miserable as
they were, were better than those they could get on the farms. The
growth of Whitehaven in the seventeenth and eighteenth centuries is, in
fact, a comment on the kind of poverty which then existed in the
cottages and hovels of what the Romantics were beginning to call a
pastoral paradise.

From all this it may seem that there was little to choose between
Whitehaven and any other industrial town of the north of England. Yet
this was not so. It retained a strong individuality, a sense of being not so
much a region as a colony, separate from the rest of the country. This
was partly due to the monopoly of the Lowther family in the town, but
the feeling of separateness was just as strong in the outlying districts
where the Lowther influence was challenged.

Whitehaven owes much to the Lowthers, the Curwens, the
Christians, the Senhouses and the Gales, for the town they built holds
on to much of its eighteenth-century mercantile and maritime
appearance. In spite of the devastated colliery landscape round about,
and in spite of the grime which has drizzled down for 200 years, the
harbour still has an adventurous, Westward-Ho look about it. From the
new loop road, just behind the plain-Jane St James's Church,[1] the two

---

[1] Inside, however, it is far from plain, with some delicate Italian plasterwork.

outer piers can be seen, enclosing fifty acres of water in their huge
crab-like claws. In a smoky winter sunset, the lights glimmer up from
the quayside, giving it the blurred beauty of an eighteenth-century steel
engraving. The lighthouses at the end of each pier were built, in fact, in
the first half of the following century, and look like white chessmen,
bishops or castles, controlling the diagonals and lines. But lighthouses,
bollards, steps and parapets, all have the same unconcerned neatness,
as if they belonged to too good-mannered a family to look awkward in
any company – and some of the company was embarrassing enough!
Then, on a brisk day in summer, with the wind on the tide, the scene
takes on the bustle of a Rowlandson print brought up to date, with
maybe one of the Marchon boats in the harbour, and lorries by the
quayside, youths fishing, children running along the very edges of the
piers, and everybody looking as if they are about to tumble headlong
into the water.

The town itself is altogether more sedate, more mundane, less
fanciful, less archaic. You must forget the usual association of the word
Georgian. Whitehaven has none of the fashionably old-fashioned
stylishness of the country town or cathedral close. Instead, it is practical
as an account book, and as orderly too, ruled in good straight lines, both
sides added up and seen to balance.

G.L.

Cockermouth

*William Wordsworth 1770–1850, was born here and so too, at Moorland
Close nearby, was Fletcher Christian, leader of the mutiny on the Bounty.
It seems likely that they were contempories for a time at the local
grammar school. While Wordsworth was buried at Grasmere, the burial
place of Christian has never been satisfactorily established.*

Cockermouth lies at the junction of the Skiddaw slate and the limestone. It
lies also at the junction of the River Cocker and the River Derwent,
hence, of course, its name. The Derwent, coming from Bassenthwaite,
reaches the town by way of the little village of Isel, with its entrancing
largely-Norman church by the bridge. Cockermouth, too, has its
Norman building – one of the castles founded by the conquerors to
secure their hold on their Cumbrian estates. Yet the impression given by
the town is less one of rural antiquity than of eighteenth-century,
forward-looking urban elegance. Perhaps sobriety would be a better
word for most of the houses, though the one where Wordsworth was
born does achieve a rather sedate kind of elegance, while one on the
opposite side of the street, called the Grecian Villa, is positively perky.
The present parish church, which has replaced that attended by the

Wordsworths, is undistinguished except in its position, high above the waters-meet, which makes the spire the most scenically effective in the Lakes. But on the whole you can understand the complacent look about the statue of the town-planning Mayor Mayo, as he divides the traffic in one of the most spacious shopping streets in Cumbria.

G.L.

Carlisle

Carlisle is one of the few places of importance in Greater Lakeland that still holds on to a mainly British name. The Romans called it Luguvalium after the Celtic sun god Lugus, and by the tenth century this element had been prefixed by the Welsh *caer*, a fortified place. The Romans had reached it in the first century, and, after the building of Hadrian's Wall, they made the city into one of the greatest military centres in Britain – the camp at Stanwix being, in fact, the largest along the entire frontier of the Roman Empire.

The original British *caer* probably stood on the knoll beside the Eden where William Rufus began the building of the castle in 1092. During the early twelfth century, Carlisle, like the rest of Cumberland, was ceded to Scotland, but after it was reclaimed for England in 1157, Edward I made it into a most formidable fortress, the king-pin of the defence of the Border.

The main gateway of Carlisle Castle is a grimly imposing block. I passed through it once, at the age of about ten, and saw the dungeons and one cell where the walls were decorated with the figures of naked women with hugely exaggerated sexual organs – perhaps the work, as I learned later, of Major Macdonald (the Fergus McIvor of *Waverley*) who was imprisoned there after the Jacobite defeat in the 'Forty Five. Carlisle, in spite of the 2,000-year ring of history behind its name, until recently was largely a nineteenth-century town. Not that it has forgotten its history. Instead, it proclaims often enough that it is a Border city, a medieval city, a martial city, but most of the proclamations are in nineteenth-century gothic.

When you emerge from the station you come at once on Carlisle's most spectacular prop of gothic scenery, the assize courts, designed in 1810 by Sir Robert Smirke, the architect of Lowther Castle, and built on the site of, and to some extent on the plan of, Henry VIII's sixteenth-century citadel. It takes the form of two enormous round towers, like the castles in a chess-set, with battlements on top, and archways on the pavements for pedestrians to walk through. That citadel must be an odd place to work in – one fancies that the tables are all oval, the desks curved and that the clerks all develop round shoulders. But it leaves you in no doubt that Carlisle thinks of itself essentially as a Border stronghold.

The older part of Carlisle lies almost entirely on an all-but-island moated round by three rivers, the Eden and its two tributaries, the Caldew and the Petteril. Remember also that the Eden is joined only a few miles back by the Irthing, and you will realize that the city stands on a great plain of alluvium washed down from the Pennines, the Lake District and the Caldbeck Fells. It is a spacious and fertile landscape. The rivers are certainly not sluggish, but they are no longer mountain streams.

Carlisle also has its place in the legends of the British hero, King Arthur. It is true that Geoffrey of Monmouth does not mention the city, nor does Wace nor Layamon, but Chrétien de Troyes, writing in the twelfth century, puts Arthur's court there, probably dimly remembering the time when Cumbria was still ruled by British kings. And later on a whole group of Middle-English romances, many of them about Sir Gawain, are set in 'Merry Carlisle' and the Forest of Inglewood.

G.L.

Penrith

My strongest impression of Penrith comes, not from my own but from another man's experience: it was the town where Wordsworth was unhappy. And it was on Penrith Beacon that he found what he thought were the initials of a murderer carved on the turf close to the spot where the body had hung in chains. Wordsworth was mistaken: the initials, T.M.P., were those of the victim: 'Thomas Parker murdered'. The name of the murderer was, in fact, Thomas Nicholson (he had been hanged at Carlisle before the corpse was suspended on the Beacon), and I am proud to think that a Nicholson, and quite possibly a distant relative of mine, may have helped to inspire one of the finest passages of *The Prelude*.[1] The town itself is as well made as a piece of eighteenth-century farmhouse furniture. It has some fine Georgian houses and probably the best Georgian church in the county.

Yet I have one memory of Penrith which even Wordsworth might have envied. On Palm Sunday, April 1966, I was engaged to read my poetry at the Newton Rigg Farm College beside the Penrith–Wigton road. The day before there had been, unseasonably, a snowstorm. Sunday, however, was a day of cloudless skies – the air still freezing but the sun as warm as in June. I was driven over Kirkstone Pass, between high barricades of snow, down the length of Ullswater to Penrith. Everywhere the snow was unscratched, unblotted, like a clean sheet of paper. Once or twice in every winter you can expect to see the fells

[1] Book XII, lines 225 – 47.

snow-covered from base to cairn under a bright winter sky, but not more than twice in a lifetime under such a floodlight of April sun. The dazzling contradiction of two seasons made the whole landscape look artificial. Around Penrith the red sandstone barns and farms were plopped out on the fields like red glacé cherries decorating a white-iced cake. My face grew damp with sweat from the heat of the sun on the windscreen, yet outside not a drop of thaw could be seen on wall or twig or grass-blade.

G.L.

Ulverston

Ulverston, for a time my own home, has deep agricultural roots as its marts and lively Thursday markets still show.

The Hoad at Ulverston looks across the salt marshes and sands of Morecambe Bay and carries a monument in the form of a lighthouse that makes it look like a town-crier's bell standing, mouth-downwards, with the handle sticking up in the air. (The lighthouse is dedicated to the memory of Sir John Barrow, born at Ulverston in 1764, who became a high official of the Admiralty, and in 1831 published the story of *The Mutiny of the Bounty*.) The whole of this section of Morecambe Bay is almost astonishingly unsullied and unspoilt in spite of the fact that industry of one type or another has been carried on there since at least the early Middle Ages.

P.L.

John Soulby, Printer

Ulverston, the modern capital of Furness – in medieval times Dalton held that honour – is a place of considerable distinction, though you can hardly tell this from the new trunk road which bulldozes its way through the centre of the town. The best of Ulverston (Princes Street and the Market Cross end of King Street) has little of the county snootiness that you often find in a Georgian country town. I think this is due to the fact that towards the end of the eighteenth century, Ulverston realized that it could not go on being just a place of merchants and lawyers and doctors, a place where the gentry of the district came in to visit the theatre and attend balls. So it developed its canal and entered the new century as the port of industrial Furness. And this time of looking both ways, to the country and to the town, is beautifully captured for us by John Soulby, father and son, jobbing printers of Ulverston between about 1790 and 1830, collections of whose work can be seen at Barrow Public Library and also at the Museum of English Rural Life in the

University of Reading.[1] Among their work you will find notices of sales of hay, wheat, clover, turnip-seed, farms, coppices, and dwelling-houses:

Shop, Barn, Stable, Warehouse and other Outbuildings, Orchard and Garden, and 4 Inclosures of Land (in good cultivation) containing together, by admeasurement, twelve Acre, Statute measure, or thereabouts, together with

1 PEW IN LOCKWICK CHAPEL
contains 7 sittings

And a parcel of peat Moss, about one customary Acre (of freehold tenure) upon Roam Moss in the Parish of Colton in the said County.

And side by side with these, you will see signs of the new Ulverston: the sale of the hull of the Sloop *Tom*, the sale of the wreck of the Schooner *Sally*, and advertisements for carters for the 'Gothwaite' (Gawthwaite) Quarries and for 'Twenty Men who have been accustomed to work in IRON MINES' for Lindal.

Later on Ulverston had its own blast-furnaces and foundry, and though the one was pulled down and the other was transferred to Millom, the town has not lost its practical, workaday look, which may discourage some people from exploring anything more than the obviously Georgian centre. This is a pity, for Theatre Street, opening off Princes Street, and the alleys off King Street, are full of twists, while the houses round the Gill, now a parking-place, have the unsmiling, straight-backed rectitude of the villages of Galloway. Then at Swarthmoor, just outside the town, there is a fine Elizabethan manor-house, once the home of Margaret Fell, whose second husband was George Fox, so that Swarthmoor Hall has become a place of Quaker pilgrimage, while the meeting house, not far away, has a simplicity and severity that is almost romantic to present-day eyes.

But the main attraction of Ulverston comes from the fact that it lies, like Kendal, at the junction of the limestone with the slate. On one side the town eases itself out into the suburbs and gardens towards the limestone of Birkrigg and Bardsea. On the other, the terraces slant dourly up the steep lower slopes of Kirkby Moors – the most westerly outcrop of the Silurian slates which make up, together with the limestone, the whole of southern Lakeland.

G.L.

---

[1] See *John Soulby, Printer, Ulverston,* printed by the University of Reading as a catalogue to their exhibition of 1966.

Barrow-in-Furness

Historically Barrow-in-Furness does not belong to the Lake District at all. In the eighteenth century, when Whitehaven was already a thriving sea port, and there were small but busy ironworks in nearly all the valleys of Low Furness, Barrow did not exist even as a village. Not until the 1840s was it planned into existence by Ramsden and Schneider and the Dukes of Devonshire and Buccleuch on the extreme tip of a long peninsula so far from the fells as to be scarcely aware of them. With the coming of the railway and the lake steamers a day trip to Windermere or Coniston became possible for most Barrow people but it was still a trip into what seemed a foreign country.

Today this is changed. This submarine building town has now absorbed a good deal of the industry of Askam, Lindal, Dalton and the rest of Low Furness, and is an important centre of employment in the area. More and more, the villages within about ten miles of Walney Channel began to depend on Barrow. Like Kendal – though without Kendal's 500-year training for the job – it was becoming the half-reluctant godfather of a large section of the Lake country.

P.L.

Sports and Pastimes

Cock-fighting

A thing which still goes on is cock-fighting. R.D. Humber, in *Game-Cock and Countryman*, tells of some of the old, almost legendary tales of cock-fighting policemen and magistrates, of daring escapes from the law at Foulshaw Moss and Blea Tarn and among the ruins of Millom Castle, and of dead cocks hidden in straw and live ones shut into milk churns and driven innocently past the raiding police. There was a time when nearly every farm in the dales had its game-cocks, and mains were fought regularly, though in secret. Today it is probably the very illegality of the sport which is its chief attraction. It is hard not to feel a kind of grudging admiration for men who, to follow their hobby, will cross half a county and gather at dawn or by the light of car-headlamps on some cold, misty moors or marshes – just as it is hard not to feel admiration for the pluck of the birds themselves. (If a game-cock refuses to fight, the owner immediately wrings its neck to teach it to know better next time.) The admiration sometimes comes from unexpected quarters. A few years ago Foulshaw Moss, immediately opposite Sandside on the Gilpin shore of the estuary, was the scene of one of the most notorious of post-war cock-fighting meetings, where the police took the names of hundreds of spectators.

'I hear you were at Foulshaw the other day,' said a constable, interviewing an acquaintance of mine.

'No, no. You're wrong. I never left the house.'

'But your car was seen.'

'I tell you, I never left the house.'

'Stick to that story,' said the constable, 'and you'll hear no more about it.' *G.L.*

Fox-hunting

Norman's sympathy lay more with the fox.
In Cumbria fox-hunting is not just a social gathering for organized

cruelty. Foxes have to be kept down somehow and it is at least arguable that hunting is the most practical way of doing so. Anyway, the graces and snobberies of county society have little to do with the fell hunts. (I do not speak of the lowland hunts, of which there are several.) The professional huntsman may wear the red coat but his followers turn out in whatever will stand up best to the weather. For the hunting has to be done on foot, and as the fell foxes mostly lie well above the plough-line and nearly always make for the tops when pursued, the followers must be ready to face wind, rain and cold, to cross slopes shin-deep in bog or snow, or to go hours through mist, guessing where the hounds are from the sound of their voices. Many times both fox and hounds have fallen over precipices and dashed themselves to pieces.

The fox, whenever it can, will make for an earth or borran. Some of these are terrifying spots – chimneys or caves, plugged with chock-stones and rubble; or crumbling mountainsides where dumps of fallen boulders are riddled with holes and tunnels; or the abandoned workings of old mines and quarries where roof and walls are liable to cave in. This is where the terriers are needed. Their job is to enter the hole and make the fox bolt, but often they fight to the death in the dark cracks of the rock. Now and again neither fox nor dog emerges, and no amount of searching with crowbar or even dynamite can catch the one or save the other.

At other times the fox takes shelter on a benk, a narrow ledge or cliff-face, where the hounds cannot reach it. Sometimes, after the hounds are called off, it cannot make its way back from its refuge and has to stay there till it starves or falls. There is a story of a man who was lowered on a rope to shift a fox from such a perch, and succeeded so well that the rest of the hunt went off excitedly, leaving the man dangling in mid-air.

Probably the best way to watch a hunt is to get well up among the fells before it begins. With any luck you may be able to view all the first part without moving more than a few yards, and if the fox gets well away you can follow on the level without having to climb. But the most popular method at present seems to be to follow by car. When the fox strikes up the fellside, the followers set off along the narrow roads and farm tracks for that spot in the next valley where it is most likely to come down. Visitors with large cars who choose to drive along these roads in the opposite direction will have a good opportunity to study the dialect. Before long, no doubt, groups of Manchester sportsmen will be following the pack by helicopter.

There are five fell-packs – the Ullswater (hunting Patterdale and Mardale), the Blencathra (Skiddaw and Borrowdale), the Melbreak (Lorton, Buttermere, Loweswater), the Eskdale and Ennerdale (the western dales), and the Coniston (Old Man and Langdale). Of them all, the Eskdale and Ennerdale probably hunts the wildest and roughest country, including Pillar and Scafell.

P.L.

A Famous Huntsman

John Peel, born Caldbeck c. 1776, buried Caldbeck 1854, tends to inspire two schools of thought: one which backs him as a great Cumbrian huntsman, and the other which says he was not quite the excellent fellow he is often represented to be. In recent years his grave has been desecrated by anti-hunt activists.

Because of 'D'ye Ken John Peel', many people think of Cumbria as the typical hunting county, with Peel himself as the master of a fashionable hunt. But there was nothing fashionable about John Peel. He came, not from the gentry, but from ordinary farming stock, living at Caldbeck, and hunting the fells round about Skiddaw with his own small pack of hounds. This was rough work – out every morning at five or six o'clock, no horses (except for the pony on which he rode to the meet), and – unless I am wrong about the 'coat so grey' – no red coats.[1] Peel died in 1854, and it was not until some years later that the song became popular, by which time the tune had lost the dotted quavers which give a lilt to the verses in the original version. John Woodcock Graves, who wrote the words of the song, liked Cumberland so little that he emigrated to Tasmania in 1833. Followers of the Eskdale and Ennerdale swear that, in any case, John Peel was not to be compared with Tommy Dobson.

P.L.

Hound-trailing

Hound trails are marvellous. An errant pack poured through my cottage living room at Oxen Park in High Furness one summer's day, completely lost. The excitement of a trail has to be experienced to be believed. And after a trail is over, there is always, it seems, a lone Land-Rover blazing up and down the countryside, an irate owner looking for the one forlorn hound that still hasn't arrived home.

Hound trails first became popular at the country sports-meetings and just about every agricultural show still runs one. Then they began to be

---

[1] Cumbrian people still argue as to whether John Peel wore a red coat or not. The evidence seems inconclusive, but for my own part I am satisfied that the 'coat so gay' of the song was really a 'coat so grey'.

Loweswater, Mellbreak Foxhounds country

held in the small towns on the edge of the fell district, and now trailing is widespread and well organized under an association founded in 1906. During summer and autumn there are trails nearly every day in one spot or another, the more successful dogs may go out two or three times a week. Form is followed very closely, with trailing-notes published each week in the local papers, while the leading hounds are listed in a championship table according to the number of wins and places.

It is, moreover, a democratic sport, drawing its followers from all the strata of local society. The leading hounds are valuable animals, but it is not beyond the means of a working man to buy a pup and rear it, and if the dog grows into a winner, it becomes the pet and mascot of the neighbourhood.

Trailing, no doubt, owes its popularity partly to the love of gambling, and there used to be heartbreaking tales, during the lean years, of miners who starved their children in order to feed dogs on eggs, cream and sherry. But it seems likely that trailing also appeals to a scarcely understood backward-look at the old dale life. The delicious names given to the dogs seem to confirm this: Starlight, Lonning Lass, Lawless, Dowcrag, Briery, Fibre Mills.

Certainly a trail is often a grand sight – the hounds are slipped in a field and up they go to the tops, out of sight much of the time, and back again in thirty-five minutes or so. They have a curious leisurely way of running, taking wall and dyke in an easygoing stride and casting a friendly eye about them. The trail is laid by an aniseed mixture, dragged over the ground in an old sock. Two men start together from a point about mid-way round the course, and make their way, each by a different route, to the starting post. Many tricks were played in the past. False trails were laid down; hounds were lured off the course and fed or given drugs to make them thirsty; some were seized, carried off by car, and put back on the trail ahead of the others. Today there is much closer supervision, and most of the trails are well watched and guarded.

P.L.

The Dale Sports

Hound trails are now one of the chief attractions at nearly all the dale sports. These may vary from village fruit and flower shows to popular meetings that draw crowds from all over the North-west. The travelling bank attends the larger shows, and ice-cream vans and tricycles roll up from the towns, with horse-boxes for the increasingly popular horse and pony jumping. The local brass band bellows like a musical farmyard, and the sound swells and fades in the wind with the smell of hawthorns and hay. Looking down from the tops, you see the crowd like wood-lice around the ring, and the marquee with its red pennons, and the cars lined up about the field. At one time these shows were favourites with all the young people from the smaller towns, but today it is probably only the dance in the evening which attracts many of the town folk. Yet the boys of the town still know how to get into the field behind the gatekeeper's back and are always ready to help to drive the animals from any one spot to any other. When I was a boy all the Millom schools were given a holiday for Green Show,[1] held three miles away. Some of the mining towns have their own sports, such as Egremont Crab Fair, with dancing in the streets, a fair queen, and a gurning competition.

Gurning consists of putting one's head through a horse-collar and pulling the ugliest face possible. And it was my privilege to know for many years one of the champion gurners of West Cumbria, of whom it was said that he had once won a competition without knowing that he had entered. He had merely been following the efforts of the other competitors with interest and sympathy.

Grasmere is the greatest of all the meetings, in its cup-like valley with the dark green of late summer slumping heavily on the woods and hills. It is held during August – often one of the wettest times of the year in the Lakes – so that sometimes the valley is swimming with water the day before, and then, in the morning of the sports, the sky clears and the sun clamps down on the meadows like a red-hot plate. Or perhaps there is that warm, pewter-coloured haze, when the clouds are low, the fells flat as wood-engravings, and there are hardly any shadows.

Whatever the weather, it cannot discourage the older dale folk to whom the sports are a passion. I knew one old man who, as a youth in the 1870s, lived just below Boot in Eskdale. He worked on the Irton estates, and after his day's work would meet his friends at the Woolpack Inn a mile above Boot village. It was the eve of Grasmere Sports, and half a dozen of them decided to go. They each went home, had supper and packed a few slices of bread, and then met again at the Woolpack. They set off over Hardknott – then, of course, only a rough, pony track – to Cockley Beck and over Wrynose into Little Langdale. It was midnight when they reached the Tourist's Rest, – now the Three Shires Inn – in the village, but one of them knew the landlord and persuaded him to let them sleep on the kitchen floor. After breakfast they went by Elterwater and Red Bank to Grasmere, watched the sports, came back the same fourteen or fifteen miles overnight, and were at work the next morning.

P.L.

---

[1] The annual show of Millom and Broughton Agricultural Society, now no longer held at the Green, but still known as Green Show.

The Guides' Race

The most spectacular event in dale sport is undoubtedly the Guides' Race. The route is always out of the field to the steepest slope nearby, up for fifteen hundred feet or so, and down again. Not all dale sports are conveniently situated for such a race, but at Grasmere and Coniston the whole fellside becomes a magnificent stadium, with an obstacle course of crags, screes, grass rakes and sheep trods, with spikings of rowan, holly, birch and juniper. The competitors walk, run, climb or scramble up as best they can, but once they are at the top, the nature of the race changes, for they come down in a kangaroo chain of leaps, jumping from crag to crag, crashing through the bushes, glissading down the screes. A man who reaches the turn with a lead of twenty yards is likely to be a hundred yards ahead less than a minute later.

P.L.

Wrestling: 'A Laal Furtle'

It is wrestling which really holds the heart of the Cumbrian.

Wrestling, in the Cumberland and Westmorland style, is the most good-natured of all forms of physical combat. It needs a calm concentration and watchfulness which leaves no place for malice or anger. If you lose your temper you will probably lose the fall. Often you will see men smiling quietly to themselves as they waltz round one another, waiting for a chance to attack, and when they fall they get up with the look of surprise that you see on the face of a very young child who knows that he cannot walk without falling but is never quite ready for the fall when it comes.

The men stand face to face, breast to breast, locked closer than lovers, each clasping hands behind the other's back, one arm above a shoulder and one below. If a man breaks hold, except when throwing his opponent, he loses the fall. The round ends when a man is down – there is no need for both shoulders to be touching the ground as in some forms of wrestling. Usually both men fall together, and the loser is the one who is below. Sometimes a skilful and agile wrestler can twist in the arms of an opponent even as he is being thrown and so end the fall uppermost. Physical strength alone is not so important as may be thought. A man who is much the stronger of the two can always win by forcing in his opponent's back, but granted that there is a reasonable balance of weight and stature, the fall will usually go to the more skilful or more enterprising wrestler.

Of the methods of attack – hipeing, inside striking, in and out, the chip, haming, hankering the heel, haunching, cross-buttocking and the like – I will not presume to speak. The terms would mean nothing to those who have not themselves tried to wrestle – not even as boys at school – and indeed, the majority of the spectators at the big meetings know little of the techniques they are watching. Dale wrestling is really a sport for the wrestler, not the spectator. It is a standard joke that if you want to see the wrestling at Grasmere you have to enter for it. This is true in more than the obvious sense. For all the spectator gets is a sight of two men staggering round one another like a couple of drunks trying to dance. The real contest is lost to him. It is not to be *seen* at all. To appreciate wrestling the mind must think in images which are largely tactile. The wrestler must fix his hold, keep his balance, and try to read the mind of his opponent entirely by touch. It is a sport for individualists; for men who want to be in it; for men who like a laal furtle.

We hear of wrestling in Cumberland as early as the seventeenth century, but the first organized meetings seem to have been Melmerby Rounds on Midsummer Day and Langwathby Rounds on New Year's Day, both of which were well established by the end of the eighteenth century. Another meeting was held in July at the top of High Street in the Ullswater Fells, where the wrestlers would have to wait for their second wind before beginning the contest. In the early nineteenth century Professor Wilson (Christopher North) helped to set up the sport at Ambleside, after which Keswick rose in importance as a wrestling centre. Finally the 'metropolitan' competitions were organized at Carlisle, the winner of which might call himself World Champion, Cumberland and Westmorland style.

We now come to a magnificent list of names which have in them the bone and breed of the dales: William Richardson of Caldbeck, Thos. Nicholson of Threlkeld, Miles and James Dixon, Harry Graham of Brigham, Robert Rowantree, William Dickinson, Tom Todd, the Rev. Abraham Brown, and many more, almost forgotten, such as those given by William Litt: '... his last four opponents being A. Armstrong, J. Frears, T. Richardson, and T. Lock, all of them good wrestlers'.[1] Litt himself was a good wrestler, and in 1811 met Harry Graham on Arlecdon Moor for a purse of sixty guineas – the largest sum wrestled for up to that date. But his fame – if we can speak of the fame of one whose name is known only to Cumbrians and not so many of them – depends not on his own prowess but on the fame he gave to others. For *Wrestliana*, his account of the early wrestling and wrestlers, is one of the classics of the literature of sport, worthy to go beside John Nyren's *Young Cricketer's Tutor*.

After Litt's time the wrestling grew even more popular, until in 1851 a championship match was held at Flan How, Ulverston, for a purse of

[1] William Litt, *Wrestliana* (Whitehaven, 1823).

£300. Then, in the latter half of the century, Grasmere became the capital of the wrestling world, dominated by the figure of George Steadman, heavyweight champion for thirty years – a massive man of over eighteen stone in his prime. Steadman's last appearance in the ring was at the age of fifty-four, in 1900, when he defeated Hexham Clarke in the final at Grasmere. Four years later he died at Brough. In photographs he looks calm and almost benign, with a huge forehead and white side-whiskers like those of a Victorian archdeacon, but the strength of the man shows in the waves of muscles along his forearm and the link-like lock of fingers on fingers. He wore the traditional costume – still worn today – of white underpants, white vest and embroidered drawers, and, of course, he wrestled in stocking feet. Steadman's son was also a well-known wrestler, and once broke the collar-bone of an uncle of mine – not, however, wrestling, but playing rugby.

P.L.

William Litt's Wrestliana

Litt was born at Bowthorn near Whitehaven in 1785. 'His parents held a highly respectable position in society, and he received a liberal education, with the object of fitting him for a clergyman in the Church of England.'[1] Study did not greatly appeal to young William, however, and he took to farming for a while, but his heart was really in wrestling. Soon he became one of the most famous wrestlers in West Cumberland, fighting his way through the ring, year after year, between 1805 and 1815. When Litt met Harry Graham in 1811 he was in poor health and wanted to postpone the match, but Graham's supporters insisted that it should be carried out, and Litt, after losing the first three falls, won seven out of the next eight. During these years in which he was winning great honour as a wrestler, farming and business were neglected. He tried to recover his fortunes as a brewer, and when this failed he went to live at Hensingham, and finally emigrated to Canada, where he died in 1847, broken down in body and mind.

When he started to write the history of the beginnings of wrestling in Cumberland and Westmorland, some people seem to have doubted whether he had the literary ability to tackle his subject. He himself had no doubt. He argues with such a critic in his preface:

'"Does not the subject require a *practical* man?" "Yes." "Thinkest thou there is one man in the kingdom who has won as many prizes as I have and can write better?"'

His confidence was justified, for *Wrestliana* is one of the classics of English sport. Moreover, it is one of the best books which has come out

[1] Jacob Robinson and Sidney Gilpin, *Wrestling and Wrestlers*, to which is added 'Notes on Bull and Badger Baiting' (1893).

of the county. It has the true Cumbrian tang in it; and the prose, in spite of some stiffness of phrase, has the physical, tactile strength of a wrestler.

C.W.

Regattas

Keswick Regatta was staged more than two centuries ago and among its enthusiastic supporters was the amazing Mr Pocklington, owner of Derwentwater's largest island.

The first attempt in Lakeland to organize an entertainment of this kind was made at Ouzebridge on Bassenthwaite in 1780, when ducks were chased by water-spaniels and a number of horses were taken out into the middle of the lake in a flat boat fitted with a plug – the plug was pulled out, the boat sank, and the first horse to swim ashore was the winner. Pocklington's Derwentwater regattas were both more spectacular and more humane. In 1782, for instance, according to the account in the *Cumberland Pacquet* (a weekly paper published at Whitehaven), a large gathering of people assembled on the shore of the lake as early as eight o'clock on the morning of the event. There were marquees in the fields and boats and barges on the water, many of them decked with bunting. At noon, Mr Pocklington's personal friends rowed out and were greeted by a salute of guns from his battery, while, at the same time, five boats set off on a race round the four islands. At three o'clock there was a sham attack on the main island, the besieging fleet coming from behind Friar's Crag, and after two attacks, 'a great variety of beautiful manœuvres', and a whole *Sacre du Printemps* of guns and echoes, the garrison capitulated. By this time it was dark. The visitors were guided back to Keswick by a string of lamps stretched from the water's edge to the town, and the day ended with fireworks and a dance – 'a chain of amusements', claimed the paper, 'which ... no other place can possibly furnish, and which wants only to be more universally known, to render it a place of more general resort than any other in the Kingdom.'

L.

A Rugby Error

I remember the village of Holme because of an incident that shows how close is the link between the Lake countryside and the industrial coast. One summer evening I was walking through the village when a man called to me over a garden wall and asked if I remembered Jim Buckett. Ten years later Lord Birkett was to ask me the same question. For in the

1890s, when Lord Birkett and the old man in the garden had been young, Jim Buckett was the star player in a Millom Northern Union Rugby team, which provided eleven of Cumberland County's thirteen men. I did, in fact, remember Buckett as a very old man, twisted with rheumatism, while my father had often told me of a cup-tie which Millom had been drawn at home against one of the powerful Yorkshire clubs. One minute from the end the visitors were leading by three points to nil when the ball was passed to Buckett, who, with his very long reach, gathered it well in front of him and went over the line. But the referee thought he had knocked-on and disallowed the try.

And now this old man began to tell me about the same match. I listened abstractedly as the smoke of his pipe floated over the antirrhinums and early michaelmas daisies. It was an old story; it had not lost much in the telling; and, anyway, I suspected that my acquaintance, like my father, was talking only from hearsay, and had not seen the match at all.

'It should have been at least a draw,' he went on. 'The referee knew he had made a mistake the moment he had blown his whistle, but there was nowt he could do about it then.'

'Did you see it?' I asked, somewhat sceptically. 'Were you a spectator?'

'I was not. I was the referee.'

G.L.

Some New Sports

Even since the time of Professor John Wilson there have been men who look on the Lakes as a gigantic gymnasium, where the visitor from the towns can find space and fresh air, and can test his skill, daring and endurance. I suppose it is the mere prejudice of one who has hated athletics since childhood which makes me detest this point of view. Too much of my youth had to be spent trying to save my life for me to see much fun in risking it on rocks or in water. Others disagree, however, and rock-climbing, skin-diving and the gentler art of sailing have become very popular. All three, of course, are holiday pastimes, appealing more to the visitor than the local man, though they now have many followers among the scientists and technicians of the newer industries.

For the marathon walkers and record breakers, I can raise nothing but a kind of bewildered grin – the two Grasmere men, for instance, who claim to have swum in every one of the district's 463 tarns; or the Heaton brothers, from East Lancashire, one of whom climbed fifty-one Lake peaks in twenty-four hours, while, later, the other climbed fifty-four.

Many of these men have a real love of the rocks and some of them have a practical knowledge which I can only envy. And none of them, in any case, interferes with the enjoyment of anybody else.

But this can scarcely be said for the speed-boaters, the water-skiers, or the organizers of motor rallies, motorcycle scrambles and go-kart races, all of which bring turmoil, noise and stink to the very spots where one goes primarily to escape them. To ban such things is not to be autocratic but merely to help the national park to carry out the purpose for which it was established. What is the point of preserving the lake shores pure and unsullied to the eye if they are allowed to sound and smell like a factory-town bus-station with a juke box and pin-table saloon next door?

P.L.

Running the Screes

This passage was omitted from later books, perhaps for ecological reasons. The tramp of feet has certainly produced amazing erosion on a number of Lakeland mountains. And, following on, an equally amazing number of people have appeared intent on repairing the paths.

To run down screes is one of the delights of the climber, when he knows how to do it – not, probably, the Wasdale screes, for there you are likely to end in the lake, and it's not shallow. They are not as steep as they look, of course. If they were, the stones would fall. Wasdale Screes, seen from across the lake, look almost perpendicular, but the angle of the slope is really less than 45 degrees – they fall 1,500 feet in about three furlongs. Nevertheless, when going over the top of a scree for the first time, it looks steep enough. The secret of confidence is simple – when in danger, when giddy, when losing your balance, just sit down. The scree will not be far behind the part of you that sits. Scree running is really a series of strides with each stride carrying you many feet, according to the flexibility of the scree. You need good boots, or your ankles will be skinned. You need good socks, too, for I have found that after running down a scree holes appear, not at the ankles, but underneath the heels and the backs of the toes. Sometimes you may want to cross a patch of scree horizontally. This is difficult, as if you slide you have to climb the height you have lost. The method is to stand perfectly upright. If you lean in towards the scree your feet will push the stones in the direction in which they want to slide; if you stand upright the pressure of your feet helps to hold the stones steady.

C.W.

The Names on the Land

Norse Words

There are signs of Norse ancestry in the Lakes which cannot be forgotten since they are engraved across the landscape like the names on a map. Fell, scar, scree, gill, tarn, beck – these Norse words at once name the landscape and bring it to the eye. They make sure that the Lake scene will not only look different from any other in England but will sound different too. Their synonyms have nothing like the same force – no one could confuse a fell with a hill. They belong so particularly to the North that a southerner uses them almost self-consciously, as if in inverted commas, while they come as easy as whistling to the lips of the Cumbrian. There are others, not quite so familiar, which have the same expressiveness: pike, gable, knot, mire, force (a waterfall), nab (a projection, as in Nab Scar on Rydal and Nab Cottage where De Quincey lived for a time). Some topographical terms have more than one meaning. Hawes or hause or hows, for instance, may be derived from Old Norse *hals* a neck or pass (e.g. Esk Hause), or from *haugr*, a hill or mound (Skiddaw), or again it may be related to the northern dialect world, *haugh*, which usually means the flat alluvial meadows beside a river.

Many of these Norse words are also known as common suffixes or prefixes in place-names – *thwaite*, a clearing, the best known of all. There must be a hundred places in the Lake District the names of which end in *thwaite*, as well as a large number of surnames – my own middle name being Cornthwaite. Then there is *biggin* (a building), *keld* (a spring), *wath* (a ford as in Langwathby), *holm* (an island, or a piece of land half-surrounded by a stream as in Holmrook or Herbertholm, the old name for St Herbert's Island in Derwentwater), *thorpe* (farm or hamlet: Crackenthorpe, the home of Wordsworth's maternal great-grandparents), *scales* (*skali*, a shepherd's summer-hut; Seascale, Portinscale), *wick* (*vik*, a creek or bay – the Vikings were the creek-men), *seat* (*saetr*, a summer-pasture farm or shieling: Seatoller).

Seat, when it is a suffix, is often changed to side – as in Swinside and Ambleside – and this may lead to confusion. On one of the bleakest stretches of the Cumbrian coast there is a very old farming settlement at the mouth of the large beck which flows from the slopes of Black Combe and through the village of Bootle. This settlement was named from the Old Norse personal name Einarr and so became Einarr's Saeter, and through various corruptions (Aynerset, Andersetta, Anerset, etc.[1]) to Annaside. The beck, naturally enough, took its name from the settlement and became Annaside Beck. But recently, people have begun mistakenly to presume that the settlement took its name from the beck, since Annaside looks as if it means 'beside the Anna', so that in the last few years Annaside Beck has appeared on maps pretentiously swollen into the River Annas.

There are many other Norse words too deeply grafted into the local names to be easily recognizable, and others – suffixes such as *land* or *ness* (a promontory) – which may come either from Old Norse or from Old English, but where the other part of the name suggests a Norse derivation. Even such English-looking words as mere and water are often found linked to Scandinavian surnames. Buttermere, Windermere, Grasmere, Ullswater, Elterwater and Thurston Water (the old name for Coniston Water) have been thought to contain respectively the Scandinavian names of Buthar, Windar, Gris (meaning swine), Ulf (a wolf), Eldir and Thorstein.

P.L.

Irish Influence

Signs of the vital cross-breeding between the two cultures, Irish-Christian and Norse-pagan, can be seen all along the west Cumbrian coast. There are many place-names, for instance, in which an Irish personal name is joined to a Norse element. Aspatria is the most notable case. Here the Irish Patrick is joined to the old Norse *askr*, an ash tree, and the whole word is turned cart-before-the-horse after the Celtic fashion. Vikings who had not lived in Ireland would have put the man's name first as in the present-day Ullswater, which is Ulf's lake. The practice was even continued by habit in names which have no Celtic associations at all. In the south of Cumberland, for instance, there is a whole batch of hamlets or farms with names of a similar form: Hallsenna, Hall Waberthwaite, Hallthwaites, each of which would probably have been called Senna Hall and so on in most other parts of England.

[1] See: *The Place-Names of Cumberland* (Cambridge University Press).

It should be remembered, however, that this Celtic-type inversion-compound is still an eccentric form, possibly adopted only by those Norsemen who had been overtouched by the blarney – those, in fact, who came rather late to the county and so had an extra generation or two of Irish mothers-in-law behind them. As a general rule the Norsemen and the Danes continued to put the defined term second, as is still the case in English. Thus in Cumbria we say Scafell and not Fell Scar, Troutbeck and not Beck Trout. And if we want to differentiate between town and lake of the same name, let us speak of Windermere Town and Windermere Lake, and not twist our tongues into the ridiculous affectation of Lake Windermere. As for such monstrous tautologies as Lake Ullswater and Lake Derwentwater, I can only say that it would be as logical to speak of Mount Richmond Hill.

The Irish influence on the Norsemen shows also in their devotion to the Irish saints. St Bega is commemorated at St Bees. St Bridget, the sister of St Patrick, can claim the dedication of the old church at Beckermet and is also remembered at Bridekirk near Cockermouth and at Kirkbride on the Solway, the latter being yet another example of a Celtic inversion. So also, at the opposite end of the county, is Kirksanton, the church of the Irish Saint Sancton.

G.L.

Dialect

If the place-names record the dead Norsemen as on a tombstone, the dialect still keeps their language at least half alive. It is not, however, true to say that there is one dialect in the district, for the speech of the coastal dales varies considerably from that of Westmorland or even of Furness. The colliery district of Whitehaven and Workington has a dialect quite of its own which sounds like a cross between Cumberland and Tyneside, while Barrow-in-Furness speaks a language not easily distinguishable from that of any industrial town of the North-west.

The true dale dialects are full of Norse words and have a clicking, cracking, harshly melodious tune in which nearly all the vowels are diphthongs or triphthongs. In fact, in three words out of four the old dalesman seems to use a sound which can perhaps be suggested by 'ee-y-an', though there are slight variations of colour which differentiate the vowel. Thus a farmer speaking to me of an unsuccessful fox-hunt said:

'Nee-y-ah scee-y-ant at ee-y-al', and there was no doubt whatever that he meant 'No scent at all'.

The dialect is dying out, and it is no good either denying this, lamenting it or trying to prevent it. In any case dialect is not held in much honour by the ordinary countryman since it is associated in his mind with poor education and the status of the farm labourer. So that the people who really value the dialect are precisely those who do not normally speak it.

P.L.

A Local Habitation

Inside the Real Millom

Norman's delightful book, Provincial Pleasures, *gives a warm insight into his home town of Millom, here named Odborough, but it is also in a wider sense about the Cumbrian way of life. The underlying humour of the music festival will be recognized by many readers both in Lakeland and farther afield. For St Kentigern's Terrace read St George's Terrace.*

The life of a small town seems to wash up and down, to sway backward and forward from generation to generation. The great industrial cities, though they may have grown up in the nineteenth and twentieth centuries, had the basic plan of their development laid down in the Middle Ages. The church, the High Street, the ford, the bridge – these drew the first lines which centuries have not been able to rub out. But the small town, with no known history behind it, is less predictable in its way of growth. From the time of the Norman Conquest until the eighteenth century, Odborough was no more than a castle, a church, and a few poor farms or cottages. Even that castle lay a mile away from what is now the town. The site of the town was then merely the Mains, the Outer Demesne, marshland and rough heath or dune, not worth the labour of digging. It stretched in a parallelogram of waste, half-overlapping the Dunner estuary. Here and there were a few dollops or drumlins of clay, left by the retreating glaciers at the end of the Ice Age, which gave round hills of fifty to seventy feet high. But for the most part, the land remained at marsh level, except at the spot where the parallelogram was hinged on to the main curve of the land. Here the rock on which the whole of the marshland lay, suddenly revealed itself, a hundred feet high, scraped to the bare bone by the ice.

It was here, with unpredictable perversity, that the first village took root. Ever since the times when the Romans withdrew from the North, this part of the coast had remained strangely isolated from the rest of England. South was the Dunner estuary and Morecambe Bay; north, the barren coast as far as the Solway; and inland were the fells. But, in the eighteenth century, with the development of the coal trade at Whitehaven and Workington, a certain amount of traffic began to trickle along the coast through Odborough: pedlars, tramps, carters with grain or coal, drovers leading Scottish or Irish cattle down to the Lancashire markets. They came to Odborough, crossed the estuary at low tide, then by Furness and Cartmel and the sands of Morecambe Bay. So an inn or two was built to accommodate them. Not, as one might have expected, on the inland sheltered side of the hill but right along the top – the road hoisting itself a hundred feet on one side and slithering down again on the other, though with a deviation of less than a furlong it could have kept to level ground. The Ship was there in 1745 and claims to have accommodated John Wesley. The Pilot inn employed a man to act as guide to travellers across the shifting sands of the Dunner.

So Old Odborough established itself – a knotty, stretched, tail-end of a street, trailing over the hump of the hill. Below it, still, was nothing but marsh, sandy pasture, and the sod-and-cobble hovels of the forty-acre farmers.

It was in the middle of the nineteenth century that the new town began – when iron ore was discovered at Odborough Point. At first, development was cautious – the prospectors had no idea of the enormous deposits of ore which lay beneath the line of the high tide. The first miners lodged in Old Odborough. The first new houses were built there, along the old road over the hill. It was no hardship to the men in those days to have to walk two miles either way to work, and they wanted the company of the older houses and inns – they did not fancy living in lonely huts or terraces out on the windy Mains, among the new sores of the mines. The railway came and set its station at the bottom of the hill, and indeed, named it Odborough Hill, after the hill rather than the town, for Odborough still remained primarily the name of the castle. The old road from the Ship and the Pilot now became the main street. Other inns were built and a bank and new houses – all of them more like farm-buildings jutting out from the hillside than the beginnings of a town. There were no terraces, no villas, no gardens. Every building was improvised; walls, gables, roof-end, porches, conglomerated side by side, haphazard as a rockery. Then the first shops appeared. Cheap and Best, anxious to stake their share in the new enterprise, opened their stores at the foot of Old Odborough, opposite the Railway Hotel.

Here the main road from Lancashire entered the town, forking left from Odborough Hill, and right, over the level-crossing towards the offices and the mines. As the manager of the stores watched the farmers driving in to market and the bosses driving in to work, he felt certain that he was right in the heart of this newly come-of-age town, with his hand on the wallet above that heart.

But the town was only at the beginning of its growth. In the 1860s new deposits of ore were discovered, and new shafts sunk. Blast furnaces were opened at the other corner of the parallelogram, looking up the estuary. Miners and labourers came in by the hundred – from the dales round about, from Cornwall and Wales and Ireland. The little houses and inns of Old Odborough were packed to bursting, and a dozen sects and dialects slashed and convulsed together. Builders came. A quarry was opened. New houses sprang up out of the stone of Old Odborough on the only land that could be bought – the half-marshland near the new ironworks. There was digging and draining, dynamiting and levelling. Streets, houses, pubs, the cattle market, the first school, the first chapels. It was as if the heart of Old Odborough, swelling and bursting from its breast, had detached itself and gone rolling down the hill, over the level-crossing to settle in the New Town.

Tommy Dale's father was among the first to realize what was happening. From the level-crossing he saw the road run through the still empty fields to the new houses midway between there and the ironworks. He saw the cattle market and the Crown Hotel take their places proud as pew-holders, beside the rectangular green that lay between Victoria Street and Albert Road. He saw the new emporium of Happy Homes Ltd, facing them from the other side of the Green. At the T-junction of Westmorland Road with Trafalgar Road the Bible Christians had begun to build their chapel, and Cumberland Road was the site for the Wesleyans, and, at the gasworks end, that for the Roman Catholics. The private railway line to the furnaces passed close by between marsh and houses: if there were to be another Odborough station it might very well be there. The as yet unbuilt-on land ran in a straight line over dead flat fields from the railway crossing to the Green; if there were to be trams, where could you find a more likely route? The Green, as Absalom Dale saw it, was the obvious civic centre of the new town. He therefore persuaded his firm to leave Old Odborough and open new premises midway between the Crown and the cattle mart – a long double-fronted shop with warehouse behind and living accommodation above.

For some years the town grew around him. The fields between the Green and the ironworks began to disappear, as the streets overstepped them on one side, and the grey dune of the slag-bank drifted over them on the other. The shop prospered. The Green assumed its right of assembly place. The fairs came there and *Maria Marten*. The club walks began there, and the Bible Christians held their big mission in a tent on the grass. On summer Saturdays wrestling matches were held, and brass-putting, and young men and girls met there, outside the cattle mart, on hiring days.

But the fourth side of the Green remained a waste lot. The town hall, which old Mr Dale had envisaged, did not appear. For there was a change coming over Odborough. The excitement of its beginnings and growth had not yet died away, but now it was more aware of itself, and more aware, too, of the world outside. What had once been a lost heath and haws now proclaimed itself as a rightful part of the British Empire and not even Livingstone, at the Victoria Falls, had made a greater discovery than this. The eyes of these new citizens of no mean city began to lift themselves above the marsh and the mines and the slag-bank to where, a quarter of a mile away, rose the nearest hill. It was the highest of the glacial drumlins, facing Old Odborough across the little valley in which lay the railway station, and part of it was already reserved as the site of St Kentigern's Church and the new graveyard. But a quarter of a mile seemed a long way from the packed and practical streets. The council hesitated.

Then, suddenly, the railway company built a bridge, and built it moreover, not on the site of the level-crossing but on the other end of the station, taking advantage of the rise of the hill. All at once the town was thrown on the wrong foot. The lane from the Crown Green which was to have been a broad, tram-thronged thoroughfare, now led nowhere. Instead, the lower slopes of St Kentigern's Hill became the one inevitable route for everyone entering or leaving New Town. The council's mind was made up for it. Where the road descended to the new bridge they levelled and terraced the side of the hill, laid down a square, and built the town hall. High above all the roofs and chimneys, the town clock displayed itself, proud as the Prince Consort. Opposite came the three banks, and on the third side of the Square, the Prince of Wales Hotel. And in the middle, with magnanimous remembrance of Her Majesty's other subjects, was placed the Queen Victoria ornamental horse-trough, where four iron lions spewed water into four stone basins.

At first the change meant little to Absalom Dale. The town was already beginning to divide itself into class-zones, and this new area had the look of the middle-class or, in a word just coming into use, of the residential. St Kentigern's Terrace, which joined the Square to the old, only half-built-up Rotting Road, was a street of bow-windows, each with its own carpet square of garden walled off from the pavement. The trade of the town still remained centred round the Green.

But as the century moved onwards, so the life and business of the town turned its back on the slag-banks and moved uphill. A Saturday market was established in the hall beneath the town clock. The Co-operative Society opened its stores at the top end of Waterloo Street, the farthest from the furnaces. One by one the bow-windows of St Kentigern's Terrace were converted into shop-fronts. The once-prosperous shops of Westmorland Road moved to new premises, or declined to pot-shops and penny sweet-shops and shops that sold

Black Combe

glasses of herb beer and hore-hound.

Absalom Dale saw it and did not understand, but his son, young Tommy, did. He saw, but he did not worry, for he had now built up a solid-as-mahogany connection among the farmers and country gentlemen, and he supplied, wholesale, every little grocer's and confectioner's shop in every village for twenty miles around. He had three horse-vans and later, three motor-vans going out into the country every day. So that now, on this New Year's just-after-Eve, the shop remains secure and prosperous in a half-derelict square. The premises of Happy Homes Ltd. have declined through half-a-dozen bankrupted haberdashery and remnant stores into the whist-and-tattle rooms of the old age pensioners, the plate-glass painted green for privacy. All the other shops are closed, and many demolished or condemned. Half the Green is enclosed as allotments – the lamplight hanging skeins of tinsel along the tin sheeting and old iron bedsteads which make up the fencing. Only the Crown Hotel, the auction mart, and A. Dale and Son (late Cheap and Best) retain the respectability of new paint and mortar.

P.P.

The New Year

The best way to see the New Year in is to be fast asleep. I do not enjoy a First of January which starts with a headache. So New Year's Eve is a night for early to bed and never care whether next year comes or not.

There is still plenty of time, however, to take a last look at last year's world before the first-footing processions begin.

I walk to the dormer window of my attic bedroom from which, like a cave-dweller, half-way up a cliff, I can watch the tidal movements of the street below. It is a warm, moist, muzzy night. A wave of Atlantic air, sweating with fogs, washes round the base of Black Fell [Black Combe] as it rears itself, unseen in the darkness, like a harbour mole above the town.

The fine rain seems not so much to be falling as to be floating, drifting, even steaming, upwards. Hold out your hand and you can feel not a drop, yet the sleeve of your coat is found to be damp. The street-lamps are no longer points or splinters of light. They are absorbed entirely into the blur of mist, so that the black cliffs of the street are lit as with a phosphorescence, a faint underwater light in which shapes undulate and bulge and only shadows have any solidity.

St Kentigern's Terrace is, at a first glance, empty. Beyond the gently shelving slope of the street, the mist swirls and brightens, to reveal, bold as breakwaters, the three banks of the Market Square. Above them, like a lighthouse, shines the market clock, seeming to have lifted itself clear of the spray and smudge of the rain. I cannot see it from here, but I do see the light from it lying flat and steady on the roofs of the house opposite, grey-washing the squares of slates, lining the edges of skylight and dormer. So that here, among the roofs, lifted high above the swish of the street, here is a solid world. The roof-line is the level of the land. Below, submarine, the streets are carved in channels up which the town's tide flows. I can hear the first murmur of it already as the ebb begins to turn at the dip of the year. The tide flows through the streets as through a delta, through gulley and creek and backwater, along the main canals of Waterloo Street and Trafalgar Road and Furnace Road, full into the harbour of the Market Square.

The market clock strikes half-past eleven. They are gathering now in the Square. Only a few people at first, clustered in the shadows of the doorways. The centre of the Square, under the spray of the lights that have replaced the Jubilee drinking fountain, is still empty. The upstairs windows of the houses behind the shops are lit, their curtains drawn. From the Victoria Hall comes a gust of trumpets, a kick and clatter as if all the old buckets and biscuit tins of the town were being rolled across a bouldery shore. The door of the Prince of Wales gapes open and out blows a breath of beer and extended licence. The gloss of the vestibule glows a clean, pale, aspidistra-green, as if electricity had never been invented and every bracket was still alight in a pride of gas-mantles.

A quarter to twelve ... the green four-face of the clock, like a huge illuminated flower-head of the wild moschatel, blooms into the rain. The Odborough Royal Temperance Band is assembling outside the Prince of Wales. Each bandsman props his music into the little stand that juts out close to the mouthpiece. An effort of cheering is heard, purposeless and forced. A late bus edges slowly into the Square, pushing its way through the crowd. A night-flying sea-bird pipes above the roof-tops.

Five to twelve. A dozen people are gathering for Watch-Night service in the Bible Christian Chapel in Trafalgar Road. The minister is bringing his short address to a close. Soon he will begin the prayer which is to lead into the New Year. Contralto Ethel sits alone in the choir, her old face wrapped like the withered outer leaves of a cabbage round a centre that is still green as a salad. The almost empty chapel is before her – Jacobean-stained pews, umbrella stands, the red hymn books in the back seat, the great brown honeycombs of the gallery.

The ten or twelve in the congregation, scattered so widely about the church that they are scarcely within shouting distance of one another, are growing restless. Wrists twitch watches into view. Without bothering to look behind at the hymn-board Ethel opens her book at the next hymn. There is no one in the congregation whom she did not know as a child, yet there is not one under fifty. The New Year is the time when you feel old. The New Year is a time for remembering.

The market clock strikes. Violet Moss's sister kisses her father. A cheer begins, raucous, ironical, from those on the edge of the crowd. The ironworks buzzer to-wit-to-whoos as the first minute emerges like a mouse from its hole. In the middle of the Square there is a dim, indiscriminate scrimmage of Happy-New-Yearing.

The crowd, arm-linked and knotted together in a bootlace tangle, tries to form a circle. 'Auld Lang Syne' is heaved into the air as if the tune were being tossed in a blanket. Daphne Huggins is swung by the armpits clean off her feet. Screams and high-heel shoes skitter across the pavement.

The six bells dive off together, belly-flapping and splashing all at once into the middle of the peal. Sudden as an explosion, the band drums up and blazes away down the Terrace into Rotting Road.

The crowd in the Square begins to whirl round and round like water in a pot-hole, continually throwing off little splashes and dribbles which trickle away down St Kentigern's Terrace or along Jubilee Road or over the railway bridge to Old Odborough. But the centre of the whirl, as if held by some half-drunken centrifugal force, still coheres in a pool of shadows and voices. Now it begins to wash down and up the Square. It forms itself into a wave, and crests and breaks and goes flowing down the Terrace back along the channels of the town. The year's first tide is on the ebb.

P.P.

Staying in Bed

The weather has changed as quick as the twist of a tap. The first ironworks buzzer wakes me at five-thirty – a long dinosaur moo, followed by two short snorts – and immediately I feel that the world has broken into a hot sweat. I put a hand out of bed and find that the wall is as wet as a fishmonger's marble slab. So is the woodwork of my bed, and, indeed, everything of metal or stone which is within touchable distance. The room is steaming like a greenhouse, and glass, wood, and iron are slobbery with water. My head, too, feels like a washtub with suddy vapour oozing from my eyes. The meteorologists will say that a warm, damp airstream arriving suddenly from the Atlantic precipitated its moisture on every surface that was still cold with the frost. For myself, it will be said that I have a cold in the head and must stay in bed.

But this does not mean that I am absent from the life of the town. For this life is like an enormous hurdy-gurdy, every wheel cogged to another wheel, so that, merely from the sounds which reach my bedroom window in St Kentigern's Terrace, I can read nearly all the turnings and whirligigging of the whole contraption.

After the ironworks buzzer there is half an hour's pause. The men are tying their bootlaces, picking up their bait-tins, swilling down hot tea and puffed or powdered or shredded maize or oats or grass-seed. ('It's a caution when you have to go out to work on nubbut a couple of fire-lighters,' says Chunker Wilson.)

Then comes a trickle of footsteps, a rippling river of rolling pebbles, gathering its tributaries from back and side street. The waters pass by and dry up. Then the mail train, at the station, applying its brakes; the post-office van bringing the letters, the boys delivering the morning papers, each letter-box clattering. Footsteps again – the high heels of girl assistants at the early-opening shops. St Kentigern's communion bell. Children's voices, the scratch and scamper of buses. Bleat of sheep and bark of dog. It is auction mart day – I had forgotten. The farmers are coming to town.

'Hello, you great big silly-looking beggar. Aren't you dead yet?' It is a greeting of pleasure and affection.

Outside the Prince of Wales I hear the voices of boys waiting with sticks to whack the cows all the way down Albert Road to the auction on the Crown Green. The market clock strikes nine, but they take no notice.

The first shopping cars. And now to the growing but barely perceptible murmur of the morning the neighbours add each his trademark tune or tinkle. Old Mr Sprout, the greengrocer, greets the street with a voice that for fifty harvest festivals has hosannahed the roof off the Bible Christian Chapel. The young manager at the ironmonger's slaps every lady's bicycle within reach into a giggle of bells and rivets. Christopher Crackenthwaite condescends to the day like a tuba-player being introduced to the new cornet.

'A large morning, Mr Wilson,' he says magnanimously.

'You've got your share of it, so what are you fratching about?' Chunker replies.

The hours gossip past till the market clock strikes twelve. Buzzers bray, buses rev up, school unbuckles its satchel, and all along the street the Yale locks snap the shops into the silence of lunch-time.

P.P.

Shops

Norman's father, Joseph, kept a men's outfitter's shop in St George's Terrace, Millom, selling everything from cloth caps to guards' worsted trousers. Home was in the house behind. During Norman's childhood the shop was lit by hanging gas globes. It was small, filled with a worsted stuffiness and, in winter, the smell of an oil stove. Later, the shop was converted into another room for the house. Today it is a café and shop, with a plaque outside commemorating the poet.

The part-time shops, taken on to pay the rent or because the woman is bored, were the beginnings of the retail fortunes of the town. Here hung the hams and sides of bacon, with black puddings, sacks of flour and dried peas, rice, oatmeal, yeast, and Yorkshire Relish. Tatters and chippings of their former prosperity are still glued to the window panes:

RY'S   C C A

and

M Z W TEE   TE

And here and there, behind counters or at the back of the shelves, lie old advertisement cards – VIROL and SWAN VESTAS and the fat-faced little Lord Fauntleroy, blowing his bubbles of Pear's Soap. As business moved towards the new centre of the town, these little shops lived on through the chronic consumption of bankruptcy. But the case, now, is different. Here a new kind of retail business has arisen, which thrives on the new spending-power of the two – or three – wage-packet homes of the workers. These shops do not pretend to the status of the Edwardian family grocer or Italian warehousemen, who liked to supply enough food at one selling to stock a household of twelve for a month. Instead they cater for the poppers-out, the mothers with just a minute to spare, the wives who want something tasty for tea. Some of them act as agents for the larger greengrocers and confectioners, selling tomatoes, bread, and cakes on commission. Others rely on prefabricated food – meat-pies in cellophane, swiss rolls in tin-foil, sausages in tomato, potted salmon, tinned carrots, tinned pineapple, potato crisps, pork and beans, salad cream, red pickled cabbage, bottled blackcurrant juice, and non-alcoholic cider. Where the term 'mixed business' used to bring an image of a dark, dusky shop in a muddle of turnips, humbugs, and hair-grips, it means today, more often, a neat little shop blooming like a florist's in all the colours of the fifty-seven varieties.

P.P.

Calico and Limelight

Between the ages of six and sixteen I missed none of the annual productions of the Odborough Amateur Operatic Society. I was taken first of all by my father, who on that one Saturday afternoon of the year, would shut up shop and go over to the hall to show the matinée patrons to their seats. Then, after having told some other responsible person to keep an eye on me, he left me – small, silent, and completely enchanted. Of the first production, in 1920, all that remains in the memory is a coffin, or maybe a stretcher, carried across the stage. But from this time onwards I attended with growing comprehension and never lessening wonder.

It was the time of the Edwardian operettas. An age which had been shelled out of existence by the war still lingered on among the amateur societies like comfrey and feverfew in the garden of a demolished cottage. Pretty little buds of melody flowered among the waste of the slump and the jazz. I remember the shoe-buckles of *Tom Jones*, with a golden retriever on the stage, petted by the chorus; the policeman of *A Princess of Kensington* who fainted flat twice in every performance; the barge that floated across the back-cloth in *Miss Hook of Holland*; *Cingalee*, with the stage darkened, and a brown-stained chorus singing to a spotlight of a moon; *San Toy*, with its knowing chinkery-tinkery, its jangle and tinsel; *The Duchess of Dantzig* and *Nell Gwynne*, with characters I knew about, Napoleon and Charles II, looking as I knew they looked and speaking as the ironmonger and the milkman spoke. I remember the fifteen-stone tenor as Oberon, King of the Fairies, singing:

I do ride upon a swallow –

('Oh, my God, you must be hollow,' said Chunker Wilson in the fish market.) I remember the beloved buffooneries of the comedian, a barber who sang like Figaro; the soubrette, who could convey in a wink a whole lost age of back-stair humour; the singing heroes whose names remain among our local worthies, legendary as John Peel, long after their voices had cracked and their subscriptions expired.

But more than all these, more than the clowning, the grotesqueries, the melodrama, I see a strange, green incandescence, painted canvas leafing and branching, a blossoming of calico and limelight. The willow pattern of China, the moonbeams of Ceylon, fade from my mind. It is a nearer-to-hand scene which remains – the glades of *Merrie England* and a *Country Girl*; oaks dropping chorus girls like acorns; lawns and rides and clearings opening into dream beyond dream of green perspectives; shadowed side-screens, thick as bracken, folded and doubled one over the other. I see ribbons and smocks and garters; ale-mugs topped with froth as Scafell Pike is topped with cloud; girls whose bare arms were a flutter of sunlight in a birch-wood. In the half-dark, when the footlights went down at trysting time, the branches were thridded with owls and squirrels and the roots smouldered with glow-worms. And all of it was lifted in a huge green wave of song – men and women singing like a gale in the forest, roaring until the boughs rocked and fern and frond blew straight into the eyes and ears of the watchers to settle in the leaf-mould of memory.

These annual events, in fact, took on a significance far beyond their artistic merit. In spite, often, of fluffed lines, delayed entries, stumbling dances, shoddy scenery, behind-stage jealousies, there was created an imaginative whole, a transfiguration of the crudest common denominator of desires. Shop-girls and typists, all of them known to everyone by their Christian names, flicking their flounces, flashing their bare legs, gathered about themselves something of the mystery of Botticelli Graces. The show had become a ritual.

As the twenties moved on, the Edwardian confidence faded. The Young Men's Self-Improvement Club was forgotten. The choral work became less conscientiously four-part. On Saturday night the comedian permitted himself the occasional swear-word. With the thirties came tap-dancing, bare midriffs, trick-lighting, and half-jazz. The old operettas were still presented from time to time, but the charm, the prettiness, the Edwardian archness had disappeared. Today it is the grandiose vulgarity of the American musicals that most of the societies try to imitate.

Yet the spirit of the movement has changed very little: Go behind the stage at Odborough, and you will find the same excitement, the same commotion, whether the show is *Floradora* or *The Desert Song, The Pirates of Penzance* or *Oklahoma*.

Opera Week Finale

It is Saturday night, now, and the backstage is crowded. Below, in the basement, a row of helpers is making tea and washing up at a trestle table. Committee men, programme sellers, mothers of the chorus, visitors from other societies, stand about chatting as at a party. The entire company is on the stage at the moment. There is a distant murmur of the orchestra, the thump of the dancers. A cymbal clangs, followed by the sound of applause. One is reminded, almost with surprise, that an audience is present, for here that audience is quite forgotten. The chorus clatter down the two winding staircases which lead from either side of the stage, girls unbuttoning their dresses and half wriggling out of them, making ready for their quick reappearance in the finale of the first act. They accept a cup of tea as they pass, and scrimmage through the crowd to the curtained recess where they change.

With the chorus out of the way for a minute or two there is room, upstairs, behind the wings. Ardent arguments are taking place in groups of two or three. There is so much noise that it seems impossible for the audience to hear what is being said on the stage. Every now and then the prompter hisses for silence. Beside her the principal scene-shifter sits on a crate of bottles, a dancing girl on each of his knees and his hands on the curtain rope. Jack Edwards stands deliberately apart, concentrating on his lines. The leading lady, in a polka of debate, is suddenly seized by the producer and pushed through the wings into the stage, where, like a duck thrown into the pond, she instantly takes to the water and begins to swim.

The beer is going round. Some of the chorus are being kissed in corners and some not in corners at all. Larking has begun. On the stage the consequential innkeeper presents to Milord on a salver a card on which is inscribed a single rude word. Milord hides a smile with a flick of his glove, folds the card, and hands it casually to the second soprano.

'Where's Bobby?' says the producer. 'He's due on in half a minute.'

The call goes down the stairs, through the basement, into the dressing-rooms, into the gents' and, failing that, the ladies'. The leading lady and the innkeeper desperately improvise a misunderstanding over chairs, which – as much to their embarrassment as to their relief – turns out to be funnier than what they ought to be doing. Bobby is discovered outside, leaning over the fence of the cricket field in the pitch dark, contemplating Jupiter. He is thrust upstairs and on to the stage, trips over his spurs, and falls with the grace of what seems to be perfect rehearsal into the arms of the leading lady. He twines his hands round her neck and hangs in a dead weight, panting to get his breath back.

'Which bloody act are we supposed to be doing?' he whispers, as the audience rumble with delight.

But, behind stage, the crisis has hardly been noticed. The show goes on like a machine, like a giant's ride in a children's playground, on which every member of the company jumps now and then for a ride, and then jumps off and lets the whole contraption keep turning without him. The chorus are back upstairs now, herded like sheep at a gate, waiting for the final entry of the first act. There is a conspiratorial glee among them, for someone has substituted a bottle of port wine for the bottle of cold tea from which the innkeeper will have to fill their glasses. The leader of the chorus, who is standing in the wings in view of the audience, is aware behind her of that which, being in view of the audience, she is unable to prevent. Whatever may be the show on the stage, behind scenes is always *Merrie England*.

This is the true significance of the amateur operatic movement. It is the descendant, in an urban society, of the primitive fertility cults. For the myth of the dying and reviving god, of the sacred marriage between sun and soil, the magical cults to bring rain and crops, all survived, until very recently, in the seasonal festivals and superstitions of country folk – May Queens, Rose Queens, Morris Dancers, Midsummer Fires, Hallowe'en, mistletoe, rice at weddings, April Noddies and May Goslings. All this is well known in the post-Frazer world. But it is not so often realized that when these customs died out with the coming of the industrial era man did not suddenly become independent of the seasons. His fundamental needs remain what they always were. He depends, as he always did, on the sun, on the forces of air and water, on the fertility of the soil, on the yearly renewal of the green world. For many men, indeed, this fact is obscured by the mechanization of society.

Farm on the road to Hodbarrow, Millom

They forget it with their minds; but in their hearts they still know it is true. The seasonal festivals may have become cheapened and commercialized, the Easter daisies drenched with petrol instead of dew and Simnel Sunday rented out to sweet and flower shops – but they still help to satisfy a fundamental human desire. For today, as much as ever, man needs to adjust himself to the seasonal rhythm of nature, to the growth of grass and tree, to the alternation of sun and wind and rain. He finds it impossible, however, to revive the old customs. Much as they may appeal to the deeper levels of the imagination, they seem to his conscious mind to be archaic, irrelevant, and even silly. But in the amateur operatic movement he can indulge in myth-making without knowing what he is doing. He can be primitive and almost up to date at one and the same time.

The resemblance between the operettas and May Day and the festivals is quite remarkable. First of all there is the central figure of the spring goddess or leading lady, chosen like the May Queen, from among the local girls, courted and complimented by the whole society, saluted with flowers and ceremoniously kissed by the chairman on the last night. Then there are her attendants, the chorus girls and the dancers, with their ribbons and posies,; her clown, the comedian; her guard, a retinue of soldiers – the 'green men' of the woods. Often there is a dog on the stage or a pony or a parrot, representatives of the natural order of beast and bird. Then, again, there is all the elaborate make-up and masking, the dressing-up and undressing, bare shoulders among the leafy boughs; there is the scenery of palace and woodlands, like the 'green booths' of the Festival of Tabernacles; and frequently there is female impersonation or a girl dressed as a boy, the confusion and interchange of the sexes – all familiar features of the old May Day festivals.

The final call has now been taken. The entire company is on the stage for the Queen. Tommy Dale wraps yet another scarf round his head, and with uplifted voice begins to praise, not the production he has just seen, but that of *The Mikado*, which he had seen (and unlike the present one, had also heard) in 1910, when the society was first founded. On the stage, the presentations begin. To the producer, to the conductor, to the prompter, and the stage manager. The principals present one another with bunches of flowers – like Russian footballers. The cheering renews itself in multiples of three. The men being to gyrate, as in the lancers, kissing each girl as they pass. The mother of the leading lady comes round with a couple of clothes baskets to carry home the presents. Jack Edwards and some of the older men have packed their cases and are ready to depart, feeling the weight of ten or twenty shows descending on them like autumn leaves. But the young girls are as wide awake as if the show were only beginning on the first night. They have not changed from their costumes of the last act, and some of them are going off to farewell parties in shops and parlours which will last until two or three in the morning. The next day they will cry with tiredness, the make-up not yet properly wiped off their eyes, and all the trouble of packing and returning the costumes and scenery yet to be done. Sunday after Opera is a blank and bleak day. But their duty has been carried out. The ritual has been performed. The return of spring has been made certain, the crops have been secured. Fertility has been promoted, and will come to some of them, perhaps, sooner than they had reckoned on.

P.P.

On the Tops

Once, the people of Odborough had known every lane and path for miles around. They would visit each at the right season – a favourite primrose patch or a holly bush as if it were old friend. During the slump the out-of-work iron men would spend hours on the Tops looking across the unsmoking chimneys to the estuary, or gathering mushrooms and blackberries and bits of sticks for firewood. Dole diet may have taken the red from their cheeks, but not the strength from their legs. Today the Tops are empty and the field-paths greened over. The better-off circumnavigate the district in cars, but the young workers are oblivious to the country. They think of themselves as townsmen and turn to scratchy imitations of the townsman's pleasures. Their girls try to dress like town girls, and display all the badges of the pavement parade – high heels, ear-rings, handbags, and cheap scent. The town girl does not enjoy privacy; she plays, as she works, in public. And after marriage there is enough privacy in kitchen or in bed and no need to search for it in the lanes or behind hedges. But for this one period of courtship, when the street is too public and the home too private, the couples break from their flock like nesting chaffinches and spread out among the fields. They explore the spots their parents talk about – Odborough pier, Oatrigg dunes, the Castle woods, and along the estuary and up into the hills. In two or three years their walks will cease, but they will carry memories of those places into their old age. And maybe one day, doing the honours to a grandson or a visitor, they will re-inspect the landscape of memory and find that time has either erased it or preserved it neat and green as a pickled onion.

They are sauntering now among the budding bread-and-cheese, with never a suspicion that it is what they pay no notice to that they will remember the most poignantly – the lark song, the lamb bleat, the king-cups in the ditch, the blackthorn in the hedge. Such things, coming without warning before their eyes or into their ears, will bring back the tingle of courtship more palpably than a midnight of willed recollections.

'Oh,' she says, pointing among the celandines, 'a bee.'

And he does not even notice the celandines, but the bee has left its buzz in his memory for ever.

P.P.

The Gala

The brass of the Royal Temperance Band blows through my window on the lift of the wind. It is the day of the Cricket Club Gala, and round the corner from the Jubilee Road, where the procession had been assembling, comes P.C. Goosefoot, leading the band.

It is a brilliant billowy day – the wind scours straight from the Irish Sea. All along the side of the road the crowd is planted like an herbaceous border, blooming with colour. The band is passing now, so that I look right down on the top of their hats and the bright blare of their trumpets. First the dancing troupes, brought in bus-loads from Furness: little girls of seven or eight in yellowish satin trousers with ear-rings and tambourines; girls of thirteen or fourteen, bosoming out their drummer-boy jackets, or in top-hats and white shorts, blasé as Burlington Bertie. Next, the first decorated car, bearing the Ironworks Queen, and after her, Miss Oatrigg, and the Temperance Band's Miss Music, and the Furness Hospital Gala Queen, and then the champion-chested professional pin-up who has come from Morecambe to crown Miss Odborough in the cricket field. More dancers; children's fancy dress – Dutchmen, Gainsborough ladies, cowboys, bridal couples, postmen, geisha girls, golliwogs, a half-cast negro girl as Miss Althea Gibson, a boy with his head in a goldfish bowl as a space man, a little girl, naked to the waist, with halves of grapefruit tied to her chest as a hula-hula dancer.

Now come the cycles and tricycles: a girl, in ballet dress, wheeling a huge swan; a boy pedalling inside Donald Campbell's *Blue Bird* ('He saw it on Ullswater!') while his mother walks beside to give a push on the hills. Next, the decorated lorries: the Crown Green Garden Party, with a striped umbrella and a trellis of paper roses and all the children of the Green supping tea out of saucers; A Day on the Shore, with ten hundredweight of sand scattered on the lorry-floor, and the children making pies and juggling with pebbles; a bedroom scene from the employees of the knitting factory in shortie-nightdresses, with candles and curling-pins and an enamel under-jar well in view; and the girls of Old Odborough new estate in bathing-suits depicting nothing but themselves. (Daphne Dempster, née Huggins, remembers how she herself had made the same bare-back parade on Coronation Day in a north-west wind that cut like a bacon-slicer clean through the coats of the standers-by.) A pipe-band, girl marchers, trade exhibits – the Furness Laundry Lovelies, Goodness Grocers Cornucopia and 'Why go around half dead when Christopher Crackenthwaite can give you a first-rate funeral?'

And now Miss Odborough, among a desultory revving of applause that seems to run alongside like a motorcycle escort. She sits rather awkwardly on her ribboned lorry wearing a velvet cape, and holding a bouquet of roses, wired stiff as a wreath. Last night, at the gala dance, she was queen of the quick-step, prettily bending from a neckline two years too low. There among all those who had voted for her and cheered her, she was happy and confident, in a shop-girl's dream that was tangible and sweet as toffee. Everything was normal, everything was what she expected, and her new role fitted her like her brassiére. But today she is asked to act an archaic part in a show that was already out of date in her grandmother's time. Her two attendants have been told to curtsey to her when she reaches the dais in the cricket field, and she knows they will giggle when they do. She herself is not giggling. She is trying to bow her head to the applause of the crowd as she has been taught, but it is a crowd of children and of the middle-aged. The young men who voted for her are not there now. They do not acknowledge her. They would scarcely recognize her, indeed, garbed as she is for this antique charade. She moves on in her car of state, fulfilling a ritual of fifty years ago, passing between walls more familiar with such scenes than are the eyes who watch her from the pavement.

The procession turns out of the Terrace, dragging behind it the ghosts of all the processions which have passed along those streets: recruiting parades, victory parades, salute the soldiers, holidays at home, coronations, jubilees, ambulance parades, May Queens, Rose Queens, club walks (the Buffs and the Blues), election campaigns, strikes, and funerals.

The red and purple and yellow, like polyanthus in a back-yard garden, blossom among the grey. So that I am reminded how, at the coronation, a shiver of blue, as if from the dipping of a score of swallows, flew along the houses at bedroom-window height. And of the parties after the war, when every street had its queen, and the cars were barricaded out and children ran races, and trestle tables were set up on the pavements, and boys swilled down dandelion and burdock till they hiccoughed 'Rule Britannia'.

John Dodder, in Rotting Road, remembers seventeen Miss Odboroughs or queens or something or other who have waved up to his window as this one is doing now. Old Mr Postlethwaite, in Trafalgar Road, remembers 'V.R.' in incandescent gas-mantles outside the market hall. Mr Dale, on Crown Green, thinks of Whit Monday Sunday school anniversary processions, led by himself and the minister, walking between the shuttered shops, silk banners waving in the wind – 'The Good Shepherd', 'Suffer Little Children', and 'Remember Thy Creator in the Days of Thy Youth'. And down in Marsh Edge Street, Mrs Grice hears the sound of the band as it wheels from Cumberland Road into Victoria Street, and she goes to her front-room window and displays the picture of King Edward VII which she had displayed when the last procession passed along that way on 26 June, 1902.

My father remembered the occasion well. It was a Thursday, and the whole day was given up to festivities. At ten o'clock in the morning the four brass bands of the town assembled outside the Jubilee Field, together with all the marchers: the Volunteers, the Cumberland and Westmorland Yeomanry, the members and officials of the Urban District Council, the school board and guardians, the friendly societies, the fire brigade, the tradesmen's association, the tradesmen and inhabitants, all of whom were 'respectfully invited to join'. Except for the very old, not a man was left indoors, and only women and children were left to watch. The little town was emptied of its folk that pious morn. After 'God Save the King', with half of them still singing 'Queen', they began strongly but silently, the bands saving their breath on the hills – over the railway bridge and up to the very top of Old Odborough. Then down they came, in triumphant blare and braggadocio, back over the bridge – the front of the procession barely missing its tail – encompassing in one great fling the whole stretch of the town, from Old Odborough quarry to Marsh Edge Street and the beginning of the new slag-bank. It was a walk then, not through a forgotten bottom-end, but through substantial terraces that still held the glint of the new-cut stone, blue as the bunting that flapped from window and lamp-post.

In the afternoon the children had their turn, being each presented first with a medal and a new penny. Then off on the same three-mile walk – Old Odborough, Albert Road, Victoria Street, Crown Green, to Waterloo Road, Westmorland Road, Marsh Edge Street, and back, with no quarter or consideration for shortness of wind or legs. They walked in Sunday schools, tactfully divided by the bands. In the first batch, St Kentigern's and the Old Church; in the second, the Primitive Methodist, the Wesleyans, and the Bible Christians; in the third, the Baptists, the Salvation Army, and the Welsh Calvinists; and finally, the Catholics, the Spiritualists, and the children unattached to Sunday schools. After tea the short legs were whipped up again for children's sports in the Jubilee Field, and the bands played in the Square, and at five o'clock hundreds of pigeons were let loose to wheel round and round throughout the whole fagged-out evening, until the light dozed off and the fireworks fizzed up above the Jubilee Hill. My father said he counted thirty bonfires.

P.P.

Bogey Burrows

In twenty years Bogey Burrows has had the job of foreman on the tip
(with the finest view, he says, from any slag-bank in England), and no
one in Odborough knows more of the countryside round about. Not
that he ever sets foot in it. The cricket field in summer and the working
men's in winter are as far as he ever goes, but he can tell you the crop of
every field on either side of the estuary. He knows, to an hour, when
each farmer begins ploughing or haymaking and when the fishermen
are out or the duck-shooters or the hounds. He watches the bracken
burning on the Tops in late spring, and times each orchard as it bursts
into blossom, and spots any new barn or cottage before the walls are
three foot high. From his hut in a corrie of the bank, he sees where the
duck fly off in pairs to nest and he watches the geese congregate in
October, and is acquainted with the movements of heron and cormorant
and the timetable of the owls. He has known swans, moorhen, coot, and
duck of a dozen kinds nest in the furnace reservoir, and watched the
pipit rear a cuckoo in the whins behind the pier, and threatened to get
the sack for any man who touched it. He knows the estuary better than
the pilot, and when the salmon are running he will scan the pools with
his binoculars as the tide ebbs and will pass on the news to his friends
the MacIntyre brothers. One of them, caught wheeling a ten-pound
salmon off the Dunner Banking in a perambulator was brought up in
court and fined forty shillings. Afterwards in the Prince of Wales, the
magistrate quietly handed him two pounds in a sealed envelope.

'And so he bloody well should have,' says Chunker Wilson. 'It was
him that got the salmon.'

P.P.

The School

The school seems part of the hill, being built of that very slate which has
been blasted away to make room for it. Looked at from the road, it is a
dibble of steep roofs, gable ends, peaked windows, porches, chimneys,
ventilators, and turrets, over which, nevertheless, it is still possible to
get a good view of a cricket match without having to pay. The
playground which once belonged to the infants is barricaded by an
outcrop of bare rock down which, already, the ivy-leaved toadflax is
dribbling a few mauve flowers. The boys' playground, on the other
hand, looks into the turf of the field, the first leaf of elder, and the huge
hullabaloo of the sky.

But when you enrolled at the boys' department, after leaving the
infants, you saw none of this. For the school had been built round a yard
or quadrangle. Maybe the intention had been to leave this open to the

sky, but in my time it was roofed in with opaque glass, so that to step inside was like stepping into one of those translucent mists of spring. You were doused in light, yet you could see nothing. All around you were whitewashed walls and above you was a perpetually cloudy sky. It was a room where there were no shadows. The space behind the blackboard was as bright as that in front. Ink-wells, rulers, copy-books, the stove, the stove-pipe, the fire-guard, stood preserved as in a jelly of light. It had its own quietness. The sound of the world outside never reached it through the surrounding rooms. The sound of other classes and other teachers seemed irrelevant to little boys who did not yet feel part of the community of the school. Hail drummed on the roof, and when it rained cans and jam-jars were disposed to catch the drips, and the desks were arranged round the pools and splashes like streets round the canals and lagoons of Venice. The room was completely without ventilation, and in winter became a refrigerator of dead-still draughtless cold. We could see our breath rising in the air like floating hoar-frost. In summer the dead air expanded as in a greenhouse, and pressed clumsily on our temples. We drowsed and snorted, half-choked by the smell of hot socks, sweat, unwashed hair, ink, chalk, and stale disinfectant. The whitewash restricted our gaze on every side, and only when a gull let on the roof and left a slightly whiter patch behind it on the white glass did we have any news of the world outside.

The old man who taught us – and who had taught my father forty-one years before – would retire behind the blackboard every now and then to chew tobacco. He taught – as, indeed, we learned – by habit. Regular as the tides, twice a day, the same words came pounding against our undefended shores, and slowly they wore away resistance, making deep grooves in our memory. Nothing that I learned in that first year, aged seven or eight, was ever forgotten.

My companions were boys of an iron time in an iron town. Born into war rations and bred on the dole, they lived in a world where poverty seemed too natural to complain about. Those from the workless homes dangled feet in huge clumsy clogs provided by the local police from their annual Footwear Ball. Their heads jerked out of the collarless necks of their shirts like a sweep's brush out of chimney-pot. The others showed varying degrees of shabby elegance and mother's pride – celluloid Eton collars with bow-ties, woollen jerseys buttoned up to the neck, and in my own case, a sailor suit. These were the sons of clerks and shopkeepers, who would slip through the secondary school as through a trap-door and escape from the town. The rest would stay. Some of them I saw nearly every day – friends and acquaintances whose lives have run parallel for forty years, never meeting and yet getting no farther apart. Others were quite lost sight of. But sometimes, in the street or at a cricket match, a face would appear which I could give no name to, could relate to no circumstance or person, and which was yet tantalizingly familiar. The brand of the old quadrangle does not easily wear off.

The quadrangle itself, however, no longer exists. Its floor is asphalted and open to the sky and forms a space between the two separate blocks of the now reconstituted school. Today it is empty. The boys, having arrived at nine o'clock, found the school closed for measles. Timothy Tyson returns home for his whip and top and then begins to spin his ambitions up and down Trafalgar Back Street, knowing that he need fear no alarms until dinner-hour, as the Rotting Road schools have not been closed. He whips steadily and earnestly, crouching over the top, not even straightening his back when he runs. The top, thin and tall as a clothes-peg, leaps high in the air at the feel of the lash, skipping twenty yards. He darts after it among the clothes-props and the washing, for it is Monday, and among the milk-carts and coal-lorries and old prams loaded with sacks of coke. He dodges round women pegging out shirts that twist like wrestlers in the bullying wind. They take no notice whatever, being used to these Lenten humours, for now is the time that the Passion symbols take the shape of children's games – the whip, the scourge, the rod. Even the crown of thorns is not forgotten nor the dicing for Christ's garment. No one has explained to the children the significance of this ritual, yet, by some seasonal intuition, they recognize March as the time for these harsh toys and strict competitive games. In the front playground of the girls' school the skipping ropes twirl salt-mustard-vinegar-pepper in a swirl of legs and gym-slips. At the back, a hundred pairs of hands are keeping a hundred pairs of tennis balls in continual pat and bounce against the yard wall. One, two, three and under, one, two, three and over, and upsey, a downsey, a curtsey, a bow, a single decker, a double decker, a butcher, a baker, a policeman, a rabbit, a thunder:

> Nebuchadnezzar the King of the Jews
> Bought his wife a pair of shoes,
> When the shoes began to wear
> Nebuchadnezzar began to swear,
> When the swear began to stop
> Nebuchadnezzar bought a shop,
> When the shop began to sell
> Nebuchadnezzar bought a bell,
> When the bell began to ring
> Nebuchadnezzar began to sing:
> Doh Ray Me Fah Soh La Te Doh – OUT

In the boys' school there is a fierce Eisteddfod of marbles, and each dinner-hour the boys run home at the crouch, chasing a spate of minties, poppies, glassies, and tullies down the groove of the gutter. Even in the new housing estates on the far side of Old Odborough, a boy no higher than the whip he holds is trying to coax and bully a huge fat top as if he were teaching a puppy to beg. The top, spun off from his hands, makes a few lazy turns and wobbles slowly over on to its side, while the boy batters it in exasperation with the wooden stick of his whip. On a broken lost pavement, close beneath the slag-bank, Diane Huggins, Daphne's younger sister, off school with ringworm, practises her way through the complicated changes of hopscotch.

P.P.

The Music Festival

Norman's fame as poet and writer was enhanced by his masterly readings of his poetry, for which he was greatly in demand. He learned much of the art as a child at concerts and festivals, backed by his father's one short piece of advice: 'Remember to speak up.' More about Norman's concert days can be found in his autobiography, Wednesday Early Closing.

In October, winter begins its seige of the town. The horizons are smudged out. Black Fell is no longer a ladder to the loft, but a stone rolled against the gateway, blocking the road. Boys forage among the turnip-smelling mists, scattering congregations of sparrows from the manure and straw and tree-fern-like forests of kale. In the allotments of Rotting Road, asters, dahlias, and michaelmas daisies are smouldering like the rakings of a coke fire, and the leaves of the white poplars, slipped loose from their branches, go planing and skidding along the pavement.

This is the time when the town closes in upon itself. The rest of England becomes foreign again. Strangers who have been made welcome throughout the summer are now reregistered as aliens. The old underground associations make their claims again in club and chapel and institute. Patterns of relationships established years ago assert their magnetic pull. This is the time when the town subdivides against itself, makes teams and takes sides. An internecine struggle breaks out – class against class, party against party, denomination against denomination. The grey fields beside the slag-banks are flocked with the winter migrants of hockey, soccer, Rugby Union, and Rugby League – the word 'rugger' is never heard in Odborough. The billiard league begins its winter run in the clubs, with dominoes and whist scampering at the side like terriers beside hounds. The darts knockout opens in the pubs. In Sunday schools and canteens there are badminton and table tennis, and the bridge cliques shuffle among the drawing-rooms of Mount Pleasant, while at St Kentigern's Young People's Fellowship, the Old Church mid-week social, the Wesley Guild, the Trafalgar Road Christian

Endeavour, the Baptist Brotherhood, and the Oatrigg Ex-U.M. Women's Bright Hour there are brains trusts, twenty questions, safety-first quizzes and beetle drives.

But the best of all the winter sports is the Music Festival. The festival has been part of my life ever since it was first founded in the early twenties. My father was on the committee from the beginning: not because he had the least ear for music, but because he was always ready to support any Odborough enterprise so long as it had nothing to do with politics. (My father believed that a man should keep his political opinions to himself, not realizing that that belief revealed well enough what his opinions were.) My mother, for her part, was one of the official accompanists. In 1923 she presented the third prize for the boy's solo to my own cousin, and it surprised me to see her shake hands with him on the platform as if he were a stranger. The next year I myself took part, singing in the Old Odborough Boys' School Choir, and the year after that, when I was eleven, I entered on my own in the elocution class. I had received no tuition, but I learnt my piece and I knew what it meant and how I meant to say it. It was a ballad of Stevenson's called, 'Christmas at Sea':

> The sheets were frozen hard and they cut the naked hand,
> The decks were like a slide where the seamen scarce could stand,
> The wind was a nor'wester, blowing squally off the sea,
> And ships and spouting breakers were the only things a-lee.

It went on to tell of a ship in a storm, close to the rocks: so close indeed, that the sailors could see the houses on shore, with the windows lit and the chimneys smoking. The wind whined and piped in my own treble; the icy spray slashed across my face as I imitated the voices of the captain and mate. And when the poem was ended, not a man of the crew felt a greater relief than I did. One of them, indeed, did not feel relief at all, for the village on the shore was his old home, and the house above the coastguard's was the house where he was born:

> And they heaved a mighty breath, every soul on board but me,
> As they saw her nose again pointing handsome out to sea;
> But all that I could think of in the darkness and the cold,
> Was just that I was leaving home, and my folks were growing old.

I won the first prize that year, and the next two years also – reciting 'Sherwood', by Alfred Noyes, and 'Off the Ground', by Walter de la Mare. Then, after missing a year, I entered again at the age of nearly fifteen when the test piece was a tiny four-stanza poem by de la Mare called 'Nod'. No chance this time of the virtuous display of memory which so impressed my uncle. No chance, either, to show my powers of mimicry or of dramatic scene-painting. 'Nod' was a quiet, sleepy little poem, and so slow that I was sure that I could have recited it in my sleep. Indeed, I was more than half asleep as I waited my turn at the side of the stage. Not from tiredness, but from nervousness, from the heat, and from the fume of hot breath and excitement which rose from the body of the hall. Moreover, I was no longer a young boy able to give his whole heart and mind to a rhyme in a story. I was old enough to be self-confident and self-conscious. I was aware of people in the audience – teachers, and my own school-fellows. I was aware of the other competitors in the same class. Some of these – the only ones, indeed, with any chance against me – were girls. They were reciting a different test-piece – something about fairy jam-making, sweet and sticky – but they competed against me for the same prize. They came from away, and I was diverted by their elocution-school accents, and especially by their pronunication of the word sugar. I was diverted, too, by their silk dresses, and by the way they fidgeted with the hem of their skirts as they recited – this was the time when hems were at their very highest. I walked out when the bell rang, with the assurance of one very much used to the job, for by this time I had recited at many concerts in every hall and Sunday school in the town.

My mind was dancing a diddering polka along the gaslights and the audience and the girls. But that did not matter: I could recite this poem by clockwork. The clock worked for two stanzas, and then stopped. I remember that I was not in the least disconcerted. My mind had come out of its dance and returned to me, and I stopped not so much because I had forgotten but because I had remembered. I was not completely aware of myself – standing on the platform, in a tense hush, and in the middle of some poem which I could not recollect. There were a score or more people in that hall who were eager to prompt me, had they dared to do so. The adjudicator, a woman, glanced at her book and read out a line. It was the first line of the stanza I had just repeated. I shook my fingers in irritated dismissal. More embarrassed, I think, than I was, she at last stumbled on the right place. I finished the poem and was awarded the second prize. I am satisfied that I had deserved no better. But the Odborough people were not satisfied. Why should boys have to compete against girls, they asked, not even saying the same pieces. And from that day to this the elocution class has been divided into two: one for boys and one for girls.

That kind of participation in the festival ended for me at the end of schooldays, but later I helped to inscribe the prize-winners' certificates – a fact doubted by those who know my handwriting – and acted as steward in mornings and afternoons when the committee members could not attend.

I remember well those opening afternoons, often with no more than two dozen people present, and the room still cold before the steam filled the pipes. The festival is held on the second floor up a twisting staircase of stone steps, in a hall as bare as a prison, with the windows set so high that not even an ostrich could see more than the chimney-pots through them. The old yellowing notices that have been used for thirty years are pinned to the window-sills: SILENCE and NO SMOKING and COMPETITORS ONLY. On the platform: a grand piano (hired from Furness), a couple of music stands, and the blackboard on which the numbers of class and competitors are pinned up. At the back of the hall in a temporary look-out tower draped with red, white and blue muslin, sits the adjudicator, by his side one of those slap-button brass bells used to summon the waitress in Edwardian tea-shops. He slaps the bell and the first competitor, who has been sitting on her hands for the last five minutes trying to warm them, trots to the piano and flops into the test piece. That first competitor is usually a girl and is always young. No one in Odborough over the age of eighteen would enter for a piano or violin class, though the singers will continue to compete until they are so old and so deaf that it is only by watching the player's hands that they can keep in time with the accompaniment.

The afternoon works its way, unenthusiastically, through the first items: piano solo, piano duet; the Class B vocal solo, open to those who have not yet won a prize at any festival and don't sound as if they ever will; the melancholy women's trio class, in which the two entries have taken more trouble to match their dresses than their voices. The adjudicator hurries on with the programme, addressing his remarks directly to the competitors and taking no notice of the few stubborn season-ticket holders in the front row. The late October dusk condenses on the window panes. Outside, the street-lamps are on, and the willows beside the hoardings wave their yellow stripes. The confectioners' shops are busy serving tea to visitors – the half-lit windows steamed, the bread sold out, the chocolate biscuits spilt on the window-bottom. A sicky, sulphury mist drifts about the street, idle as the drifting schoolgirls, whose breaths are seeming frosty in the glow of shops and lamps. Small children, half-tangled in their own stockings, begin to sludge over the bridge to first-house pictures. A bus up-ends its load of workmen into the Market Square, while another waits to take a billiard team to Furness. No one, it would seem, thinks of the festival at all.

On Saturday night, however, it will be different. That is when the choirs came out and the soloists compete for the gold medal. The hall is packed, and the audience, excited, back the local favourites as if they were horses. They applaud the adjudicator and listen to his comments, but it is the marks for which they are waiting. Sometimes a competitor will be unsatisfied with the result, and once a tenor came round to the committee room threatening to knock the adjudicator's head off:

Christopher Crackenthwaite threw him down the stairs. Others attend carefully to the advice given, and some, at least, profit by it. Just before the war the gold medal at the Odborough Festival was won for some years in succession by a young contralto from further up the county. She was later to be known as Kathleen Ferrier.

P.P.

Male Voice Choirs Night

Saturday night is, above all else, the night for the male voice choirs. They come in buses and sometimes by special trains – business men's choirs from Furness, club choirs from the iron towns, and choirs of miners from the colliery coast. The Odborough Working Men's, conducted by Christopher Crackenthwaite, gathers not at the hall, but at the club, for a final run-through. More than once, when a choir from away has failed to turn up, a message to the club has brought the men in such a hobble and scurry down the street to the hall, that not even Christopher's skilful dilly-dallying with the piano and the music stands could give them time to get their breath back. Bobby Beck, the little barber with the sweetest bass voice in the Lake Counties, loosening his throat with a bottle of beer at the back entrance to the hall, is picked up by one of the choir and carried like a baby up the steep steps.

The men crowd the ante-rooms behind the stage, wrestling, larking, teasing, hardly giving an ear to what the other choirs are doing. But when their turn comes to sing, each man becomes prodigiously serious. The Furness conductor – the only one to use a baton – marshals his men as if they were soldiers on parade, pacing the distance between basses and tenors, grading voices by strength as chorus girls are graded by height. The miners' conductor, a great gorilla of a man, bullies and bashes the music out of his singers by brute force. Christopher Crackenthwaite, holding himself very still, seems to mesmerize his men, spreading his fingers like Svengali. They lean forward in an hypnotic hush, necks stretching, eyes periscoping up – the dwarfish club-foot alto in the front row; the six-foot baritone, who always take his teeth out to sing, hidden away at the back. Jack Edwards, who can be relied upon to keep a grip on the pitch when all the rest are slithering away, makes up the left flank. There are not more than two or three of these men who can read a note of music, and not one who would ever look at a line of poetry. Yet, when they sing, both music and poetry are achieved. From the terse, distorted mouths comes a single controlled line of melody; from the goggle-eyes comes a dream, a nostalgia, a fantasy, simmering up as from an underground lake of symbol. After a pause, they scrum down and worry the heart of 'Tiger, Tiger'. The suppressed savagery of each subterranean soul gushes to the surface like struck oil. For a little while Christopher Crackenthwaite lets the geyser spout, then, with the flick of a finger, cocks it into silence. The hypnosis is over. The baritone, turning round on the audience, slips his teeth in; and the alto hobbles off, slapping backs, or, when he can't reach them, bottoms; Bobby Beck, skimming off the stage like a whippet, has his bottle out of his pocket before he is half-way through the door.

Now is the time for the adjudication. The men surge on the stage again, eager and noisy as a football crowd. At each commendation they laugh or applaud and turn to one another. A good word for the altos and half a dozen lean over to shake Clubfoot by the hand. Christopher Crackenthwaite alone remains calm, magnanimously conceding an occasional criticism by an inclination of his head. The adjudicator passes on to the other choirs. With each word of praise the Odborough faces darken; with each adverse comment they brighten again. The adjudicator conceals his final decision, raising hopes and lowering them, till his listeners are as flurried as gulls swooping for biscuits. Now all the jokes which he has used at festival after festival are brought out again.

'A pianissimo is like charity in the Bible ...'

('Wait for it. Wait for it. Shut up, Bobby, you silly sod, he's got his eye on you.')

'... covereth a multitude of sins.'

The choirs bawl with laughter, and none bawls louder than Odborough, whose pianissimos, as the men well know, are as cultivated and cared for as early rhubarb. The adjudicator consults his figures, and at once there is a groping for programmes and pencils. The silence ticks like a time-bomb.

We need not wait to hear the result, however. For if Odborough win, the shield will be displayed in the photographer's studio in Rotting Road; if they do not, the choir will cancel its celebration hot-pot supper and begin to practice double-time for Blackpool. It is no good complaining that the festivals belong to the world of football pools rather than that of music, for without them there would be no choirs at all. It is the sport that binds the men together, and enables them – for a few moments at least – to hear the submerged music in their own souls. That children's days at the festivals encourage the display of parlour-tricks is, admittedly, true. Yet for many children in towns like Odborough the festivals are the only chance they ever get to hear the piano played properly or the voice used as it should be used. Wireless and the gramophone are no substitute. In any case, why should we ban all competition from children's music? Do not larks compete in singing?

P.P.

*

In Odborough a man may seem a long way from the centre of things, but he is closer to the heart of things.

P.P.

The Explorers

Journalists and Diarists

Apart from a few attempts by local landowners and antiquaries to make some topographical or historical survey of the area, the Lake District does not come into English literature until it was discovered by visitors from the outside world. The first of these, journalists and diarists like Daniel Defoe and Celia Fiennes, hardly knew what to say. Indeed, the charm of Miss Fiennes's writing lies in that very fact. She was never at a loss for words, but they had to be her own words – she had no ready-made conventional vocabulary with which to describe what she saw.

William Gilpin was the man who supplied the convention. He was Cumberland-born of a family long-established in the county, but he spent most of his life as a schoolmaster and parson in the south of England, and, on his retirement, set out to teach the people of his time how to look at and appreciate the world around them. It was Gilpin who popularized the term Picturesque, which meant, quite literally, a way of looking at a landscape *as if it were a picture.* Gilpin was a man with an acute visual sense, but, as more and more people read him and more and more tourists came to the Lakes, the 'Picturesque' hardened into a habit. Everyone now knew exactly what to say, and the same adjectives began to echo from book to book like the sound of the horns on Ullswater: grand, sublime, horrid, stupendous, irregular, precipitous and the like. To us, Gilpin and the travellers who succeeded him sound artificial, exaggerated, yet they record, sometimes very vividly, what the Lake District looked like to the men of the late eighteenth century. For, though the fells and dales may not have changed a great deal, the way we look at them has changed enormously.

The main reason for that change, of course, is the poetry of William Wordsworth. Wordsworth broke down the picture-frame and saw the Lakes, not through Gilpin's, but through his own eyes. At the same time, he expressed what he saw, what he felt, what he experienced, so passionately, so intensely, that, once we have read him, the Lake District can never look quite the same again. With Wordsworth, the mountains of Cumbria passed into world literature, became, like the music of Beethoven and the paintings of Turner, symbols of the power, the vitality, the force of nature and super-nature which haunted and compelled the imagination of the nineteenth century.

And because of Wordsworth, directly or indirectly, an oddly varied but influential group of poets and prose-writers settled in Keswick. Ambleside, Windermere and Coniston – S.T. Coleridge, Southey, De Quincey, Harriet Martineau, Christopher North, with many lesser figures, and, a generation later, John Ruskin. For a time the Lakes became one of the power-houses of the Romantic Movement, and helped to change, not just the course of English literature, but the way people live in the Lakes. The Lake Poets, in fact, became part of our social history.

It would be possible to compile an anthology of the Lake District entirely from the work of Wordsworth. Even at his second-best, his powers of description are usually more accurate, more perceptive and far more felicitous in expression than those of almost anyone who has succeeded him.

The Lake District:
An Anthology

The Lakers

The Lakers are those persons who visit the beautiful scenes in Cumberland and Westmorland by distinction styled the Lakes.

(*European Magazine*, Vol. 34, 1798.
Review of *The Lakers, a Comic*
Opera in Three Acts. Clarke, 2s.)
L.

Daniel Defoe's Unpassable Mountains

Defoe, c. 1660–1731, published A Tour through the Whole Island of Great Britain *between 1724 and 1727.*

Among the first to take part in the discovery of the Lakes was Daniel Defoe – if, indeed, he ever reached Cumberland at all. For Defoe was such an accomplished liar, his imagination was so vivid, his news sense so sure, that there is no need whatever to doubt the authenticity of his account merely because it may be fiction. Even if Defoe himself never saw Windermere we may be certain that what he says about it would be precisely what a middle-class man of his like would have said if he had been there. And what he did say was chiefly confined to the potted char. His remarks on the mountains are more interesting and more famous:

Here we entered Westmoreland, a country eminent only for being the wildest, most barren and frightful of any that I have passed over in England, or even in Wales itself; the west side, which borders on Cumberland, is indeed bounded by a chain of almost unpassable mountains, which, in the language of the country, are called Fells.

Now these lines have often been quoted to show how false and absurd was the eighteenth-century attitude to mountain scenery. In fact, they show only that Defoe was a good journalist. He was not struck dumb with horror as many have tried to make out; he was merely determined to see that his readers got their money's worth. His steady use of superlatives, instead of seeming to exaggerate, has quite the opposite effect of sober realism. In fact, it was no great exaggeration to say that Westmorland was the most barren and frightful country *of any that I have passed over in England*. He was making comparison not with the Alps, but with the Midlands and the South Downs. Moreover, the word barren had not, for him, the emotional force it has for us. It did not call up vast landscapes of desolation; it meant merely country on which nothing profitable would grow, and what, for an eighteenth century businessman, could be more frightful than that?

L.

Celia Fiennes Stares Hard

The robust Celia Fiennes, 1662–1741, travelled through every English county, mostly on horseback, and wrote her observations as a series of Journeys. *She rode north in 1698 and remarked that in the Lake District she had had to have her horses reshod every two or three days, so rough was the going.*

Celia Fiennes aimed her story at no one. It is purely personal, entirely without purpose – the overheard mumblings of a talkative old maid. She took her 'Great Journey to Newcastle and to Cornwall' in 1698, about twenty-five years before Defoe, but in many ways she anticipated the later travellers more than he does. It is not that she is more interested in landscape, but she is more interested in herself. Defoe travelled, in the first case, to collect information for a minister of state; Miss Fiennes travelled only for her own entertainment. The scene around her mattered less for its own sake than because it could divert and amuse her. She is an extraordinarily interesting character: prudish, strict, exacting, and possibly sharp-tongued, and at the same time hardy, determined, and adventurous. To travel all over England in the reign of William and Mary demanded not only courage, but great physical toughness, yet Celia Fiennes was something of a hypochondriac, and became an expert visitor of 'spaws', where she went, not for cards and dancing, but for almost brutal treatment in icy-cold water. The Lakes, unfortunately, had little of this sort to offer, which may be one of the reasons for delay in their discovery by people of quality; for the visiting of watering-places was not just a fashion in medicine, it was a relic – though far removed – of the old pilgrimages to holy wells and miracle-working fountains.

Miss Fiennes's account of her visit to the Lakes is specially valuable because she was unprepared by the writings of others. She comes with no preconceived ideas; she did not feel that any particular reaction was expected of her. Her mind was entirely free from the suggestions of guide-book stars; she had neither to notice them nor to avoid them. Moreover, she knew of no prescribed grading of subjects. To her the purchase of curios made of 'canal coal' at Wigan was quite as worthy of comment as the crossing of Kirkstone Pass. She had little of the later preoccupation with scenery, and would ride for miles without noticing anything which stuck in her mind, yet when her interest is really roused she can be a most perceptive reporter, especially (and here she may be compared with later women travellers) in matters of inns, cooking, and housewifery. Thus she enjoys the potted char from Windermere 'big as a small trout rather slenderer and the skinn full of spotts some redish, and part of the whole skinn and the finn and taile is red like the finns of a perch, and the inside flesh looks as red as any salmon'[1]; and, since rye bread makes her sick, she is relieved to find that she can digest the Westmorland clap-bread, which played an important part in the diet of the Lake counties.

Her route, unlike her prose, was straightforward enough. From Lancaster (where her horse stumbled in the street) she went through Kendal to Windermere, over Kirkstone into Patterdale, and thence to Penrith and on to Carlisle. In all her descriptions of the fells it is noticeable that she is quite uninfluenced either by Italian painting or by English poetry. Probably, being a Puritan, she had not read even such a poet as Spenser; certainly she arrived in the district quite unrehearsed in vocabulary. Such stock terms as cataract and precipice do not come easily to her mind, and this conditions her actual vision, for, instead of being able to fit the scenery into accepted categories, she is forced to stare hard and try to take each object to pieces and put it together again, like a savage trying to understand a watch. The extraordinary circumlocutions caused by this effort, together with the natural garrulity of a seventeenth-century Gertrude Stein, make her style as hard to follow as the course of a straw in a rocky stream, but they do tell us what

[1] *The Illustrated Journeys of Celia Fiennes*, edited by Christopher Morris (Macdonald & Co./Webb & Bower, 1982).

she really saw and not just what she expected to see. In the whole history of Lake travel, there are few people who have described their first impressions with such honesty and such charm:

> at last I attained to the side of one of these hills or fells of rocks which I passed on the side much about the middle; for looking down to the bottom it was at least a mile all full of those lesser hills and inclosures, so looking upward I was as farre from the top which was all rocks and something more barren tho' there was some trees and woods growing in the rocks and hanging over all down the brow of some of the hills; from these great fells there are severall springs out of the rock that trickle down their sides, and as they meete with stones and rocks in the way when something obstructs their passage and so they come with more violence that gives a pleaseing sound and murmuring noise.

The attraction of Celia Fiennes's account of the Lakes lies in its spontaneity. She had little idea of what she was going to see and none at all of what she ought to feel about it. She had no thought of publication, and her work was not in any sense an advertisement, so that we can see in her journal perhaps the last truly unconditioned reflex to Cumbrian landscape.

L.

Thomas Pennant Takes in the Lakes

Pennant, 1726–98, was born in Flintshire, a naturalist with a keen enjoyment of travel. He visited Lakeland twice, in 1769 and 1772, and for a long time his name and his writings were repeated by the Lake travellers to whom he seemed a pioneer.

In the 1760s and early 1770s, aesthetic enjoyment of scenery had not yet replaced the inquiring curiosity about the physical world which excited so many eighteenth-century travellers. And chief among such was Thomas Pennant, who today is remembered as the man to whom Gilbert White addressed some of the Selborne letters. At the bottom, he was a humanist, interested more in men than in mountains. He had all the typical eighteenth-century pride in England's expanding trade, and he was supremely confident in the greatness of his age and in the soundness of the English social structure. But though he was a humanist he was no humanitarian. He had common sense but little imagination, and he had some of the hardness which is often to be found below the elegance of his time. At Whitehaven workhouse he could 'look with pleasure' on the sight of old people, idiots, and 'even infants of three years of age, contributing to their own support, by the pulling of

Ullswater from Howtown

oakum', and at Carlisle he received a similar pleasure from 'twelve little industrious girls spinning at once at a horizontal wheel, which set twelve bobbins in motion.' He had a strong distrust of all extravagances in thought, word and emotion, and in this was curiously unlike most of those who were to follow him to the Lakes. He had learned the jargon, of course. He knew when to call a scene 'horrid' or 'stupendous', but the words had no emotional content for him – they were merely the accepted terms for describing that sort of scenery.

On his first tour of Scotland, in 1769, Pennant passed through the Lakes only on the way back, by which time he was obviously tired by his long journey. He had had enough of marvels, and hurried through Carlisle and Penrith, anxious to get home to his children, 'after an absence' (as he naïvely and not very convincingly says) 'equally regretted by all parties'.

On his second visit, in 1772, his mind was set once again on Scotland and the Hebrides, but this time he called in at the Lakes on the way up. He travelled as before through Lancashire as far as the county town, but planned the rest of his journey so that his new route did not coincide with his former one till he reached Carlisle.

After crossing Morecambe Bay he came to Furness and thence to Coniston. This was the first English lake he had seen at close hand and he seems rather puzzled at what to say, not knowing whether to use his superlatives or to reserve them for places more celebrated. 'The scenery', he says, choosing a word which is not really one of the more conventional ones, '... is extremely noble', but he seems glad to direct his attention to the slate quarries and the price of fish. Neither Esthwaite nor Windermere impressed him greatly, though he inquired again about the fish and tells us that there are wild cats in the woods – but at Derwentwater he was faced with what was already accepted as the scenic climax to the Lakes, the 'Elysium of the North'. Here he is clearly much more enthusiastic and his prose begins to warm up into passages which were to be quoted over and over again in the years which followed. But, though he is quite sincere (which is more than could be said of many of his readers), he could not keep up that strain for long, for he was exhausting both his sense of rapture and his rather small vocabulary. Luckily, there was more to interest him. He turns from the lake and mentions, with his usual delight at any piece of stray information, that it is not long since the stipend of the vicar of Crosthwaite (the parish church of Keswick) 'was five pounds per annum, a goose-grass, or the right of commoning his goose; a whittle-gait, or the valuable privilege of using his knife for a week at a time at any table in the parish; and lastly, a hardened sark, i.e. a shirt of coarse linnen.'

He now had the good fortune to meet Dr Brownrigg, a man after his own stamp, who was then retired and living at Ormathwaite near Keswick. Brownrigg, next to John Dalton the most distinguished chemist Cumberland has yet produced, had been in practice as a surgeon at Whitehaven where he invented an instrument 'for the more immediate extraction of drowning bodies from the water'[1], and began important experiments with fire-damp and other poisonous or explosive gases which caused so many accidents in the mines. Nor was Pennant his only visitor that year, for Benjamin Franklin stayed there, preoccupied, quite literally, with the problem of pouring oil on troubled waters. He, Brownrigg and the Rev. Charles Farish of Carlisle carried out experiments on Derwentwater, and one wonders if anyone protested when the three of them rowed out from Friar's Crag and tipped barrels of oil on to the choppy surface of the lake. Perhaps there were oil casualties among the water fowl even as early as the eighteenth century.

As a writer Pennant is neither lively nor original. Defoe could make the eighteenth-century scene come alive in a few sentences, and Miss Fiennes, with her trails and tangles of words, could always make at least herself come alive. Pennant had not this gift. Too often he descends into a sort of gentlemanly journalism. Yet of all the early travellers in the Lakes, he is the one for whom I feel the most sympathy. His interests were confined almost entirely to the natural and material world around him, but they were the beginnings of a great new awakening to the physical and spiritual predicament of man. His view was limited, but it was a real view; he saw only in part, but what he did see was really there. He did not invent his own landscape, and his very lack of imagination, his literal and materialist way of thought, represents the basic, objective view of the Lakes to which every now and then we must return to renew our sense of perspective. Pennant's mountains may not point to heaven, but at least you can stand on them.

L.

William Gilpin: A Picturesque Survey

Gilpin was born in 1724 at Scaleby Castle near Carlisle. He took a degree at Oxford and after years of being in charge of a school in Cheam, Surrey, he set out to study 'Picturesque' landscape material, which he had gathered when touring the Wye, the Lakes, Wales and Scotland.

The cult of the Picturesque was primarily an attempt to educate the eye to a new way of looking at the natural world. In its simplest and purest sense the word had none of the implications of rusticity and quaintness

---

[1] William Hutchinson, *History of Cumberland* (Carlisle, 1794).

which it has today. It just meant the art of seeing the world aesthetically. People had got into the habit of using the eye mainly for information, mainly in order to know. The Picturesque trained them to use it for sensation.

William Gilpin was among the first to realize that what was beautiful or sublime in nature did not always come off in art, to explain which he invented a third category which he called Picturesque beauty, meaning, quite simply, that form of beauty 'which would be effective in a picture'. Gilpin became the travelling salesman of the Picturesque.

He set off in May 1772 from Cheam and passed through the Midlands, visiting and criticizing several of Capability Brown's 'embellished' estates, and passing through Manchester and Preston to Lancaster. He approached the Lakes by Kendal and Ambleside, and sailed up and down Windermere, noting the changes in distance and prospect as he moved along the surface of the water. He had no eye for detail, but he did have a lively interest in what might be called the series of dissolving views which is revealed as a bay slides out from behind a promontory, as the shores approach each other or open apart, or as hills emerge above hills or sink and recede in the distance. The landscape, if it is only a picture, is at least a moving picture. From Windermere he passed over Dunmail Raise, along Thirlmere, then still treeless and bridged about the middle, and on to Keswick, whence he made excursions to Lower Borrowdale, to Buttermere and Crummock, and to Bassenthwaite. He views Derwentwater appreciatively but critically, and does not fall into the raptures of many of the other visitors. He quotes the famous saying of Charles Avison, organist and composer, of Newcastle-upon-Tyne: 'Here is beauty indeed – Beauty lying in the lap of Horrour!' He tells also the rather odd story of an artist who painted a series of views of the lake from St Herbert's Island, and then hung them around the walls of a circular room, 'whence, as from a centre, he might see it in rotation'.

Borrowdale, however, made rather more of an impression on him. Here, he went first as far as Rosthwaite, and thence by the track that curves behind Grange Fell, into the small Watendlath valley, and his story of this journey was so often quoted and repeated that the phrase 'Which way to Watendlath?' has become almost a local proverb. And it is, indeed, a curiously intriguing phrase and one which, if spoken in the presence of Wordsworth, might have led to a poem, another 'What, are you stepping westward?'

> 'Which way to Watenlath?' said one of our company to a peasant, as we left the vale of Borrodale. 'That way,' said he, pointing up a lofty mountain, steeper than the tiling of a house.
>
> To those, who are accustomed to mountains, these perpendicular motions may be amusing; but to us, whose ideas were less elevated, they seemed rather peculiar ... To move upwards,

keeping a steady eye on the objects before us, was no great exercise to the brain: but it rather gave it a rotation to look back on what was past – and to see our companions below *clinging*, as it appeared, to the mountain's side; and the rising breasts and bellies of their horses, straining up a path so steep, that it seemed, as if the least false step would have carried them rolling many hundred yards to the bottom.

The last lake he visited was Ullswater. He got a glimpse of the King of Patterdale, fishing on the lake, collected a few stories about thrifty curates and great storms and then passed along to Carlisle and the Border. He had been only five days in the Lakes and his impressions were bound to be superficial, yet for two or three generations people would look at those scenes through his eyes. He had made, in fact, the first Picturesque survey of the district.

Gilpin's limitations are obvious, yet he avoided most of the absurdities of his contemporaries. He has little of the traveller's usual wish to astonish those who stayed at home, and seems deliberately to keep his enthusiasm in check (if, indeed, he was capable of much enthusiasm), and to remind the reader that not every scene in Cumbria is 'correctly Picturesque'. This cold, analytical approach may suggest that he was incapable of accurate observation, but this is not quite true. Whenever a scene has a picturesque effect which particularly interested him, he takes careful notice of the physical details which produce that effect. He notices, for instance, the variations of light on the side of a mountain, and how the surface which seems flat and dull at one time of day, can take on an exciting texture of gleam and shadow as the sun shifts to another angle. He notices too, how great tides of shadow wash round the bases of the mountains and in the clefts between them, ebbing and flowing with the sun. He was much concerned with light, and his comments on the surface of the lakes have an accuracy and understanding quite astonishing for one who spent so little time among them:

> In clear windy weather, the breezy ruffled lake ... is a shattered mirror: it reflects the serenity; but reflects it partially. The hollow of each wave is commonly in shadow, the summit is tipped with light. The light or shadow therefore prevails, according to the position of the waves to the eye.
>
> There is another appearance on the surfaces of lakes, which we cannot account for on any principle either of optics, or of perspective. When there is no apparent cause in the sky, the water will sometimes appear dappled with large spots of shade ... The people will often say, 'It will be no hay-day, today, the lake is full of shades'.

It is in his love of certain effects of light – particularly of mist, vapours, shadows and twilight – that Gilpin approaches closest to one aspect of romanticism. He was the forerunner of those who look to art to escape from the world of physical necessity into a blurred, hazy, intangible world of the imagination. He was, in fact, one to whom distance lends enchantment to the view, because distance moves out of fact into fancy.

L.

Thomas Gray: Through a Looking Glass

Gray, born in London in 1716, is best known for his Elegy, *one of the most popular poems in the English language. His first attempt to tour in Lakeland in 1767 was abandoned, but two years later he tried again and wrote his* Journal in the Lakes.

In the popular literature of the Lakes, Gray has been made the butt of all those who think themselves better men because they can climb Scafell or walk across Striding Edge. As early as 1787 James Clarke, in his *Survey of the Lakes*, was spreading the story that Gray was so terrified by the precipices of Skiddaw that he drew the blinds of his chaise. Others told how he had been equally terrified when crossing Windermere by boat. Both stories appear to be false.

Gray's ten days in the Lakes were well planned for one who did not want to exert himself overmuch. He arrived at Penrith on 30 September, climbed the Beacon Hill, and the next day visited Ullswater, returning to Penrith for the night. On 2 October he went on to Keswick and stayed there several days, visiting Bassenthwaite, Borrowdale, the wad mine, and the Druid circle at Castlerigg, and spending the rest of the time sauntering through the meadows and beside the lake. On the 8th he left by Dunmail Raise and Grasmere for Ambleside, but continued as far as Kendal because the best bedroom at the Ambleside inn was 'dark and damp as a cellar'. At Kendal he spent two nights, taking a trip to Sizergh before going on to Lancaster, and thence by Ingleborough and Settle, through Yorkshire to join William Mason in Derbyshire.

Throughout this tour he carried with him a Claude-glass, described by Mason in his memoir of the poet (1775) as 'a plano-convex mirror, of about four inches in diameter, on a black foil, and bound up like a pocket-book'. On clear days a dark glass was used; in dull weather, one laid on silver foil, or tinted to give the classical golden glow of Claude. 'The mirror', says Thomas West, 'is of the greatest use in sunshine; and the person using it ought always to turn his back on the object that he views. It should be suspended by the upper part of the case, holding it a little to the right or left (as the position of the parts to be viewed requires) and the face screened from the sun.'

The primary effect of the glass was to reduce the landscape to the size of a postcard, so that the shape, balance, and perspective could be seen at a glance. The advantage to artists is obvious (indeed, some of them still use a similar device) and it is possible that the drawings of Gilpin, both in their oval shape and the carroty colours of the aquatints, were in part an imitation of the image in the mirror. Moreover, it deflated and simplified the scene. Detail was lost; movement, except on the scale of a large storm, was scarcely perceptible; and the whole smell and taste and feel of a place were bled away till it became merely a design under glass, a dead world, indeed a world that had never lived.

Gray certainly enjoyed this toy, which, he says, 'played its part divinely' in lower Borrowdale, and the view from the Parsonage at Crosthwaite is specifically described as 'a picture in the glass'. But he was not restricted to this view. He could put down the glass and look about him, often with a clarity of vision for which he has not often been credited. It is true that he rarely focuses his eye or his interest on a small object, or on one that was near at hand. He notices that at Grange in Borrowdale the Derwent shows under its bridge 'every trout that passes', but, to our loss, he gives us none of the botanical notes and comments which so often fill his letters from Cambridge or London. Even as late as October there must have been many flowers of the dales and mountain pastures which were still to be seen and recognized – golden-rod, lady's mantle, betony, white deadnettle (Gray would probably have called it the white 'archangel'), lousewort, and grass of Parnassus, together with the peculiar bitter-orange seeds of bog asphodel, the berries of rowan, tutsan and bird-cherry, and all the brown rag-mat of dying leaf and fern. Of this he mentions only a few lichens and the gale or wild myrtle, yet we have many glimpses that are clearer, cleaner, truer, with more line and edge to them than anything which had been written before. There is Ullswater, 'smooth as a blue mirror', with 'white farm houses looking out among the trees, and cattle feeding'; there is, at seven in the morning, the hoarfrost 'which soon melted and exhaled in a thin bluish smoke'; there is Saddleback, 'whose furrowed sides were gilt by the noon-day sun, whilst its brow appeared of a sad purple from the shadow of the clouds as they sailed slowly by it'. Nor does he restrict his notice entirely to the countryside, for outside Kendal he is intrigued with the tenter grounds, where the bleached cloth was stretched to dry, and, in a delightful phrase, says of the houses of this town that they 'seem as if they had been dancing a country-dance, and were out: there they stand back to back, corner to corner, some up-hill, some down, without intent or meaning'.

Whenever he settles himself to sketch a complete landscape he does so with a real sense of composition, giving us foreground, and middle distance, with side-screens and back-screen, arranged formally yet not artificially. In his picture of Ullswater, for instance, the eye is led from the lake up through lake meadows to the lower hills and then checked, encircled and enclosed by the fells so that it cannot overrun its subject. Yet, unlike Gilpin, he does not sacrifice everything else to the art of formal composition. The landscape is simplified, but it is not distorted; it retains much of its true character and colouring. Indeed, if Gilpin's descriptions often resemble his own vague and misty aquatints, Gray's are more like the type of colour print with which we have become familiar in the better type of railway poster – stylized, romanticized, yet with a certain, almost photographic literalness. At the same time, they are drawn with true feeling, with genuine and not prefabricated excitement, and with delicate shading of poetry. Gray had not Wordsworth's gift of seeing in the forms of nature a tremendous and transcendental significance, but he could look at them straight and could delight that they were what they were.

L.

Well Muffled and Cautious

For Gray a landscape was not merely a scene, but an environment. He could not feel, as Wordsworth could, that he himself was part of that environment, absorbed into it, sharing its life, yet he did feel that it was all round him, encircling him and bending over him. It was the element in which he moved, as a bird moves in air or a fish in water.

It is perhaps significant that he came to the district in October, which may seem a strange choice for a man of delicate health, until we remember that October, in its brown autumnal varnish, is pre-eminently the month of the Picturesque. It is also the month when a view is almost tangible. In the turnip-purple mist that rises from the stubble the senses are intermingled. You *smell* the brownness, you *feel* the manure-smells, the harvest- and orchard- and dead-bracken-smells, and the yellow light drifts round your head like mist.

Gray was 'no lover of dirt', nor of damp. We often catch his fastidious and hypochondriac shudder at the soft humidity of the Lake air, and he obviously approved of the local description of Derwentwater as 'the Devil's chamber-pot'. As he walked, well muffled up, stepping cautiously, even his feet collected sensations which contributed to his experience, noticing, for instance, at Dunmallet, that the meadow is 'spongey' to stand on. It is, however, his sense of the height and steepness of the scene, rather than of its texture or mass, that makes his *Journal* memorable – his sense of the lift, the jaggedness, the gothic upsurge of the central dales. The mountains seemed to him to have an inexplicable malice which made itself visible in the shape of overhangs of rock, filling his mind with fear of falling stones. His awareness of the landscape was intensely physical, but, unlike that of John Wilson and of modern hikers and rock-climbers, it was entirely passive. He did not try to impose his own personality on it, he did not try to break it to his will. Instead, he endured it, suffered it, felt it directing itself against him, impinging on him, leaning over and overshadowing him.   L.

Echoes of William Hutchinson

The historical sense, one of the main ingredients of the Picturesque, was left out of Gray's *Journal*, but the omission was made good by two other travellers Hutchinson and West, each of whom was both an historian and a connoisseur, though otherwise they had little in common.

William Hutchinson (1732–1814) was a solicitor at Barnard Castle, with ambitions both as an imaginative writer and as an antiquary. He made a good many tours through the Border counties, and published valuable histories of Durham County (1785) and of Cumberland (1794), the latter of which is, in fact, a Picturesque work.

Hutchinson made two visits to the Lakes for his *Excursion*, the first in 1772, when he was accompanied by his brother, a frail, melancholy-looking young man, who died the same year. They travelled by Bowes and Brough to Penrith, visited Ullswater, on to Keswick, where they climbed Skiddaw, and thence to Ambleside, Kendal, and home by Kirkby Stephen. The ascent of Skiddaw was enlivened by a thunderstorm, in which Hutchinson revels like a Wagnerian at *Tristan*, giving us a rather incredible picture of the guide, lying on the earth, 'terrified and amazed … accusing us of presumption and impiety'. On the second visit, in the following year, taking the same route as far as Keswick, and climbing Skiddaw this time on horseback (a procedure he does not recommend), he passed through Cockermouth to the coast, then north to Carlisle, and back by the Roman wall. As he went through Cockermouth it is possible that Wordsworth, then three years old, may have been playing in the garden behind the house in the main street.

The new complexity of response which Hutchinson brought to the Lakes, his virtuosity on the five-manual organ of the senses, can be seen in the account of his favourite, Ullswater. The party of which he was a member started from Askham, beside the River Lowther, so that they first saw the lake from the hills which lie between Lowther and Pooley Bridge. Then, having reached the shore, they left their horses at an inn, and went aboard one of the pleasure barges placed there by the Duke of Portland. Rowed by four men, they ascended as far as Watermillock where they landed to picnic. The lake, which before had been ruffled by the wind, now 'became a shining mirror', with the water so transparent that they could 'perceive the fish and pebbles at the depth of six or eight fathom'. They set off again, passing 'Gobery Park' (the Gowbarrow Park of Wordsworth's daffodils), and Hutchinson, who all the time has been looking about him with excited interest, now begins to feel the full evocative power of the scene, to move, as it were, from the swell to the great. As they sail along, one peak is disclosed behind the other, the prospect continually unpacking itself like a parcel. The clouds hang about the mountain, jutting out from its sides, or descending up and down, in the strange way clouds behave above the lakes. I myself, very early one summer morning at Cockley Moor, above Airey Beck, have seen a new lake of mist, identical with Ullswater in size and shape, lying some fifty or a hundred feet above it, as if it had grown a second storey.

Then, leaving the gentlemen on shore, the barge put out into the lake to rouse the echoes, for which purpose it was fitted with six brass cannon, mounted on swivels, while some of the men had French horns to add to the harmony. The passage in which Hutchinson describes these echoes is one of the most famous in all Lake writing, and will go on repeating itself in guide-book after guide-book, reverberating like the sounds it describes. It is the climax of what we might call the sensational approach to the Lakes – the moment before the wave breaks, before the bubble bursts, before the swing swings back:

> The report was echoed from the opposite rocks, where by reverberation it seemed to roll from cliff to cliff, and return through every cave and valley; till the decreasing tumult gradually died away upon the ear.
>
> – The instant it had ceased, the sound of every distant waterfall was heard, but for an instant only; for the momentary stillness was interrupted by the returning echo on the hills behind; where the report was repeated like a peal of thunder bursting over our heads, continuing for several seconds, flying from haunt to haunt, till once more the sound gradually declined – again the voice of waterfalls possessed the interval – till to the right, the more distant thunder arose upon some other mountain, and seemed to take its way up every winding dell and creek, sometimes behind, on this side, or on that, in wondrous speed, running its dreadful course – when the echo reached the mountains within the line and channel of the breeze, it was heard at once on the right and left, at the extremities of the lake – In this manner was the report of every discharge re-echoed seven times distinctly.

It is impossible not to like Hutchinson. There is a boyish eagerness about him, an almost adolescent acceptance of a new world of the senses. His intellect was not profound, but it was lively. If he was not one of those who opened new vistas of experience for humanity, he was still, within his limitations, adventurous, enterprising, never disappointed, never bored.

L.

West's Guide to the Lakes

Thomas West, 1717–79, was a Catholic priest who lived at Tytup Hall near Lindal-in-Furness, where he wrote The Antiquities of Furness. *Later, at Ulverston, he published his* Guide.

Father Thomas West was much more of a true historian, but he had nothing of the charming eagerness of William Hutchinson. By his time the Picturesque was already becoming a planned pleasure, a Butlin camp of the sensibilities, with all its possibilities tasted, tested, tried, recorded, and mapped out. The Lakes soon were to become less of a discovery than a fashion, and West himself did much to bring about this change through his *Guide to the Lakes,* published in 1778. He died in 1779, but the guide was reissued the following year, revised and enlarged by William Cockin of Burton-in-Kendal, who also added an appendix which is a most important anthology of pre-Wordsworthian writing on the Lakes, and it was here, rather than in the original editions, that the majority of the tourists first met Gray's *Journal,* Brown's *Description of Keswick,* and Dalton's *Descriptive Poem.*

West has the merit of knowing the district he describes, but he catches little of the adventure and excitement which we feel with Gray or Hutchinson. His *Guide* helps the traveller to find his way, tells him what to look for, but it never makes the scene appear before his eyes. He wrote at a time when the vocabulary of Picturesque travel had already hardened into a convention, and, while this spared him the effort of searching for the right word, it meant that his language is too blunted to have much effect. His rivers invariably 'serpentize', his mountains are 'most horrid and romantic'. Moreover, he was not really happy among rocks and crags. A dale without a lake meant nothing at all to him. The centre of his interest was always water, and he would jump from the lake to the next with scarcely, a glance at the intervening country. With Gilpin as guide, he directed the traveller to a progression of 'stations', or, as we would call them, viewpoints – each lake being divided into Station One, Station Two, and so on – comparing one view with another, judging them like exhibits at a flower show.

We can illustrate West's method of quoting from his account of Coniston which he approached from Ulverston, reaching the lake at the southern tip. He gives his directions with characteristic detail:

STATION 1 ... From the rock, on the left of the road, you have a general prospect of the lake upwards. This station is found by observing where you have a hanging rock over the road, on the east, and an ash-tree on the west side of the road. On the opposite shore, to the left, and close by the water's edge, are some stripes of meadow and green ground, cut into small enclosures, with some dark coloured houses under aged yew trees. Two promontories project a great way into the lake; the broadest is finely terminated by steep rocks, and crowned with wood; and both are insulated when the lake is high. Upwards, over a fine sheet of water, the lake is again intersected by a far-projecting promontory, that swells into two eminences, and betwixt them the lake is again caught, with some white houses at the feet of the mountains.

There is nothing slipshod or haphazard about that. West is obviously determined that no one shall miss any detail of the view, yet he never catches the imagination, and succeeds in giving only what Gilpin would have called a catalogue and not a landscape. For all this, his stations are chosen with knowledge and care and the next one, from the 'far-projecting promontory' just mentioned, has already been canonized by the National Trust. It is that small headland, about a mile and a quarter from the foot of the lake, where a fist of reddish rock thrusts out of the cuff of the shore to make a miniature Hebridean island of tiny cliffs, screes and ledges, with bracken and elder, heather and wild thyme, a picnic-sized back-of-beyond. 'From thence,' says West, 'the coast is beautifully diversified by a number of green eminences, crowned with wood; and sequestered cottages, interspersed amongst them, half concealed by yew trees, and, above them, a wave of rocky spiral mountains dressed in brown vegetation, form the most romantic scenes.'

West tried to dress to a fashion he did not really understand, so that his work lacks the vitality which we find in writers much less informed. Already, by 1778, he was demonstrating the deadening results of the conventional response.

L.

Bold Joseph Budworth

Budworth, 1756–1815, wrote for the Gentleman's Magazine *under the pen-name 'a Rambler'. In 1792 he published* A Fortnight's Ramble to the Lakes. *Its third edition, in 1810, included* A re-visit to Buttermere.

Captain Joseph Budworth strode into the literature of the Lakes like Long John Silver into *Treasure Island*. Like Silver he was purposeful, independent, cheerfully arrogant and superbly alive. Like Silver, too, he was something of a cripple, though it was an arm that he had lost and not a leg. While he is before your eyes you can look at no one else.

The people he meets are acted off the stage or are remembered because of what he said of them. Even his occasional affectations, his delights and shudderings, seem to be merely freakish disguises of his own true personality.

Budworth's reactions to the Lakes are perhaps the freshest and most spontaneous since those of Celia Fiennes. In spite of his one arm (he had lost the other at the siege of Gibraltar), he was essentially a whole man, having the energy which was lacking in Gray, and the balance and animal spirits which were lacking in most of the rest. He could at times invent his own little pretences, but he was never one of those who cried, as he himself tells: 'Good God! how delightful! – how charming! – I could live here for ever! – Row on.' Such sham ecstasies provoked him to nothing but scorn. He would like to paint Kendal, he says, but the roads were so ill-paved that he could mind nothing but his feet. In the same way his descriptions often have a little hard knob of reality, which tells us more than a hundred stock epithets. Grasmere, for instance, has a 'green rump-shaped island'; Ullswater, seen from a spot on Helvellyn where Place Fell interrupts the view, has the shape of a pair of breeches; while Red Tarn is like a Bury pear.

Moreover, unlike West, he did not go from view to view without noticing what happened in between. For quite a lot happened, especially food. The route from Ambleside to Keswick did not just include Dunmail Raise, it included a mid-morning breakfast of mutton-ham, eggs, buttermilk, whey, tea, bread and butter, and cheese – and all for sevenpence. Many of the early travellers had enjoyed the trout and the potted char, but none, we feel, brought such an eager appetite as Budworth. His pleasure still hangs to the pages like the smell of a savoury, while he licks his lips over a meal such as that at Robert Newton's in Grasmere:

> Roast pike, stuffed
> A boiled fowl
> Veal-cutlets and ham
> Beans and bacon
> Cabbage
> Pease and potatoes
> Anchovy sauce
> Parsley and butter
> Plain butter
> Butter and cheese
> Wheat bread and oat cake
> Three cups of preserved gooseberries,
> with a bowl of rich cream in the centre:
>
> For two people, at ten-pence a head.

After this he set out to climb Helm Crag, and it is not surprising that the hill looked formidable, and 'not less so, to speak in plain English, from having a complete bellyful'.

Buttermere Valley

Budworth was not content to stay at lake level. As well as the usual Skiddaw, he climbed Helvellyn, Coniston Old Man, and Langdale Pikes, and he was the first of all the travellers to begin to see the fells as a physical challenge. He did not face that challenge as boldly as Christopher North, but he was able to accept physical effort, if not with enjoyment, yet with a cheerful toughness. When he tells of his struggle to climb a frozen grass slope near Scale Force, you are conscious not only of pride in his endurance, but of a certain heightened physical awareness, a translation of the hill from terms of visual scenery to the tactile impression of feet and legs and muscles:

> I made many efforts to overcome the glassy hill; and although I had sharp nails in the balls of my shoes, and large stubbs to the heels, with a pike to my hazel stick, my efforts were useless; I tumbled twice, and slid bodily down the hill again ... Although the surface was ice, the rough grass and water oozing through had made it both hollow and rotten. It soon got over my shoe-tops, and up to one knee, and then I felt myself conquered, gave up the pursuit, and determined to bear a great disappointment with due meekness.

Here at last is a landscape you can really touch, can really get hold of. Budworth is exaggerating – the average youth hostel schoolgirl of today would be up that slope with a sandwich in one hand and ordnance map in the other. But he is exaggerating in a new way. Quite unlike Gilpin and Hutchinson, he is not making the view conform to a preconceived image. Instead, he is exaggerating as a sportsman exaggerates. His descriptions are like fishing stories – lies told within a certain convention, certain accepted limits, which are understood by the listener as well as the teller. He is not so much deceiving as spinning a yarn.

Budworth is distinguished from all others of his time not only by his physique but by his quick interest in people. He made friends with the landlords of all the inns, and gathered the local gossip from them. He wished, he said, to 'give free scope to everyone he spoke to', so that an old grandmother at Dunmail Raise proved that she had 'the clack of her sex', and told him that she had been too often on Skiddaw in her youth to be ill in her old age. Even his guides, Paul Postlethwaite and Robin Partridge, obviously liked him, though they may have laughed at him many a time behind his back.

Yet inevitably he was a man of his time, and his view was not free from the distortion of the Picturesque. Just as he had exaggerated about the mountains, so now he struck an attitude about the people. Against the evidences of his own sense, he had to feel that the Cumbrians were a strange, primitive, pastoral race, far away from everyday problems, far away from the vices and corruptions of civilized society, shut off from the rest of the world (as John Housman said) 'by those natural barriers infinitely stronger than the great wall of China'[1].

The primitive was the Picturesque view of man: Rousseau's dream of a noble savage realized in a people who were not quite savages. Because of this, when Budworth watched a village wedding, somewhere between Leeds and Kendal, and when he attended a dancing-class at Heversham, he reported both of them in the tone of a lady traveller describing racial customs of the Balkans. Because of this, again, when he saw a young girl serving at an inn in Buttermere, he indulged in a sentimental daydream which was to distort the shape and course of her life and to make her name known throughout the country.

L.

The Beauty of Buttermere

This famous story created a sensation in its own time, at the beginning of the nineteenth century, and even today it still attracts readers – and writers, as in Melvyn Bragg's The Maid of Buttermere *(Hodder and Stoughton, 1987).*

Mary Robinson, daughter of the landlord of the Fish Inn, Buttermere, was first seen by Budworth in 1792. She was then about fifteen, shy enough to keep out of his way at first, and for a man like Budworth, in early middle-age, she had all the sentimental, might-have-been, poignantly sensual charms of adolescence. It is possible that he scarcely spoke to her, for he gets her name wrong in the first two editions of his book. Yet he wrote of her in self-indulgent and unguarded praise.

> Her hair was thick and long, [he says] of a dark brown, and, though unadorned with ringlets, did not seem to want them; her face was a fine oval, with full eyes, and lips as red as vermillion; her cheeks had more of the lily than the rose; and, although she had never been out of the village (and I hope will have no ambition to wish it), she had a manner about her which seemed better calculated to set off dress, than dress *her*. She was a very Lavinia,
> > 'Seeming, when unadorn'd, adorn'd the most.'
> When we first saw her at her distaff, after she had got the better of her first fears, she looked an angel; and I doubt not but she is the reigning Lily of the Valley.

Now, without casting doubt on Mary Robinson's good looks, we can easily see that those lines are almost pure fantasy. The wish that the girl should never leave her own valley gives Budworth away. He wanted

[1] John Housman, *Topographical Description of Cumberland, Westmorland and Lancashire* (Carlisle, 1800).

her to live out for him the myth of the primitive; he wanted her to act his own dreams. Unfortunately, his very words destroyed his hopes, for when *The Ramble* was published, it drew everybody's attention to the girl, and sent all the Keswick tourists to Buttermere on the chance of seeing her. Many of them paid attentions that were not wanted. J. Grant, who went in 1797, tells of a friend who left some black stockings in her empty shoes, and when he returned the next year found that she had not dared to wear them, fearing that someone might come back to claim them. Budworth, who could be thoughtless but never mean or callous, realized that he had been rather a fool, and in January 1798, on his second visit to the Lakes, he called again at the Fish Inn. Here, 'taking the opportunity of our being alone', he revealed his identity, and gave Mary a little homily on the dangers of vanity. Strangers would come, he said, some of them with 'very bad intentions', and he hoped that she would never suffer from them. She was, he added rather naïvely, not really so handsome as he had thought she was, and was glad to have had the chance to undo any harm caused by his former flattering report.

He returned home, published an account of his visit in the *Gentleman's Magazine*, and sat back with an easy conscience, congratulating himself on having carried out a moral duty which ('taking the opportunity of our being alone') he had rather enjoyed. But his complacency was not justified. In July 1802 there arrived at the Queen's Head, Keswick, one calling himself the Hon. Alexander Augustus Hope. This man, a rather flashy but evidently well-to-do tourist, soon wormed his way into the local society, making friends among others with Mr Crump, the Liverpool businessman who built Allan Bank and rented it to Wordsworth. Before very long he found his way to Buttermere, then famous for its char-fishing, and immediately included Mary in the sport. They were married at Lorton on 2 October, and, as the girl was something of a celebrity, the wedding was reported in the newspapers, where it came to the notice of people who knew that the real Colonel Hope had been abroad all the summer and was then in Vienna. Inquiries were made and a warrant was issued, and 'Hope' was formally arrested, but was allowed to fish on the lake in the charge of a constable, from whom he managed to escape, crossing over Sty Head Pass to Wasdale and Ravenglass, where he hid for some days on board a small ship. Eventually he was captured in South Wales and taken to Carlisle for trial, by which time it had been discovered that his real name was John Hatfield, and that he was a bigamist with several children by his first wife. The case aroused enormous interest, and when he was found guilty and condemned to be hanged on 3 September 1803, the county rustled with rumours of a pardon or of the postponement of the execution. Large crowds gathered around the gaol. Wordsworth and Coleridge, who were passing through Carlisle at the beginning of their

Scottish tour, tried to obtain an interview with the prisoner, who would agree to meet only the former, though Coleridge seems to have caught a glimpse of him as he walked in the yard, with chains on his legs, taking exercise and air. One of the bystanders told them that Hatfield's fate was a warning against meddling with pen and ink.[1]

At the execution, which took place on the banks of the River Eden, Hatfield behaved with all the courage and bravura of a French aristocrat or an English highwayman. He dressed carefully, showed great politeness to the chaplain who attended him, gave his last half-crown to his executioner, and asked that his body should be buried at Burgh-by-Sands. Mary, who had had a child about this time, later married a local man and settled down to what seems to have been quite a happy marriage.

There would be no need to retail this rather squalid little story were it not for the immense excitement which it caused throughout England. It was repeated in dozens of letters and magazine articles and journals. It was written up on a broadsheet and acted in London as a melodrama. Nor was it just a seven-days wonder, for as late as 1841 it was the subject of a novel, *James Hatfield and the Beauty of Buttermere*, set in the over-manured ripeness of the high Victorian landscape. Now when a story appeals even to the less discriminating readers of two ages so different as that of the Prince Regent and that of the Prince Consort, we can be sure that it must have some inner vitality or significance. There can be no doubt, I think, that the people of the Industrial Revolution saw in the tale of Buttermere, consciously or unconsciously, a kind of allegory. To them Mary represented the sweet natural innocence of man living in an almost classical landscape, a modern Golden Age of shepherds and mountains. Hatfield, on the other hand, stood for the corruption of that new society, which was destroying the peasantry and the rural way of life, and imposing a new economic compulsion on all classes of men. He stood, also, for the evil in human nature, an evil which men were to believe in less and be aware of more. The Buttermere story, in fact, was popular because it was both a social allegory and a moral allegory. It was a story of the Fall, in which modern man could identify himself both with Mary and with Hatfield, both with the tempted and with the tempter, with humanity and with the devil.

L.

[1] See: Dorothy Wordsworth, *Recollections of a Tour made in Scotland*; and also James Denholm, *A Tour to the Principal Scotch and English Lakes (1805)*.

Down the Tourist Trail

Holidaymakers

The romantic need which drew more and more people to the North-west was satisfied in many ways – the lakes, the dales, the legends and even by strange occurrences. And as the number of visitors grew, so did the note of commercialization begin to sound.

By now we have heard practically all the themes which go to make the full chorus of the early Picturesque. There is the scientific curiosity of Pennant, the pure aesthetics of Gilpin, the romantic aesthetics of Gray, and the aesthetic sensation of Hutchinson. There is also Gray's imaginative response to history, together with the antiquarianism of Hutchinson and West, and their interest in local customs and the like. This pattern of interests, this counterpoint of curiosity with connoisseurship and of imagination with the senses, remained for many years the aim and object of tourists in the Lakes. But as visitors became more frequent and the district better known, as the tour became less of an exploration and more of a routine, we find that these main themes diminish in scope and in pitch. The curiosity of the scientist becomes a mere itch for oddities; the artist's careful assessment of the landscape in terms of visual beauty and design becomes a mere taste for prettiness; the painstaking (if rather amateur) research of the historians becomes a mere eye for a monument and an ear for a legend; and the genuine virtuosity of sensual response cultivated by such men as Hutchinson becomes a mere search for thrills. After 1790, the tourists were no longer pioneers or explorers; they were holidaymakers.

L.

The Mountain Snob

The travellers of the late eighteenth century visited only a part of the area, and those of the nineteenth century still less. Indeed, the fashion has been largely to concentrate on more and more intensive exploration

314

of a continually shrinking area. For as the roads have improved and brought coaches and hotels to the lower dales, the mountain-snob[1] has moved upwards and inwards. Long ago he deserted the pastoral lakes, Windermere and Esthwaite, leaving them first to the pony-cart and then to the limousine. Already he is snooty about the larger villages, and soon he will retreat, like a melting glacier, to the daleheads, or become one of those who deny the true name of Cumbria to anything below 2,000 feet.

L.

Playing the Tourists' Own Game

Pocklington Island in Derwentwater attracted the attention of early tourists, though rather less for its beauty than for the excesses of its eccentric owner.

In the time of the tourists the largest islands of Derwentwater and Windermere carried the names, respected and respectfully, of Mr Joseph Pocklington and Mr John Christian Curwen.

Curwen's Island or Christian's Island is the large low whaleback of land which lies almost opposite to Bowness Bay, and is known today as Belle Isle instead of by its old name of Long Holme. The first attempt to improve the island (made by a Mr English in the middle of the century) provoked much censure, but in 1789 the ownership passed into the hands of the Curwen family, who planted with discretion, and built the odd, but rather amusing, circular house which evoked, much praise from those who were not yet converted to the gothic.

The unfortunate Mr Pocklington, however, came in for practically no praise, perhaps because he had no powerful Cumbrian family behind him, like the coal-owning Curwens. It is true that the man had no taste at all. His buildings were laughably ugly and were stuck all over the place like decorations on a Christmas cake. He did not even confine his embellishments to the island. At one place he cut off the branches of an oak, shaved the bark and whitewashed the trunk, so that it stood in the meadow like the ghost of a tree. While at the Bowder Stone, says Don Espriella, he 'erected an ugly house for an old woman to live in who is to show the rock, for fear travellers should pass under it without seeing it ... [and] dug a hole underneath through which the curious may gratify themselves by shaking hands with the old woman'.[2]

Yet in spite of this, it seems surprising that he provoked such censure from the tourists, for he entered so wholeheartedly into their own game, getting far more fun out of his island than did Curwen at his sedate seat

[1] 'The mountain-snob is a Wordsworthian fruit' – W.H. Auden.
[2] Don Manuel Alvarez Espriella, *Letters from England* (Robert Southey, 1807).

Derwentwater

on Windermere. Derwent Island, as it is now most unimaginatively named, is at the lower end of the lake, side by side with Friar's Crag, and so close to the town of Keswick that one feels it ought to be under the jurisdiction of the parks committee. It has had several names. In the late eighteenth century it was known not only as Pocklington's Island but as Paradise Island, though the sight of Mr Pocklington himself, naked as Adam and with a suitable Eve, is one of the few possible attractions which he does not seem to have thought of. Before this it was Vicar's Island, from a presumed connection with Furness Abbey; and earlier still it held the splendid Norse name of Hestholm, stallion island.

In spite of Pocklington's silliness, there seems to have been a childlike charm about his dolls' village during the few years that it lasted. For the house itself, there is little to be said, but half-hidden away at various points on the island were several more entertaining contrivances. First of all, there was the church, built, as Budworth says laconically, 'as an object'; a fort and a battery, fitted with cannon for echoes; a boat-house looking like a Primitive Methodist chapel; and, most endearing of all, a Druid circle fifty-six feet in diameter, planned on the model of Castlerigg.

With all this to choose from, what right had the tourists to be ungrateful? Pocklington's fancies might be naïve, but at the bottom they were no more ridiculous than the attitudes and cadenzas of many more learned and more respected men. He was, moreover, curiously uninhibited and generous both of enthusiasm and of money to a project like the Keswick Regatta which he helped to establish during the 1780s.

The commerical note sounded in the *Cumberland Pacquet*'s report of Pocklington's regatta activities was to grow louder and louder. Mr Pocklington's fleet on Derwentwater, the Duke of Norfolk's pleasure barges on Ullswater, and Mr Curwen's seventeen vessels with rowers in scarlet were reserved for friends of the owners; but soon everyone could find water-transport at a modest cost. Hutton, the museum-keeper, plied a boat for hire at Keswick; the White Lion at Bowness and the New Inn at Coniston each had boats for the use of residents. The King's Arms at Patterdale provided not only a boat but a small cannon for the echoes, which was discharged 'at trifling expense'. Nor did you need to be a nobleman to be received with a military salute. You did not need even to be rich, for Lodore tactfully provided two cannons, one for four shillings and one for half a crown ... though, as Don Manuel Espriella very understandably said, 'when one buys an echo, who would be content, for the sake of saving eighteen pence, to put up with the second best, instead of ordering at once the super-extra-double-superfine?'

L.

The New Lakes Industry

The first tourists had appeared. Wordsworth's Guide *eventually would follow ... but who could have envisaged that it would all lead to today's 12 million annual visitors? The early commercial undertakings seem strangely innocent now.*

Gradually the towns began to adapt themselves to the new industry. Penrith had a start on the others, for it was on the main route to Scotland, and the last stop before Gretna, so that the inns had always to be prepared to put up runaway couples. In winter there was a regular card assembly together with many private parties; and in summer there were bowling-greens, which, as Clarke says, afforded 'exercise and amusement to such of the males as have no better employment'.

In contrast, Keswick and Ambleside and to some extent Kendal catered not so much for the passing traveller as for the true Lake tourist. Ambleside, early in the nineteenth century, had Green's exhibition of drawings and aquatints. Kendal had one museum, Mr Todhunter's, and Keswick two, Hutton's and Crosthwaite's, of which the later was on much the larger scale. It was housed in a lofty, imposing building, fitted with 'a number of little reeds fixed to the foot of the window-sash, through each of which, by applying your eye, you are directed to principal objects on the lake'. Inside was an astonishing assortment of oddments and oddities gathered rather as a sheep gathers bits of briar and twig and barbed wire in its wool. There were fossils, shells, stuffed birds, petrifactions, local antiquities, and various curiosities and monstrosities scraped together from all over the world – including a set of musical stones collected from the River Greta, the straw hat of a sailor who was with Bligh on the *Bounty*, two barnacles from the bottom of Captain Cook's ship, a piece of bamboo brought back from India by Captain John Wordsworth, and a lamb with claws instead of hooves and with wool of three colours. ('A racoon broke loose from Mrs Bradyle of Conniside [Conishead] Priory, and was missing a fortnight, he was seen amongst the ewes, and it is the general opinion that he copulated with them.') In spite of the sniffs of the virtuosi, the museum was extremely popular, and in 1793 could claim to have been visited by '1,540 persons of rank and fashion'. Each week their names were printed in the *Cumberland Pacquet*, and throughout their stay in Keswick they were greeted by Crosthwaite's barrel-organ whenever they passed down the street, while strangers had their attention drawn to the museum by the sound of an enormous brass gong.

L.

Spying Out the Needs of Tourists

Peter Crosthwaite, one of Lakeland's extraordinary characters, was the son of a farmer of Dale Head in the parish of Crosthwaite, and as a boy had been apprenticed to a weaver. Later he went to sea, and served with distinction but little reward in the gunboats of the East India Company which later became the Indian Navy. He left the service when he was thirty-one, and after twelve years or so as an excise officer he decided to retire to Brown Beck, in the Naddle valley, where his father had given him a small estate. The solitude of Saddleback and the Naddle fells, however, did not suit his enterprising and ingenious spirit, and within a year he had moved to Keswick and began to assemble his museum. It was a venture which he tackled with an obvious opportunism and a batty enthusiasm which must have made him quite the most intriguing curiosity in all his collection. Nor were his activities confined to his own house. By right of his naval experience he was promoted admiral of Pocklington's fleet on Derwentwater, he made surveys of the Lakes, and kept detailed observations and measurements of rain, wind, and weather. When a canal was contemplated to link Bassenthwaite Lake with the sea, he surveyed the whole route at his own cost. He was continually spying out the needs of tourists and anticipating their demands. In 1786, for instance, he made a zigzag path to the top of Latrigg, doing most of the work with his own hands or with the help of his son. About this time, too, he arranged for three men to build the first beacon on Skiddaw, and in 1796 he persuaded Mr Robinson of Buttermere (the father of Mary, the Beauty of Buttermere) to construct steps in the rock for the convenience of tourists visiting Scale Force. Today, however, he is known chiefly for his maps of the Lakes, sold at the museum along with prints, guide-books and an improved Æolian harp of his own design. These maps, with their undoubted charm, are a revealing memorial of this second phase of Lake travel. In their proportions they are reasonably accurate, marking the sites of West's stations, the inns and the farms, and giving also depths of the lakes, direction of the current and the like. Again, they are decorated, after the manner of an old sea-chart, with drawings of antiquities and gentlemen's seats, and views of the fells which look exactly like municipal flowerbeds piled high with shrubs. Yet the old adventure is gone. The mountains no longer contort themselves into strange shapes, the rocks do not 'impend'; the lakes and becks do not disappear into dark, unknown dales and gills of deep and dubious hachuring. All is now mapped and measured. There is no more mystery in the Lakes, but only a calculated curiosity, a polite and paid-for pretence.

L.

Gold in the Hills

If we are to believe the first visitors, the inhabitants were amazed at the strange interest in their county. 'Ith neome oh fackins' said Budworth's young guide in pure Cockney Cummerset, 'wot a broughton you here?' There is the story of a man who bought a plot of land at Grasmere. 'He paid too dear for it, Sir,' said a 'poor unrefined rustic' to Mr Grant. 'Had I been in his place, I would have bought another estate among the mountains, at the same price, and twice the value; but Mr Olive is a neat nacky man like, and thinks it fine diversion to look at the water coming down the fells, when there's a flood like, and that's all he has for his money.'

This point of view did not last long and there were many who saw that there was gold in the hills. Very soon the children were waiting to open the gates for carriages and we hear of one lad running indignantly after the gentry to demand change for a bad ha'penny. Moreover, the dale folk had a shrewd eye for the affected response, the pretended ecstasy. The very name by which the tourists were known, the Lakers, has an underlying irony, since 'laking' or 'laiking' is the dialect word for playing, and, more particularly, for playing as children play. Already, Picturesque travel was beginning to look rather naïve; sometimes there was seen a rather sophisticated smile among the tourists.

L.

The New Tourists

After Wordsworth the true Picturesque was dead. Excited journals were no longer published: fanciful drawings were no longer engraved. The Lake books of the eighteenth century were written by strangers, but those of the nineteenth, by residents – men, often, who had given many years to the patient and unspectacular study of their district. There was Jonathan Otley, swill-maker and watch-repairer, born in 1766 near Loughrigg Tarn, whose studies led Professor Sedgwick to the Lake rocks. His *Guide*, first published in 1823, is the basis of all sound factual writing on the district. There was William Green, of Manchester, a surveyor, who gave up his profession and settled at Ambleside as an artist. His *Tourist's New Guide*, published in 1819, is the first of the highways-and-byways type of book, leading the reader up every dale and every pass with the certainty of a man who knows his way blindfold. Green's work as an artist was appallingly industrious and almost completely uninspired, yet he set a new standard in topographical literalness – a standard which has been maintained by most succeeding artists to the almost total loss of every other merit. The larger subject obviously beat him – fells becoming mere outlines, flat and empty as a transfer pattern, but there is charm and what Keats might have called a 'low surprise' in his lovingly conscientious studies of boulders, walls, bridges and odds and ends of rock.

The tourists of the mid-nineteenth century were quite happy with this literalness, but they were not satisfied by it. They needed something more. Times had changed and so had they. They belonged, now, to the middle classes rather than to the gentry; they came from the industrial towns rather than from the country estates and the university cities; they were business people rather than intellectuals. Above all they belonged to a busy, prosperous, self-satisfied generation, and they were not in any way in revolt against that generation. They no longer came as explorers searching for the wild, the primitive, the edge of civilization; but rather as good, honest, practical men, giving their families the benefit of their initiative and sobriety. Yet the plain hills were not enough. They needed the extra glow, the extra excitement which they had neither the imagination to discover for themselves nor the training to learn from art. And they found it in Wordsworth.

In dealing with Wordsworth so far I have taken care to avoid the heart of his vision; his religion of nature, his 'mysticism', pantheistic or sacramental, whichever you will. It is a subject obviously beyond the scope of this book [The Lakers], which is concerned with a fashion, with popular fancies and foibles rather than with the more profound thought of the age. Yet Wordsworth's poetry now began to affect that fashion. For the agnostic, the earnest high-principled materialist of the Victorian age, it threw a glimmer of the transcendental over what was still rather a purposeless creed, an empty house rather than a new building. For the rest, it covered hill and dale, farm and inn, wagonette and picnic-basket, with the fat, yellow, comfortable warmth of religiosity. The Picturesque, which had once been aesthetic, was now moral.

The last taint of this attitude has probably disappeared from the cities, but it still lingers faintly in the small towns of the Lake border. How many boys, and, more specially, how many girls, have been prejudiced against the Lakes for life because they were preached to them as something they *ought* to enjoy, something which would do them more good than Blackpool or dancing or the cinema?

L.

Rest Cures and Refuge

Visitors in Ruskin's day turned to the Lakes for comfort and rest, no longer demanding the stimulus and excitement which had been the joy of the earlier travellers. The first great thrust of the Industrial Revolution had overstretched itself; the muscles were beginning to sag, the energy to fail. In the parlours, the drawing-rooms, the pews, all was still comfortable and secure; but in the back-alleys, the rotting cottages, the slave factories, there was the strain and anger of a society at one and the same time vigorous and stunted, opulent and starved. In spite of all the clangour of the railways, the grasp and grab of trade, the grandiloquence of empire, the flags, the dividends, the harvest festivals, the brass bands, the gold watches and Prince Albert himself, there was hidden somewhere in every Victorian a tired, rather frightened, rather lost little dog that wanted to crawl under the table and sleep. So the Lake tour became a rest-cure rather than an adventure, and the hills became a refuge rather than a discovery.

L.

Victorian Tourism

By the time Ruskin came to the Lakes the Victorian tourist trade had already reached its height. Keswick and Ambleside were well supplied with old and new hotels, and a completely new town had arisen at Windermere – a town of boarding-houses and shops, an inland watering-place with neither the raffishness of Brighton nor the honest vulgarity of Blackpool. Everywhere wealthy new residents were building their villas, in a style derived, for the most part, from the Elizabethan, but transformed by the dark green stone into something very different from Compton Wynyates. The steep gable roofs, the dark crag-like walls, the window-sills of grey limestone or purple sandstone, would scarcely accept the discipline of architecture, and after a few years of weathering they seemed to slump back again into rock like the artificial screes beside a quarry. The woodwork, often curled and scrolled, on porch and window and gable-end, seemed to try to bind the stone together, fencing and shelving it as with a dour, sour romanticism; while huge black rhododendrons unfolded shadows thicker and fatter than their own leaves. There might even be a motto on a stone sun-dial or a wrought-iron gate set in rolled-back walls. But the stone refused to play. It belonged to the chronology of the rock, and would not wear the fancy-dress of this century or that. It hunched itself against the rain and let the years grow over it like moss, and very soon it looked as old as the Old Man.

The age, however, was able to display itself more fully on the water, where, fortunately, it could leave no permanent mark. Steamers sailed to regular timetables on Windermere, Ullswater and Derwentwater, and a steam gondola made trips on Coniston timed in connection with the trains. Windermere now held an annual regatta, a set of races for sailing-craft, less boisterous and less ingenious than Pocklington's frolics on Derwentwater. Maps, engravings, postcards, guide-books were available everywhere, the books often packed with advertisements. Visitors were reminded that 'White and Sound Teeth' were indispensable to 'Personal Attraction', health and longevity by the proper mastication of food. Notepaper could be obtained headed with tiny prints of views of the Lakes – nearly a hundred views to choose from, or sold assorted in packets. For three and six you could buy a 'scientific souvenir' of 'Ferns From The Lakes', with 'specimens carefully mounted and enclosed in a tasteful cover'. Somewhere a few of these must still remain – scaly spleenwort or rustybacks now rusty all over, and the feathery barren fronds of parsley fern now dry and brown as its own spore branches. The glass case was beginning to be lowered over the Lakes.

L.

Floating Island

The tourists were in search not only of the scenery but of the eccentric, whether it be the phenomenon of a floating island, an oversize boulder or the characters that each age seems to generate.

It is much more than a matter of accident that this north-west part of England has come to be known as the Lakes rather than the Mountains. Yet, to those who live there, it is the mountains rather than the lakes which determine its character. To them, the lakes, attractive as they may be, are passing floods, older than man, no doubt, but almost temporary compared with the enduring fells. To the visitor, on the other hand, the lakes have an immense fascination; no valley, they feel, is complete without one. The Picturesque traveller gloried in water – lakes, ponds, rivers, cascades, clouds, floods, water in the sea, water on the land, water in the air. He loved islands, especially the Floating Island of Derwentwater which, of all the water fancies, was the most exciting. I say 'fancy' deliberately, because, as the island appeared only for a week or two at a time and sometimes not for years at a stretch,[1] few of the travellers ever saw it at all. For the majority it rose and fell only in imagination, drawing about it the mists and mystery of all those strange islands that float through the legend and history of the world, from Circe's Isle to Prospero's, from the Isles of the Blest to Juan Fernandez. To them it was a magic island, an island of fancy, and it is with this fancy that I am now concerned, rather than with the observable facts.

Of the few tourists who did see the island, William Hutchinson, in his excursion of 1773, was the first. He writes:

---

[1] G.J. Symons in *The Floating Island of Derwentwater* (1888) estimates that the island rose about forty times between the years 1753 and 1888.

We next visited a very extraordinary phenomenon, an island about 40 yards in length and thirty in breadth, grown over with rushes, reeds, grass, and some willows – We would have landed upon it, but as the water was said to be forty fathom deep in that place, and the attempt rather hazardous, we desisted, and had not the means of enquiring particularly as to its nature – This island rose about 4 perpendicular feet above the surface of the water, on which we were told it floated; – from its magnitude we were not able with one boat to try whether it would move, from the perpendicular line of its then station, or whether it was bound to and connected with the bottom of the lake by the roots of any aquatic plants which appeared upon its surface.[1]

That has a completely authentic sound. There are the measurements, and the presence of those amazingly quick-growing willows. There is the Defoe-like touch of the attempt to move the island, to make it swing round on its anchor, as it were. That, surely, would convince anyone. But oddly enough it did not convince Hutchinson himself. When he visited Derwentwater the year after that, the island had not risen, and he concluded from this that it did not float at all, but merely rose above the surface of the lake when the water-level was low. It is strange that this writer, who rarely hesitates to exaggerate, should be so cautious when he had the evidence of his own eyes. Indeed one feels that many of the travellers wrote of the Floating Island as if they were afraid of being laughed at when they returned home.

L.

The Bowder Stone

One sight that never failed to rouse the visitors' wonder was the Bowder Stone of Borrowdale. This stone is a large boulder, deposited by a retreating glacier at the end of the Ice Age. There are many such in the Lakes and, compared with others, the Bowder Stone is less spectacular in its situation, being in the dip of a valley instead of the brow of a hill, but it is by far the daddy of them all in size, balanced on its narrow base, as Mrs Radcliffe says, 'like the roof of a house reversed'. As a stone it is no more remarkable in shape or substance than the millions of smaller stones in all the becks of Cumbria. The early travellers did not look at these stones, but they *did* look at this one and so were able to see, magnified till it was big enough to attract their attention, something of the beauty of form, colour and texture which was lying around them everywhere in the dales.

At first glance, the stone seems a freak of perspective. You see what

[1] William Hutchinson, *Excursion to the Lakes* (1776).

might be a perfectly ordinary fragment of volcanic rock, but you see, as it were, a rabbit's-eye view of it. It blocks the entire mouth of the burrow along which you are walking. The boulders and rocks round about are like gravel or the most minute shiverings of scree, and the birches are like summer grasses, glossy and lish in the stem and flecked and feathery with seed.

When we read the eighteenth-century accounts of the Bowder Stone, we are entertained again and again by attempts to explain it. Obviously it was much too heavy to have been moved by human means, nor could one imagine any flood which could sweep it along the river-bed. Henry Kett, a contributor to Mavor's *British Tourist*, thought that it had fallen from the rocks above, and managed to persuade himself that he had spotted the 'large vacant place from which it had broken off'. Yet even if one admitted this, it seemed hard to believe that the stone could have rolled so far, to say nothing of its finishing perched on one point like a gigantic top. How, then, could it have come where it was? Their answers, as unscientific as Old Moore's Almanack, seem to me oddly imaginative. They did not say that the stone had grown out of the ground, as had been said of Stonehenge; but they did say that it had always been there, had never been anywhere else; that it was by itself and of itself; that it was, in fact, 'a separate creation'. James Clarke, speaking of this and other similar boulders, called them self-stones, a phrase which hangs about the memory as a cat hangs about a house after its owners have left. Unscientific it may be, geologically absurd, astronomically preposterous, but I cannot help feeling that in some strange inexplicable way it may yet be true.

L.

The Phantom Army

This ghostly visitation is reported to have been seen on three occasions, 1735, 1737 and 1745. Unlike most 'ghosts,' the phantom army appeared in daylight.

The phantom army of Souter Fell is a legend which contained much for which the travellers were seeking. To begin with, though it had the tone, the timbre, of a medieval romance, it was set in the near-present, the mid-eighteenth century, and because it was founded on evidence at no more than secondhand, it seemed almost contemporary, almost subject to verification, belonging among the curiosities rather than the folklore. There were good reliable-sounding names like that of William Lancaster to witness for the event, and even that of Daniel Stricket, who – and this should dispose of any further doubt – was an auctioneer.

It is not likely that any of the tourists really believed the story, but it had just that apparently objective, quasi-scientific sound which made it plausible in that quasi-scientific age. There was a queer suggestion of mirage, perhaps a time-mirage, by which the people of Souter Fell had been able to see an event that had not then taken place.

Here is William Hutchinson's version of the story:

> On Midsummer eve 1735, William Lancaster's servant related that he saw the east side of Souter Fell, towards the top, covered with a regular marching army for above an hour together; he said they consisted of distinct bodies of troops, which appeared to proceed from an eminence in the north end, and marched over a nitch in the top, but as no other person in the neighbourhood had seen the like, he was discredited and laughed at. Two years later, on Midsummer eve also, betwixt the hours of 8 and 9, William Lancaster himself imagined that several gentlemen were following their horses at a distance, as if they had been hunting, and taking them for such, paid no regard to it, till about ten minutes after, again turning his head towards the place, they appeared to be mounted, and a vast army following, five in rank, crowding over at the same place, where the servant said he saw them two years before. He then called his family, who all agreed in the same opinion; and what was most extraordinary, he frequently observed that some one of the five would quit rank, and seem to stand in a fronting posture, as if he was observing and regulating the order of their march, or taking account of the numbers, and after some time appeared to return full gallop to the station he had left, which they never failed to do as often as they quitted their lines, and the figure that did so, was generally one of the middlemost men in the rank. As it grew later, they seemed more regardless of discipline, and rather had the appearance of people riding from a market, than an army, though they continued crowding on, and marching off, as long as they had light to see them.
>
> This phenomenon was no more seen till the Midsummer eve, which preceded the rebellion, when they were determined to call more families to be witness of this sight, and accordingly they went to Wilton Hill and Souter-Fell-side, till they convened about 26 persons, which all affirm they then saw the same appearance, but not conducted with the usual regularity as the preceding ones, having the likeness of carriages interspersed; however, it did not appear to be the less real, for some of the company were so affected with it as in the morning to climb the mountain, through an idle expectation of finding horse shoes, after so numerous an army, but they saw not the vestige or print of a foot.[1]

L.

---

[1] William Hutchinson, *History of Cumberland*.

A Joy to Tourists: The King of Patterdale

The mountains have always been rich in characters as grotesque and individual as the crags they lie among – from the two Quakers of Kendal who called themselves Adam and Eve and went naked in the streets, to the old man of next door to living memory in my own town, who used to carry his Sunday dinner each week to a certain spring below Lowscales near the Duddon estuary, saying that the water there was better than anywhere else. The little fell farms, ten acres of ploughland and a warren of bracken and rock, bred such men as naturally as it bred foxes, though, with the disappearance of the statesman holdings, they were growing rarer by the end of the eighteenth century. One, however, survived and was a continual joy to the tourists – John Mounsey, the King of Patterdale. His very title fascinated them. It had a faint suggestion of the Scottish clans, of ancient allegiance and patriarchal pride; it corroborated their conception of Cumberland as a little world apart, appealing both to their sentiment and their sense of humour. Joseph Budworth represents the old man as a miser, gradually putting together a fortune by the most fantastic means. He grazed ponies on the common land, and worked them till they had not an ounce of strength left; he let out fields for a rent of dinners and suppers to save having to feed at home; he always carried bread and cheese in his pocket to avoid having to pay at an inn. Once, says Budworth, when he was transporting a load of slate by boat on Ullswater, he was wrecked on an island in a storm and remained there for two days with one labourer for companion. This other man had brought no food, so when the king felt hungry he would go to the other side of the island and there eat his bread and cheese while pretending that he had only gone to see if the weather were likely to change. It is a story compounded obviously enough of gossip and leg-pulls, but it carried here and there a genuine stamp. 'He sometimes has been heard to complain', says Budworth, 'that a man should be cut off in the prime of his life, at eighty or ninety years – for if he could live to the age of Methusalem, he might save a little money.' Here surely is the voice of a true dalesman, more subtly ironic and more profoundly content than Captain Budworth could ever guess.

L.

Will Ritson: A Considerable Liar

Much has been written about this canny dalesman. He was landlord of the Huntsman's Inn – now the Wasdale Head Inn – and to his stone-flagged kitchen in the last century came the new daring breed of climbers, as well as many others, including writer and poet Christopher North.

Ritson claimed that Wasdale had the highest mountain in England, the deepest lake, the smallest church and the biggest liar – himself.

Exaggeration is a convention in northern conversation which often bewilders southerners. Will Ritson, was famous for such stories. He told of an eagle with a broken wing which was put in a chicken run and mated with a foxhound bitch to breed winged hounds that hunted along the screes. It is a long way from that story to the sagas, but the fantastic touch is there and the homely touch, too.

It is said of Will Ritson that he entered a competition at the dale sports for the man who could tell the biggest lie, but when it came to his turn he asked to withdraw.

'Why?' he was asked.

'Because I cannot tell a lie.'

He won. And there, too, is the shrewdness which was often found in the Norse tales.

P.L.

Poets and Writers

A New Race in the Lakes

There are two sorts of tourists: those who return home and those who stay, and the latter are the more destructive. There is a sort of man who can come into a district that is new to him and can take root there; can learn to accept its tradition, to adapt himself to its people, to assume, like the birds and the lepidoptera, a protective colouring. But there is another who remains all his life a stranger, a foreigner, looking on from the outside, trying, perhaps unconsciously, to make the people and the land adapt themselves to him. And of such a sort, except for Wordsworth, were the Lake Poets. They were not indigenous. They were never acclimatized, they never really established themselves. They caught and flourished for a while like the seeds of an exotic plant brought accidentally in the packing-straw of a merchant steamer. Then, after a prodigious season, they withered and died. They remained always separate, alien, self-conscious, and they bequeathed this self-consciousness to the generation which followed. From this time onwards, the Lakes began to change. The main tourist centres became cosmopolitanized, mongrelized. The clean slate of the dale villages were smarmed up with a coat of Victorian paint. The voices were different, the smell new; and slowly, almost imperceptibly, hotels and shops and boarding-houses began to be touched up, faked and frilled into a faint resemblance of seaside promenades, hydropathic spas, or continental health resorts. The dalesman skulked back to his farm; the quarryman migrated to the mines on the coast. A new race colonized the Lakes: the moneyed intellectuals, the professors, the retired clergymen, the not-quite-so-retired businessmen. They gave us some of our most brilliant figures of the last century, but they changed the character of the district more dramatically than any factory or dam.

L.

William Wordsworth

From time to time a man is born who changes the whole course of literature for a century or more. Such a man was William Wordsworth. He was born in 1770 in Cockermouth.

Wordsworth's father was agent to Sir James Lowther, who owned or controlled half the coal and iron in Cumberland; and later on his son John married Isabella Curwen of Workington Hall, daughter of the man who owned most of the other half. His uncle, Richard, was Collector of Customs at the port of Whitehaven. It is quite wrong to think of Wordsworth as one born and bred among the fells, 'far from the taint of sordid industry', to use his own words. One of his earliest recorded memories, the lovely description of bathing in the Derwent,[1] is clearly that of a child to whom the fells still seem to belong to the distance, while the immediate foreground is made up of the smaller realities of house, terrace, mill-race and the yellow 'grunsel' (he means ragwort) growing by the river. At Cockermouth the Wordsworth children must have found themselves betwixt and between socially as well as geographically. They could not call themselves gentlefolk, yet, since their father was agent to one of the most unpopular men in Cumberland, they would hardly mix freely with the Cockermouth children. For a short while William attended the grammar school (now pulled down) which stood in the churchyard, but he seems to have made no friends there. When their mother died, in 1778, the Wordsworth children left Cockermouth, and William and Dorothy went to Penrith, to the home of their uncle and aunt, William and Dorothy Cookson. From then onwards the poet's boyhood memories centred round Penrith or, much more, round Hawkshead, where he was sent to school in the following year. He began his life, however, at the perimeter of the district, awkwardly situated between the dales and the mines, between the old way of life and the new. When, eventually, he settled at Grasmere, it was an act of protest, a deliberate turning away from the kind of society the Industrial Revolution was producing.

G.L.

Not of the Dales

The first thing to remember is that Wordsworth was a native of the district, an out-and-out northerner of largely Scandinavian stock. His father's family came from Penistone in Yorkshire, and his mother, Anne Cookson, was the daughter of a mercer in Penrith, himself of Yorkshire

---

[1] *The Prelude*, Book I, lines 282–300.

descent, who had married one of the Crackenthorpes of Newbiggin Hall. Now the Crackenthorpes were true Cumbrians, almost certainly derived from the Vikings who colonized the dales in the eighth and ninth centuries:

> Christopher Crackenthorpe men did me call,
> Who in my time did build this hall,
> And framed it as you may see
> In one thousand, one hundred, thirty and three.

(The words were carved on a wall at Newbiggin Hall by someone who faintly anticipated Wordsworth's genius.)

But the poet was not himself a man of the dales. He was born at Cockermouth, which stands where the River Cocker flows into the Derwent, in the broad country that looks west to the sea, north to Carlisle, and south to the fells of Crummock and Buttermere. In Wordsworth's time it was a busy market town, with the streets and warehouses packed tight in the angle between the two rivers, and a thousand or so inhabitants crowded into narrow courts and alleys. John Wordsworth, as law agent to the rapacious Sir John Lowther, lived in a large modern house inset a few yards from the High Street. At the back was a walled garden, leading to a paved terrace about twice the length of a cricket-pitch, from which you could drop a conker into the river. Here, in this almost urban landscape, among the limestone walls, the blossoming trees, and the riverside gardens, Wordsworth felt his first, breathtaking animal response to nature:

> Oh many a time have I, a five years' child,
> In a small mill-race severed from his [the Derwent's] stream,
> Made one long bathing of a summer's day;
> Basked in the sun, and plunged and basked again,
> Alternate, all a summer's day, or scoured
> The sandy fields, leaping through flowery groves
> Of yellow ragwort; or when rock and hill,
> The woods, and distant Skiddaw's lofty heights,
> Were bronzed with deepest radiance, stood alone
> Beneath the sky, as if I had been born
> On Indian plains, and from my mother's hut
> Had run abroad in wantonness, to sport,
> A naked savage, in the thunder shower.

The limestone walls clearly showed that this was not the dale country. Their trimness, their astonishing whiteness shining from the deep green grass could not be found where Skiddaw was no longer distant.

Moreover, they pointed west, to the ore-bearing limestone which ran through Cleator Moor and Egremont almost to the sea, so that not very far from Cockermouth were iron-mines and collieries and the industrial coast of Whitehaven and Workington. Thus Wordsworth's life from the beginning was closely associated with industry and the sea.

L.

The Sea Rejected

William's sister Dorothy, on a visit to the Moresby area, saw the sea for the first time and burst into tears.

William rejected the sea together with the evocative horrors of the coal-mines, and the romance of trade. He had no deep interest in history or in folklore, in ruins or monuments or the preoccupations of the antiquary, while regattas and museums and the tricks of the tourist could be tolerated merely as toys. He rejected, in fact, all the stock paraphernalia of the Picturesque; rejected its sham ecstasies, its titillation of the senses, its self-abuse of the fancy. To use nature as a stimulus for a razzle of the spirit, a subjective self-indulgence, seemed to Wordsworth not just deceptive, not just silly, but sacrilegious.

Nevertheless, he admits that for a time he was tainted with the 'strong infection of the age', and because of this had partly lost his youthful awareness of the 'impassioned life' of Nature:

> … Nor this through stroke
> Of human suffering …
> But through presumption; even in pleasure pleased
> Unworthily, disliking here, and there
> Liking; by rules of mimic art transferred
> To things above all art.

L.

Sketches of a Master

At the time of his greatest creative power, Wordsworth gave little thought to landscape, in the ordinary sense of the word. *The Excursion* had its long elaborate panoramas, but before this, in his best poetry, detailed landscape is rare. His work resembles the sketches of a master rather than a completed canvas. The multiplication of detail took too much time, it blunted the vision, and he rarely resorted to it except in the later years when there was no vision to blunt. As in Milton's *L'Allegro*, we are often left with the impression that we have been shown

Fells at the head of Wastwater

a landscape when in fact we have built our own landscape out of the one
significant feature which has been offered to us:

> What's Yarrow but a river bare
> That glides the dark hills under?

Often, when we are given a succession of such features, the effect is
stereoscopic. For Wordsworth rarely paints on a flat, static, surface; his
pictures move and grow, develop and flower. Even in a comparatively
casual poem like 'Fidelity' he can convey an impression of
multi-sensual, multi-seasonal complexity which catches at your lungs
like a mouthful of cold air:

> There sometimes doth a leaping fish
> Send through the tarn a lonely cheer;
> The crags repeat the raven's croak,
> In symphony austere;
> Thither the rainbow comes – the cloud –
> And mists that spread the flying shroud;
> And sunbeams; and the sounding blast,
> That, if it could, would hurry past;
> But that enormous barrier holds it fast.

That is just plain description, but at his greatest, Wordsworth, like
Blake, was gifted with double vision. With Blake, the one vision
subdued the other: the eternal shone through and superseded the
temporal. With Wordsworth, temporal and eternal existed simultaneously, and both had the same shape. The object becomes the image, it is
lifted to a higher power of significance – the fells looming above the boat
on Ullswater, the owls beside Esthwaite, the 'tumultuous brook of
Greenhead Ghyll'. Yet always the image remains true to the same laws
which governed it as an object: the new significance does not distort the
old. Often, indeed, object and image, material fact and symbolic
meaning, reflect backwards and forwards, each illuminating the other.
There is a wonderful example of this two-way traffic of allegory in
Resolution and Independence. It is early morning, and the poet, in a mood
of despondency, comes across an old man gathering leeches on the
moor beside a pool 'bare to the eye of heaven'. He describes the man in a
series of similes, which open each into the other, like a system of valleys
among the hills:

As a huge stone is sometimes seen to lie
Couched on the bald top of an eminence;
Wonder to all who do the same espy,
By what means it could thither come, and whence;
So that it seems a thing endued with sense;
Like a sea-beast crawled forth, that on a shelf
Of rock or sand reposeth, there to sun itself;
Such seemed this man.

It is a magnificent image, conveying the loneliness, the poverty and ruggedness, even the grandeur, of the old man, and almost equating him with the landscape, making him part of the background against which he is seen. And at the same time, it is a most superb evocation of the rocks themselves, while the shapes of the sea-beasts seem to hint at the theory of the Ice Age and the geological origin of the erratic boulders.

L.

The Saving of Wordsworth

Dorothy Wordsworth's vision was shared also by William and Coleridge, each after his own character. Vision is perhaps a misleading term. There was nothing mystical about Dorothy's view of nature. It was a matter not of revelation but of intuition and the senses, of physical perception and sympathetic insight intensified and heightened, but not changed, not different in kind from that of ordinary people. Her view, therefore, is one which we can all share, but only fitfully, only in momentary flashes. We can see the 'gemlike brightness', the 'visionary gleam', more clearly in her prose or in her brother's poetry than in the world itself. When we look round not with their eyes but merely with our own, the trees are just green again, the sky is just blue. The world in which we live, compared with the world which they show us, is one where the sun has gone behind a cloud.

Indeed, this is precisely what the world was like for William Wordsworth himself during the greater part of his life. The senses, the nerves, could not respond for ever to the immense demands made upon them. Dorothy lapsed into near-imbecility, William – to whom the view had nearly been a vision – stiffened his sinews and, almost deliberately, hardened his arteries. He gained his soul but he lost the world.

He lost, that is to say, the world that he had once known, but he had not lost the world that we all know. 'The light that never was on sea or land' was gone for ever; but the sea and the land were still there. In those difficult years when he began to realize that his vision and his creative powers both were ebbing, he turned to the external world with a new need, a new gratitude, almost a new passion. That world was no longer 'an unsubstantial, faery place'; it was a world of 'rocks and stones and trees'. A world, in fact, of *things*. His mind attached itself to solid objects, as a creeper attaches itself to a stone wall. He began to observe and record their appearance with a new accuracy, photographic rather than imaginary.

'Their perpendicular sides', he says, speaking of the slopes of the fells, 'are seamed by ravines ... which, meeting in angular points, entrench and scar the surface with numerous figures like the letters W and Y.' We know that this is true, and we are glad to have it pointed out, glad, at any rate, to be reminded of it; but it tells us nothing that we could not have discovered for ourselves. It is true to the letter and not to the life.

Yet it was the letter which saved him; saved him not as a poet but as a man. Saved him from years, perhaps, of disillusion, of disappointment, of spiritual impotence; saved him, perhaps, from the despair which threatened Coleridge and the stupor which overcame Dorothy. No doubt, in the popular view, despair, madness, or death would be a more appropriate end for a poet, but we have no right to make such a demand or to complain that Wordsworth chose otherwise. The strain of those fifteen or twenty years – the privations, the frustrations the self-dedication, the searchings, the strivings, the headaches, the sore eyes, the colossal effort of creation – left him exhausted, anxious, uncertain. He put out a hand to steady himself, and he grasped the solid world – a gate, a wall, a tree, a crag, a mountain. He had turned from the mystery to the fact.

L.

The Guide

Wordsworth's *Guide*, or, to give it its first title, *A Description of the Scenery of the Lakes*, was written in 1810, when Wordsworth was forty – a time when poetry had not yet entirely left him though its visits were intermittent, undependable, and rare. No longer could he take an everyday incident, a commonplace scene, and brood over it till it assumed a universal significance. He tried, many times, but, now, too often it was the significance which was commonplace while the description was inflated and grandiose.

In the *Guide* he did not try. Instead of describing particular scenes and searching for a meaning that he could not find, he was content to generalize. His generalizations, however, unlike those of the eighteenth-century poets, were not abstractions, formal symbols, almost ideographs; they were the careful accumulation and organization of remembered particulars. He spoke first of all of the structure of the district: the valleys and ridges radiating from a centre. He spoke of the varying effects of light and of season, and of the differing surfaces and upholstery of fell and flank. He constructed lists of reminiscences, as Cowper did, remembering, for instance, the colour of the trees in winter – the oak, still with its russet leaves; the birch bare, 'with its silver stem and puce-coloured leaves'; the dark green holly conspicuous in the woods now that the other trees no longer have leaves to conceal it. He begins to catalogue the visual memories of forty years; to tabulate and index, to make mental cross-references.

Its first appearance was quite fantastically inappropriate, for it was written as an anonymous introduction to *Select Views in Cumberland, Westmorland and Lancashire*, a book of drawings by the Rev. Joseph Wilkinson. Now of all the prints and engravings of the Lakes which appeared round about this time, these of Wilkinson's seem to me incomparably the worst. Many of the others were more fantastic, with mountains fuming like volcanoes, crags spearing the sky, and great geysers of waterfalls spouting from every cleft and crack in the rocks. Often, though they might be labelled Derwentwater or Windermere, they had nothing about them which could be identified, and were, in fact, largely ideal or invented landscapes. This was not the case with Wilkinson's, which were among the first to pay close attention to topographical accuracy, often recording easily recognizable subjects – a bridge, a house, a bend in a river. But they were stone dead. The fantasies of the early artists nearly always have charm, often spirit, and sometimes imagination. We know that they are excited, even if it is hard to tell what they are excited about. Wilkinson's, on the other hand, record a flat, dull, colourless, lifeless scene – a scene in which the mountains hang as listless as the backcloth at an amateur operatic production; in which the trees look as if they had been cut out of paper and stuck on; in which every lake has a boat or a sail, but the water is as stiff and sticky as a cold rice-pudding.

As might be expected, Wordsworth soon realized that the drawings were poor company for his *Description*, so he reprinted the latter in 1820, as an appendix to *The River Duddon and Other Poems*, and in 1822 as a separate volume: *A Description of the Scenery of the Lakes in the North of England, Third Edition*. This volume, which included a map and *Illustrative Remarks upon the Scenery of the Alps*, was reprinted several times, and then, in 1835, Wordsworth produced his final text, called *A Guide Through the District of the Lakes*.

The book was now frankly intended for the tourist. There were hints to him about the time of year in which he should visit the Lakes, together with a suggested itinerary and an account of two excursions, to Ullswater and to the top of Scafell, adapted, somewhat clumsily, from Dorothy's journal. To this the publisher had added a list of inns, distance between towns and so on. It is obvious that Wordsworth was now much more tolerant of the tourists, partly, no doubt, because they showed more interest in his poetry than did the local inhabitants. Partly, too, because, as he grew older, he had moved away from the people, the life of the dales and small towns, to the life of the gentry, of country houses, of wealthy residents and fashionable visitors. He was rather like a man who, by mixing almost exclusively with foreign immigrants, begins to lose his native accent even in his own home.

The 1835 *Guide* was the final form of Wordsworth's own text, but the book went through yet another change, and a very significant one. In 1842, with the poet's permission, it was reissued by Hudson and Nicholson of Kendal. This version, which is often known as *Hudson's Guide*, was very popular and went through several editions. The basis of the book is Wordsworth's original *Description*, printed in full, but the Notes for Tourists have now been expanded until they fill about half the whole. Wordsworth himself seems to have had some say in the compiling of these notes, and he also persuaded his friend Professor Sedgwick to contribute three letters on geology, while another friend, the blind John Gough, supplied lists of plants discovered in each area. In addition, the publishers added 'Itineraries' and 'Admeasurements of Distance', taken chiefly from Green's *Guide*, together with four diagrams drawn by Mr Flintock of Keswick, designed to help the visitor to recognize the mountains as seen from one or two selected viewpoints.

As edition followed edition, still more notes were added, so that the volume did not reach its full and final shape until after Wordsworth's death. The fourth edition, for instance, of 1853, contains two more geological letters from Professor Sedgwick, together with lists of fossils and shells, and a chapter on the derivation of local names.

It is easy enough to say that to some extent Wordsworth was conforming to the interests and habits of the tourist, but it is more important to notice that in his progress from general description to factual data he was pointing the way for his successors. The man who had once attacked the geologist with heavy-handed irony in *The Excursion*, now helped to present to the public the first scholarly study of the Lake rocks. The Picturesque traveller was already an anachronism, and the future lay with the geologist, the botanist, the archaeologist and the anthropologist. The fells were solid again.

L.

The Old Man of Rydal

To most people in the Victorian age, Wordsworth was a moral teacher, colour-washing a few simple platitudes with a Turnerian glow. His 'natural piety' became merely the sort of piety which seemed natural to them. To most people today, he is the arch-hiker, the lover of hills and daffodils. It is not, one feels, a reputation that would make a poet popular. Yet a most astonishing thing has happened, as was shown quite clearly during the centenary year in 1950: for Wordsworth has become part of the general furniture of the average modern mind; he has become the stock figure for the poet. It is not that he is read very much, but that one or two of his poems, in particular 'I wandered lonely as a cloud', have become the accepted types of what a poem is expected to be. The romantic conception of the poet – the revolutionary, the passionate young man, dying of tuberculosis or getting killed in a battle for freedom – this has been replaced by the figure of an old man at Rydal, listening to the cuckoo and stroking the heads of buttercups.

L.

Harriet Martineau and Wordsworth

This formidable Victorian writer was born in 1802 at Norwich and had already lived one life and fulfilled one career before she went to Ambleside in 1845, aged forty-three. Here she built the house where she was to work for thirty more years, producing books, essays, political tracts and newspaper articles. When she died in 1876 she left her own dispassionate obituary, already written. Her house, the Knoll, has become two private houses.

Harriet Martineau did not really get on well with Wordsworth. She knew him at the most unhappy time of his life, when he was half-blind with grief at the death of his daughter. Moreover, conversation between them was always difficult – she with her ear trumpet and he without his teeth. Difficulties apart, her nature could not adjust itself to his. She was practical about the everyday business of living but indifferent to money. With Wordsworth it was just the other way round. When she moved into her new house he came and planted a stone pine for her, then took both her hands and gave her some advice. She would get many callers he said – at Rydal Mount at least five hundred total strangers turned up every summer – and she must deal with them as he did: tell them that if they wanted a cup of tea they were welcome, but if they wanted anything to eat, they must pay for it. Miss Martineau, however, had not Wordsworth's lofty unconcern about the impression he made, and after having been accosted beside the flowerbeds and stared at through the windows, she decided that she must leave Ambleside for a month or two each year during the tourist season.

L.

Dorothy Wordsworth

Dorothy, 1771–1855, was born in Cockermouth and had the distinction of being friend and companion to two great poets, her brother William and Coleridge.

Among all the immeasurable mileage of Lake District prose, Dorothy Wordsworth's Grasmere journals are supreme. Of course, she did not think she was writing prose at all. She had her own delicate felicities – speaking, long before Keats, of 'that noiseless noise which lives in the summer air' – but she did not try to gather and shape her phrases into full periods. When she did try – as, for instance, in the draft which she prepared for possible publication of her *Recollections of a Tour made in Scotland* – she was altogether more stodgy, more conventional both in phrase and in point of view. But here, in the journals, her hands have the quick, living nervous movements of an artist sketching from life. The movements are not a definition of the image, a line drawn round the thought – they are part of the physical act of seeing. They are not observation but experience. Here is the Lake District as it looked, as it felt, to one exquisitely gifted person 180 or so years ago.

In these journals we feel the integrity, the immediacy of those first years at Grasmere – not only the birds, the birches, and the breezes of summer, but the cold beds, the scrappy meals, the long journeys over the Raise to Keswick, battling against the hail, or crawling on all fours to keep on the road in the dark. On Dorothy, more than on anyone else, that time made great demands. There was the washing and baking, the endless copying of William's poems, unexpected visitors arriving any day and at any time of the day. There were the long walks on the fells, the innumerable shorter journeys to Ambleside and the farms for letters or for food. And all the while she was struggling between two loves, and understanding the nature of neither. For William, straining himself ill with his poetry, she ached with a tenderness which was half-maternal, half-incestuous. When he sat late in the garden she would throw a cloak to him through the window, and afterwards take his bread and milk to bed, and when he was away she would cherish even a half-eaten crab apple that he had left behind. Her love for Coleridge, on the other hand, though it was more normal, was more secret because of his marriage. She hardly acknowledged it even to herself, and certainly hid it from her brother who seems to have suspected nothing, though he resented Coleridge's attentions to his sister-in-law, Sarah Hutchinson.

All the time, too, she was feeling the full, sensual shock of the world around her, standing naked in a great downpour of impressions, feeling the impact with every nerve, soaking in the ecstasy at every pore. Not even her love could distract her – in fact, it made her more sensitive. She did not know what she was loving – Coleridge, William, the birds and the grass became all one in her longing and sometimes loneliness. She touched even the wind with the hands of a lover:

Afterwards William lay, and I lay, in the trench under the fence – he with his eyes shut, and listening to the waterfalls and the birds. There was no one waterfall above another – it was a sound of waters in the air – the voice of the air. William heard me breathing, and rustling now and then, but we both lay still, and unseen by one another ... The lake was still; there was a boat out. Silver How reflected with delicate purple and yellowish hues, as I have seen spar; lambs on the island, and running races together by the half-dozen in the round field near us ... As I lay down on the grass, I observed the glittering silver line on the ridge of the backs of the sheep, owing to their situation respecting the sun, which made them look beautiful, but with something of strangeness, like animals of another kind, as if belonging to a more splendid world.[1]

There is so much in that passage which is typical of Dorothy Wordsworth. First of all, the intense personal feeling, the projection of an inner emotion into the world around her without ever distorting that world. The objects are seen like pebbles, as if through clear water, and the water does not alter the fact of the pebbles. And when she liked she could conjure up her images with astonishing economy – 'The lake was still; there was a boat out.' No one, indeed, in the whole of English literature has such a gift of evoking the natural world, of bringing it before our eyes, merely by naming it. The journal is full of examples: 'A beautiful evening. The crescent moon hanging above Helm Crag'; 'A very wild moonlight night. Glowworms everywhere'; 'Catkins are coming out; palm trees budding'; 'The ground thinly covered with snow. The road, black, rocks bluish.'

Then, when she wishes to fill in a detail, not John Clare, not Crabbe, not even her own brother, can catch the likeness more vividly or more swiftly. But she was no naturalist. She was not able to distinguish between the song of the thrush and that of the blackbird, she confused the yew with the juniper, hart's tongue with adder's tongue, and she scarcely knew more than a score or two of wild flowers by their names. Yet she has that quick, confident eyesight by which a botanist can recognize a flower ten yards away at a mere glance, a glimpse of cut or colour, just as one recognizes an acquaintance in the dusk by a gesture or the shape of a shadow. Plants and flowers existed for her not in a blur of prettiness; they were all clear and bright and individual, the crisp of a petal, the curl of a leaf, each a personality to be admired, a friend to be greeted. There was ivy, 'twisting round the oaks like bristled serpents'; there was the single bud of the honeysuckle, close to the wall and away from the wind, 'as snug as a bird's nest'; there were the oak trees, 'putting forth yellow knots of leaves', and the pilewort, or as we would

---

[1] *Grasmere Journal*: 29 April 1802.

call it, the lesser celandine, spreading on the grass 'a thousand shining stars'. There were the effects of weather and atmosphere which she noted and recorded as carefully as a young mother recording the weight of her child: 'Nab Scar was just topped by a cloud which, cutting it off as high as it could be cut off, made the mountain look uncommonly lofty.' Or the harsher more spectacular effects of winter: 'The snow hid all the grass, and all signs of vegetation, and the rocks showed themselves boldly everywhere, and seemed more stony than rock or stone.' And again, with a queer wincing tenderness, a longing as if to warm the world at her breast: 'We stopped to look at the stone seat at the top of the hill. There was a white cushion [i.e. of snow. N.N.] upon it, round at the edge like a cushion, and the rock behind looked soft as velvet, of a vivid green, and so tempting! … A young foxglove, like a star, in the centre.'

L.

Robert Southey

Norman saw Southey as more of a Laker than a poet.

There is something false about the very term Lake Poet. It began as a sneer, and it has ended as a vague proprietary title, a trademark, by which certain writers attain the rank of local worthies without one's needing to read them. And on none of them does the name ring more falsely than on Robert Southey. You might almost say that his only claim to the title was a residential qualification. For he was never a poet, and very little of his long and honourable labours had anything to do with the Lakes. Yet, of that group of literary settlers, he was – oddly enough – the central figure. No doubt it was the presence of Wordsworth which drew them in the first place, but it was Southey, more than Wordsworth, who took on himself the position of literary host, Lord High Admiral of the Water Poets. Southey, in fact, became himself one of the picturesque features of the district, and helped to add a new brash of colour to the banks of the Greta.

In the forty years that Southey was to spend in the Lakes, he became one of the most industrious, most conscientious and one of the most admired writers of his day – but he never became a Cumbrian. He was respected, trusted, honoured, but he had few local friends. His son, himself the vicar of a Cumberland parish, says that he scarcely got to know twenty of the ordinary Keswick people even by sight. In his old age, he would walk the roads screened within himself by short-sightedness, surprised and bewildered if anyone spoke to him. He was always the off-comer, always the new tenant.

The country never became part of his life as it did with Wordsworth.

He never learned to take it for granted, to become part of it himself. He always felt that he needed to explain himself, needed to justify himself, he always felt obliged to show the sort of enthusiasm which is expected from a tourist when he has returned from a new holiday resort. Wordsworth rarely tried to persuade people to visit the Lakes. If they came they were welcomed, but he did not really worry whether they came. But Southey was always persuading, one might almost say always advertising. As he grew older and more famous, he took to himself, in De Quincey's words, 'the duty (for such he made it) of doing the honours of the lake'. When friends or relatives came to stay with him, he would climb Skiddaw with them, or Great Gable, and there would be picnics, boating, and visits to the island that was now no longer Pocklington's. Sometimes the Coleridges, Southeys and Wordsworths would meet at some appointed place about half way between Keswick and Grasmere. Sometimes there would be stately excursions to Lodore; sometimes the visitors were satisfied to play about in the garden, trying to build stepping-stones across the Greta. Among them were a good many of the famous. Samuel Rogers came before Southey settled there. So, too, did Charles Lamb, and was persuaded to forget his prejudices and admit that Skiddaw was 'a fine creature' and that after all there was such a thing as the romantic, which he had doubted before. Hazlitt came soon after Lamb; Shelley called when he was in the district, and left Southey feeling as if he had seen the ghost of his younger self. Keats passed by, but did not call. The eleven-year-old John Ruskin, touring the Lakes with his parents and his cousin, attended Crosthwaite parish church solely in order to catch a glimpse of the poet:

> His hair was no colour at all by the way,
> But half of't was black, slightly scattered with grey;
> His eyes were as black as a coal, but in turning
> They flashed, – ay, as much as that coal does in burning!
> His nose in the midst took a small outward bend,
> Rather hooked like an eagle's, and sharp at the end;
> But his dark lightning-eye made him seem half-inspired,
> Or like his own Thalaba, vengefully fired.

To all of them, whenever they called, whether the time was convenient or not, whether he was idle or whether he was busy, Southey was always courteous, always hospitable, and (though he did not show it) nearly always glad when they went.

Southey was the spiritual antipodes of Wordsworth. Wordsworth's manner of thought was intensive; he prowled around the scenes of his boyhood till he had scratched up every bone that might be hidden in memory. But Southey was in spirit a traveller. He saw the most clearly at the first sight, and, as the view grew more familiar, it blurred and faded.

The northern fells

Glimpses of Portugal remained vividly in his mind throughout his life, but the mountains of Cumbria were seen so often that he ended by not noticing them. It was only when he conversed with a stranger, with one to whom the view would be new, that he recaptured something of his former enthusiasm. He might be writing a letter about Spanish literature or Brazilian politics, and then suddenly he wants to persuade his friend to come to Keswick, so down goes a set piece of description: sunset over Derwentwater, or snow on Skiddaw. There are passages of more tender description, too, both in the letters and in *Sir Thomas More*, where the scene is overlaid with the associations of many visits and many friends. Indeed, More's ghost chose to visit him in just those places where he would most often walk with the children or with visitors – Walla Crag, the Druid Circle, Applethwaite and Threlkeld Tarn, now known as Scales Tarn. Southey's best descriptive prose comes almost always when he is writing as a newcomer, a foreigner – curious, critical, excited by the novelty of it all, but not personally involved.

L.

Samuel Taylor Coleridge

If Southey was a Laker rather than a poet, Coleridge was a poet rather than a Laker. In the years which he spent among the Lakes he seems to have been aware of them only in flashes – flashes, indeed, of intense perception, but flashes which seem scarcely relevant to the workings of his mind at this period. Much of the time he could not really be bothered with the Lakes. He had come to them too late, for he no longer needed the continual stimulus of natural forms: indeed, the excitement they produced in him was only bearable in short spells, in holiday diversions. He had much else to worry about during those years at Keswick – the disruption of his marriage, his own ill-health, and the fear that poetry had left him. The greatest of his Lake poems, 'Dejection', is the expression of that fear and a lament for the loss of his lyrical genius.

His main contribution to Lake literature is seen less in his own work than in that of the Wordsworths. And more in Dorothy's than in William's. Of course it is impossible to measure the full influence of Coleridge on his friend, yet, on the whole, it seems to be a matter of stimulus and encouragement rather than of example or guidance. The main characteristics of Wordsworth's style can already be seen in the poems he wrote long before he made friends with the other poet. But Dorothy was a more susceptible pupil. She learned to look as Coleridge would look, and to feel as he would feel. Her journal is full of glimpses seen as if through his eyes.

Coleridge's first visit to the Lakes seems to have been made in the late autumn of 1799. He was at Bristol during October when he heard alarming reports of Wordsworth's health and immediately set off north to find out what was the matter. The Wordsworths, just then, were staying with the Hutchinsons at Sockburn near Northallerton, and by the time Coleridge reached them, William was better and the two of them set off on a short walking-tour, accompanied part of the way by John Wordsworth. First they visited Haweswater, Windermere, Hawkshead, and Grasmere, spending several nights at Robert Newton's. Then, by a curiously tangled route, they looped round the north-western lakes, including Buttermere, where they probably stayed the night and presumably met Mary Robinson, back to Wasdale and over Sty Head into Borrowdale, and by Matterdale to Ullswater.

Coleridge took notes of this journey and may have intended to work them up into a Tour. He had read Gilpin, and perhaps, like Southey, he may have read Celia Fiennes in manuscript. But, at the time, he does not seem to have thought seriously of settling in the Lakes. Wordsworth, however, did. While he was at Grasmere he wrote to Dorothy telling her that he had seen a small house which they might take. Two years later they moved in, and the next year Coleridge followed them to the North and made his home at Greta Hall.

L.

Coleridge on a Walking Tour

In the first week of August 1802 Coleridge slipped away on a walking-tour, the journal of which is one of the most delightful, yet also one of the least known, of all Lake writings.

He set off from Keswick on Sunday 1 August, taking with him a shirt, two pairs of stockings, tea, sugar, pens and paper, and a book of German poetry wrapped in oilskin and carried in a knapsack. One of the aims of this journey seems to have been to examine the library presented to St Bees School by Sir James Lowther, so he made towards the coast, by Gilpin's route of Newlands and Keskadale to Buttermere:

> Conceive an enormous Bason mountain-high of solid Stone, cracked in half and one half gone; exactly in the remaining half of this enormous Bason, does Buttermere lie, in this beautiful and stern Embracement of Rock. I left it, passed by Scale Force, the white downfall of which glimmered through the Trees that hang before it like bushy Hair over a Madman's Eyes, and climbed 'till I gained the first level.

He made next by Floutern Tarn towards Ennerdale. Red Pike, above Crummock, was 'a dolphin-shaped Peak of a deep red'; Great Borne on Herdus was 'a roundish-headed green hill'; while in the country below

Mellbreak, which looks down towards Loweswater, he found 'a wild green view all around me, bleating of Sheep and noise of Waters'.

He moved on, passing the precipices of Herdus Scaw, and noting every shape with the greatest precision. Ennerdale Lake, seen from above at the lower end, is 'shaped like a clumsy battledore – but it is in reality fiddle-shaped'; Burnmoor Tarn, between Wasdale and Eskdale, is 'flounder-shaped'; on Buttermere Hause the ridges are 'long arm-shaped and elbow-shaped'.

He spent the night at a farm near Ennerdale, and next day went on to Egremont and St Bees, where he found wretched lodgings in a pot-house, sleeping in his clothes, and paying elevenpence for gin and water, bed, and breakfast. Even the library turned out to be of no value (which was hardly surprising considering whose gift it was), and the next day, 'a wet woeful oppressive morning', he trudged back rather miserably to Egremont. But after a better night there, he moved on to Calder Abbey, noticing the 'red freestone, which has the comfortable warm Look of Brick without its meanness', and then on by Gosforth to Wasdale, where he had been before, with Wordsworth. Excited as a boy playing truant, he turned his visit into a high adventure.

He approached the dale this time from the right direction – that is, from the bottom, and not from Sty Head. The lake itself was too regular, 'exactly like the sheet of Paper on which I'm writing', but beyond it was that fantastic rubble cliff:

> ... two-thirds of its height downwards [i.e. from the top to two-thirds of the way down – N.N.] absolutely perpendicular, and then slanting off in *Screes* or Shiver consisting of fine red streaks running in broad Stripes through a stone colour – slanting off from the perpendicular, as steep as the meal newly ground from the Miller's spout. So it is at the foot of the Lake; but higher up this streaky Shiver occupies two-thirds of the whole height, like a pointed Decanter in shape, or an out-spread Fan, or a long waisted old maid with a fine prim Apron, or – no, other things that would only fill up the Paper.

We can see here exactly how his mind worked in observation. First the fact, the accurate defining image – then, as he grows more excited, the image is touched with fancy, and then, at the very moment when fancy threatens to overthrow the fact, Coleridge breaks off. Fancy may explain and elaborate fact, but it is not allowed to usurp.

Wasdale seemed to bring energy and youthfulness to Coleridge. He spent the night at Thomas Tyson's, below Kirk Fell, and the next morning, Thursday, 5 August, set off to climb Scafell. As he climbed, he looked along the three western dales, Eskdale, Miterdale, and Wasdale, to where the three dale rivers joined at Ravenglass in 'the *Trident* of the

Irish Channel'. It was a new experience for him, in Cumberland, this close cousinship of mountain and sea, and perhaps it reminded him of Somerset. His temperature rose with the altitude instead of falling with the barometer. He climbed almost to the summit and then found a wind-break among the rocks, where, like a painter, he jotted down shapes and sizes while he could still see them:

> And here I am *lounded* [i.e. sheltered. N.N.] – so fully lounded – that tho' the wind is strong, and the Clouds are hasting hither from the Sea – and the whole air Seaward has a lurid look – and we shall certainly have Thunder – yet here (but that I am hunger'd and provisionless) *here* I could lie warm, and wait methinks for tomorrow's Sun, and on a nice Stone Table am I now at this moment writing to you – between 2 and 3 o'Clock as I guess – surely the 1st Letter ever written from the Top of Sca' Fell!

So far as Coleridge was concerned, it might easily have been the last he wrote anywhere. He was, he admits, something of a gambler, and when he had climbed a hill by the circumscribed route, he liked to abandon that route on the way down, following wherever his fancy led, and trusting that he would reach the bottom safely. This was what he did on Scafell, and was led into a breakneck descent which set up tremulous agitation in his plumpish and ill-conditioned body. And Coleridge conveys so well the breathlessness, the perturbation, the shock and shake and shiver of it all, that his prose takes us down with him, bumping and bouncing, slithering and sliding, in what is perhaps the earliest recorded rock-scramble in the Lakes. There is little description here, and no horror-mongery. Coleridge's ambition did not aim higher than a chatty journal to be read by the Wordsworths, who, at this time, were in France on a visit to Annette and the poet's daughter. Yet in no other passage of Lake prose is physical sensation evoked so tangibly.

L.

Wilson the Reversible

John Wilson, 1785–1854, alias the formidable Christopher North of Blackwood's Magazine, *lived for some years at Elleray, a cottage below Orrest Head, overlooking the length of Windermere. Elleray today forms part of a school.*

John Wilson came ripping and roaring into the Lakes like two men, like two different men; not so much two-faced as reversible, like one of those comic faces which one way up is a wide-browed old man and the other way is a wide-jawed old woman. The way his family saw him, he was a young poet, with blue eyes, £50,000 and a leaning towards platitude and piety – one not so much married to his muse as engaged to her. This was the man whom Crabb Robinson called 'the female Wordsworth'; the man who walked the lonnings praying audibly for miles on end; the man who moped about churchyards, sentimentally eyeing a young girl, in the last stages of consumption, looking on the spot where she was to be buried. Years later, when the wealthy poet had turned into a comparatively hard-up journalist, this was the man who could describe Windermere and Grasmere in a mixture of half-chewed, half-digested sentiment, archness, gusto and genuine enjoyment.

Such was 'Mr Wilson of Elleray', as Wordsworth called him when he introduced him to De Quincey, but turn him the other way up, and John Wilson changed into Christopher North, the man who leaped across the Cherwell, who followed cockfights and boxed with cobblers and planned to explore central Africa with Mungo Park; the man who, according to rumour, had run to sea, had lived among gipsies, and had been a strolling-player, a barn-stormer, up and down the villages and small towns of England.

If, as some say, Christopher North was Wilson as he wanted to be, then Wilson must have been North as he really was. Yet, in fact, the one was a pose as much as the other. The innocuous poet of 'The Isle of Palms' no doubt felt sincere enough, but he grew into one of the most unscrupulous journalists of the day – one who was at least partly responsible for the atrocious *Blackwood's Magazine* attack on Keats; one who could offer to review Coleridge favourably in one magazine and then go and blackguard him in another; one who could attack Wordsworth under an assumed name and defend him under his own. It is a portrait very different from that of the genial literary sportsman who, according to Canon Rawnsley, still remained in the memories of the Westmorland people until the end of the nineteenth century.

Yet perhaps Rawnsley was not altogether wrong. In spite of the pink poems, the sentimentality, the religiosity, the Lakes brought out all that was truest in Wilson's character. Christopher was only one limb of his character, but here, among the mountains, that limb could grow into a giant. Christopher was essentially physical in his nature, not intellectual, and his prose has more stamina than style, yet he often reveals flashes of insight, or, more truly, of *out*-sight, that surprise and captivate. The manner is atrocious – a swill of rhetoric, facetiousness, affectations, invocations, and self-conscious croakings in the vernacular – yet the very enthusiasm makes it bearable, at least for a page or two. He can coax and wheedle as flagrantly as a seller of vacuum cleaners:

> Windermere! Why, at this blessed moment we behold the beauty
> of all its intermingling isles. There they are – all gazing down on

their own reflected loveliness in the magic mirror of the air-like water, just as many a holy time we have seen them all agaze, when, with suspended oar and suspended breath – no sound but a ripple on the Naiad's bow, and a beating at our own heart – motionless in our own motionless bark – we seemed to float midway down that beautiful abyss between the heaven above and the heaven below ...

Or he could be as hearty as a commercial traveller with a snappy line:

So ... let us descend to the White Lion – and enquire about Billy Balmer. Honest Billy has arrived from Waterford – seems tolerably steady – Mr Ullock's boats may be trusted – so let us take a voyage of discovery on the lake. Let those who have reason to think that they have been born to die a different death from drowning, hoist a sail. We today shall feather an oar. Billy takes the stroke – Mr William Garnet's at the helm – and 'row, vassals, row, for the pride of the Lowlands' is the choral song that accompanies the Naiad out of the bay, and round the north end of the Isle called Beautiful.

L.

Thomas De Quincey

De Quincey, 1785–1859, held Wordsworth in such high esteem that it almost prevented him from ever meeting the great poet.

To De Quincey, when he first came to the Lakes, the mountains, the dales, the meadows and meres meant nothing but Wordsworth. Southey, Coleridge, John Wilson, each had his own independent reason for coming, but with De Quincey it was Wordsworth first and Wordsworth all the time. He wrote to the poet impetuously in 1803 when he was seventeen, describing himself as 'ready (I speak from the heart) to sacrifice even his life'. Wordsworth replied cautiously, no more than a vague invitation to Grasmere which De Quincey twice tried to accept in the next year or so. Once he turned back at Coniston, and once he got as far as Hammerscar, where he could look into Grasmere and across to the lake with 'its solemn ark-like island' and the woods on the far shore. Each time his courage failed him, but in 1807 another opportunity arose. Coleridge, who was then staying at Bristol, had been engaged to give a series of lectures in London, and was therefore unable to travel to Keswick as had been planned. This left Mrs Coleridge and the three children without an escort for the journey, and De Quincey, hearing of their predicament, offered to accompany them in a post-chaise. The journey, with a stay at Liverpool, took ten or twelve days, and the party reached Grasmere on a late winter afternoon in December.

De Quincey's description of that first meeting with Wordsworth belongs among the classics of English prose. In fact, his portrait is one of the few that we have in which the poet seems to move. There is an immense amount of information about Wordsworth, masses of correspondence, diaries, memoirs, and innumerable accounts of tea with the old man of Rydal. But the features are set in that familiar, stiff expression; the figure is rigid as a daguerreotype. There is never a smile, never a gesture; scarcely an anecdote that is revealing, scarcely a remark that is memorable. Rarely, outside his own poems and his sister's letters, do we get a glimpse of the living man who inspired (one might almost say 'exacted') such devotion and loyalty for so many years. Not that De Quincey's portrait reveals a lovable personality. He wrote with understandable resentment at the lack of response to his proffered discipleship. For Wordsworth is one of the supreme examples of the egoist in poetry. He could not be bothered with disciples; he could not be bothered with admirers, except when he wanted criticism or encouragement. He knew that he had to drive all his faculties, all his powers of experience, for the one purpose. The poetry justified the egoism. And afterwards, when there was no more poetry to speak of, the egoism continued as a habit.

But the personality in De Quincey's portrait, if it is not lovable, is certainly alive. Wordsworth, coming quickly through the gate of Dove Cottage, 'a tallish man', holding out his hand; Wordsworth, dragging his delicate visitor round Grasmere and Rydal, six miles in the pouring rain of midwinter; Wordsworth, hacking his way through his friend's books with a buttery table-knife – these are sketches on which the ink is not yet dry. From De Quincey we can gauge the enormous power of the poet's personality, that sense of adventure, of new beginnings, new potentialities, which, to his contemporaries, seemed to give his work the force not just of prophecy but of revelation. We know that this is so, of course. We read in the textbooks that Wordsworth revitalized poetic diction and opened new spheres of experience to the poet. But a true appreciation of this is blocked off by the dead weight of the respectability of Wordsworthianism – the Sunday school recitations, the picture postcards of Dove Cottage, the dreary centenary processions of daffodil-carrying children. Yet here, in this meeting of 1807, the urgency and excitement of Wordsworth's early poems still blow about the heads of his listeners like a mountain wind.

L.

Two Approaches to the Picturesque

The great function of the Picturesque was to teach men to use their eyes and to use their imagination, but they muddled that task by confusing what they saw with what they imagined. They used imagination, in fact, not to create but to distort; they used it to tamper with the material world, the world of the eyes, to trick it out and trinket it up with flashy, worthless spangles and crackers. De Quincey returned to the true purpose of the Picturesque, using his eyes to feed his dreams, creating a world of the imagination which followed its own logic and its own laws, free of the necessity of material causes, yet never posing as a substitute for the material world. Wordsworth worked in the opposite way, using his imagination to feed his eyes, and concentrating all his insight, all his wisdom, on the solid material world of the senses, the world of rocks and stones and trees. Both were true to their vision; neither tried to deceive himself or his readers.

L.

Harriet Martineau's Guide to the Lakes

The Guide *ran into five editions in her own lifetime.*

It was not until five years after the death of Wordsworth that Harriet Martineau published her own *Complete Guide to the Lakes* – with separate editions for the Windermere and the Keswick districts. It is, as we might expect, a work which shows a goodish knowledge of the topography of the district, and absolutely no knowledge at all of its real character. She took on the job rather reluctantly, persuaded into it by a local bookseller, but set about it with her usual gumption. She hired a wagonette and toured the entire district with six friends, testing the routes and passes, trying all the inns, and being agreeably surprised at the cheapness of the latter until she found that the friend, who was in charge of the arrangements, had been bargaining for reduced terms on the strength of the coming guide. The book is competent and readable, for Miss Martineau knew how to give life and point to her argument by anecdote and scraps of autobiography. But after nearly ten years in the Lakes her view of them was as scrappy, as superficial, as that of a weekend visitor. As she rode in her wagonette over Whinlatter or Cold Fell, or up Borrowdale or along Ullswater, she saw just what the visitor saw, she asked the same questions as he did, though, unlike him, she remembered the answers. Indeed, much of her book consists simply of the organization of such answers:

> When the turn to the left, which leads up to the chapel, is reached, the stranger must alight and ascend it. He is ascending Rydal Mount; and Wordsworth's house is near the top of the hill, – within the modest gate on the left. By kind permission of the lady

now residing there, strangers may obtain entrance to the poet's garden on two days in the week, Tuesday and Friday.

The *Guide* is remarkable, however, not for what Miss Martineau says about the Lakes, but for what she says about the people. It is not to be expected that she understood them, any more than she understood the fells, but she saw clearly the social conditions in which they lived. She was not to be humbugged into thinking that here was a new Arcady, with its people still living miraculously in the Age of Gold. She knew very well that they were living in the nineteenth century, that they belonged to the age of industrialism, and that it was impossible to isolate them from the rest of their time. To do so, to attempt to deny the dalesman his rightful part in the economic development of the country, would bring him to poverty and bankruptcy. Already the old self-supporting statesmen were dying out, and the old home manufacture was dead. Cottages were falling into ruins, fields were untilled, land was undrained.

The unhealthiness of many settlements is no less a shame than a curse, for the fault is in Man, not in Nature. Nature has fully done her part in providing rock for foundations, the purest air, and the amplest supply of running water; yet the people live – as we are apt to pity the poor of the metropolis for living – in stench, huddled together in cabins, and almost without water. The wilfulness of this makes the fact almost incredible; but the fact is so.

For all this she saw only one remedy: the Lakes must no longer be cut off from the rest of England, living in almost medieval squalor so as not to disturb those immigrants who could afford the comfortable new villas. The Lakes must accept the railways, against which Wordsworth and others had been campaigning; they must seek new markets outside the district; they must open their villages to new trades and their minds to new ideas. No doubt, she exaggerated the good which would come from increased communication with the outer world; no doubt, she overestimated the understanding and intelligence of the townsman; but at least she realized that to condemn the people of the Lakes to an unnatural, archaic existence in an artificial, preserved countryside was both economically absurd and morally wrong. To subjugate man to the scenery was to de-humanize him, to treat him as no more than a thing. To reduce the world to a mere picture was the primary heresy of the Picturesque; to reduce man to the scale of that picture was its ultimate folly.

L.

John Ruskin: The New Sage of the Lakes

Ruskin, 1819–1900, had a lifelong love of the Lakes but did not settle in the district for many years. Then, in 1871, he bought Brantwood overlooking Coniston Water, converting and extending the roughcast Cumbrian cottage into a paradise where he spent the rest of his life. And there he became the New Sage of the Lakes, the Old Man of Coniston. He died within days of his eighty-first birthday and is buried in Coniston churchyard.

Ruskin belonged to a generation which had no need to discover the Lakes for itself. He grew up among people to whom mountain scenery was the most natural of joys – like water, food, sleep, grass and the seaside. His father was a wine merchant who in summer would take with him his wife and son as he travelled by coach about the counties, calling at the great houses for orders. In this way, the boy made his first visit to Keswick when he was only five years old, so that the view from Friar's Crag became one of his earliest and most precious memories. Other visits followed quickly, and by the age of eleven he was ready to start on a long poem, the *Iteriad*, a jaunty mock-picturesque travelogue describing the scenes he was one day to know much better. But already he knew them astonishingly well. He was no poet, not even at twenty, so that it is not surprising that he was none at eleven; his lines have the hippety-hop of the horse-trap on a paved street, and his language is just what he had picked up from his reading. Yet already he has learned to see. Arthur Young, Ann Radcliffe, Adam Walker had puffed and blowed and staggered and swooned all over Skiddaw without one of them noticing nearly as much as he did of the bare summit, the screes, or the long crest of the ridge running off from the peak:

> How frowned the dark rocks which, bare, savage and wild,
> In heaps upon heaps were tremendously piled!
> And how vast the ravines, which, so craggy and deep,
> Down dreadful descending divided the steep! ...
> Then turned we around to the maze of the mountains,
> All teeming and sparkling with thousand bright fountains:
> Where the brow of Helvellyn superior tow'r'd –
> Where the beetling Scafell so tremendously low'r'd –
> Tost confus'dly in clusters all barren and grim,
> While the clouds o'er their sky-braving battlements skim;
> Till, their scarce-discerned outlines all misty and grey,
> On the distant horizon they faded away.[1]

He returned twice, some years later, during undergraduate vacations

---

[1] Ruskin: *Iteriad*.

– searching for garnets with Wright, the mineralogist of Keswick; studying the Westmorland cottages and sketching the chimneys of Coniston Old Hall. In 1847, then aged twenty-three, he was at the Salutation Inn at Ambleside, feeling so despondent that from his boat on Windermere the water appeared leaden and the hills low. The following year he was back again, on his honeymoon, but in no better spirits, and when next he returned, in 1867, he was in appearance and outlook almost an old man; famous, worn-out, weary and profoundly unhappy.

There have been many attempts to explain the tragedy of Ruskin's life – the impotence of mind or body which lost him his wife, and left him aching for love yet unable to take it; which made him idolize girlhood and adolescence till he could break his heart over a child and canonize her, after her death, with the incense of madness. These we need not consider now. Yet Ruskin was yet another of the sexually deprived or distorted who found consolation and comfort in the feminine hollows and roundnesses of lakes and hills and the masculine verticals of crags and trees. Few of his readers could understand this, yet, oddly enough, it was this very tragedy, this weariness and despair, which caught the sympathy of the Lake visitors. They, too, turned to the Lakes for comfort and rest, no longer demanding the stimulus and excitement which had been the joy of the earlier travellers.

And when, in 1871, Ruskin bought Brantwood without even coming north to look at the place, he was making the sort of gesture which many people of his time longed to make but could not.

There is, of course, little connection between the Lakes and the bulk of Ruskin's work. His immense studies of mountain forms were carried out in the Alps, not in Cumbria. Nevertheless, he is perhaps the culminating figure of the Picturesque, for in him are combined its three main phases – the æsthetic, the scientific, and the moral.

L.

Tomorrow

The Future of the Lakes

What is going to happen to the Lakes?

Let me say, first of all, what I do not want to happen. I do not want the Lakes to be turned into a museum. I do not want to see them smothered in good taste, embalmed in admiration. I do not want the dales to be bought up and managed by townsmen until the local people become entirely dependent on town money and live like Red Indians in a national park reservation. I do not want to see the clutter and coarseness of farm life cleaned up and whitewashed into the prettiness of the weekend cottage. I do not want the Lakes to be transformed into a series of coloured transparencies, where not a wall nor a roof strikes the wrong tone and the view is as neat as a postage stamp. I do not want to see the fells become like Arthur's Seat in Edinburgh – preserved, patrolled, tarmacked, tidied, molly-coddled and dead.

Today society has changed. The Lakes are no longer a place apart. Post-war prosperity, extra spending money and the vast spawning of cars have brought urban England roaring up to our borders. It is not just that immense numbers of people now come to the Lakes, for the fells are big enough to take more without being crowded. (Though, of course, it is going to be increasingly difficult to provide all the car-parks, caravan sites and holiday accommodation which will be needed.) It is rather that tourism is becoming the dominant industry of the area. At one time the tourists were received in farms, villages and towns which made their living in their own way – from sheep, wool, quarries, mines and the like. They were glad of the extra money from the visitor but they did not depend upon him. Today the visitor is beginning to own the place and, if we are not careful, the whole area will be turned into one vast holiday camp. Nobody wants this to happen – least of all the visitor who comes to the Lakes because he likes them as they are. But the ruthless pressure of profit pushes us continually in that direction.

P.L.

The Farmer First

Of course, the only real defence against the erosion of tourism is the survival of a living community, long-rooted in the locality, making its own way and at least partially independent of the visitor. I think that all that can be done should be done to help the hill farmer, both by the Ministry of Agriculture and by the local authorities. Where the interests of the farmer conflict with those of the tourist, the farmer should be given first consideration every time. I think that the Lake District Special Planning Board should try to see that life is made practicable and reasonably profitable for the men who still choose to work in the dales. They should get electricity and water; their roads should be good enough for tradesmen's vans and other services. There should be good bus transport, good schools, village halls and the like. I should like to see the Friends of the Lake District as anxious to encourage industries in the dale villages as they are (quite rightly) to discourage unsightly camps on the lake sides. And I would be ready to accept even a certain amount of ugliness, if necessary, in order that the dales might be kept alive.

P.L.

Final Word

No doubt, this is a transition stage. One day we shall achieve a new synthesis of the scientific and the imaginative vision. We shall be able to see the atoms swirling round in our own thumbs; we shall no longer shudder when we think of bacteria in our blood. When this happens our view of the external world may be clearer, richer, and of greater significance. Then, perhaps, we may be able to look at the fells of Cumbria with a new understanding, a new confidence. For they rear themselves in the middle of our civilization like an ancient boulder lying in a garden. An archaism, belonging to the world of nature as it was long before man came to look at it; belonging, also, to the world which will survive man. They are a sign both of what man comes from and what he is up against. They may be mapped, footpathed, signposted, planted with conifers, gouged with quarries, titivated with tea-shops. They may even, in some gigantic explosion, be blown out of shape. Yet they will remain the same, for they are a fact, a fact we cannot alter and perhaps cannot even understand. They are the past which shaped us and the future in which we shall have no shape. To talk of preserving them is both irrelevant and irreverent. All that matters is how long they will allow us to preserve ourselves.

L.

Works by Norman Nicholson

Topography and miscellaneous

Cumberland and Westmorland (Robert Hale, 1949)
Greater Lakeland (Robert Hale, 1969)
Portrait of the Lakes (Robert Hale, 1963)
Provincial Pleasures (Robert Hale, 1959)
The Lakers (Robert Hale, 1955)
The Lakes (*Portrait of the Lakes* renamed) (Robert Hale, 1977)

Books of Poetry

A Local Habitation (Faber and Faber, 1972)
Five Rivers (Faber and Faber, 1944)
No Star on the Way Back, ballads and carols (Manchester Institute of Contemporary Arts, 1972)
Rock Face (Faber and Faber, 1948)
Sea to the West (Faber and Faber, 1981)
Selected Poems (including works by J.C. Hall and Keith Douglas) (John Dale and Staple, 1943)
Selected Poems (Faber and Faber, 1966)
Selected Poems 1940–1982 (Faber and Faber, 1982)
The Candy-Floss Tree (including works by Gerda Mayer and Frank Flynn) (Oxford University Press, 1984)
The Pot Geranium (Faber and Faber, 1954)

Plays

A Match for the Devil (Faber and Faber, 1955)
Birth by Drowning (Faber and Faber, 1960)
Prophesy to the Wind (Faber and Faber, 1950)
The Old Man of the Mountains (Faber and Faber, 1946)

Fiction

The Fire of the Lord (Nicholson and Watson, 1944)
The Green Shore (Nicholson and Watson, 1947)

Criticism

H.G. Wells (Arthur Barker, 1950)
Man and Literature (S.C.M. Press, 1943)
William Cowper (John Lehmann, 1951)
William Cowper (Longmans Green for the British Council, 1960)

Books edited

A Choice of Cowper's Verse (Faber and Faber, 1975)
Anthology of Religious Verse (Penguin Books, 1942)
The Lake District: An Anthology (Robert Hale, 1977)
The Lake District: An Anthology (Penguin Books, 1978)
Wordsworth: An Introduction and Selection (Phoenix House, 1949)

Autobiography

Wednesday Early Closing (Faber and Faber, 1975)

Readers who would like to know more about Norman should turn to their library service for an excellent study, *Norman Nicholson*, by Philip Gardner (Twayne Publishers Inc., New York, 1973)

Finally, my grateful thanks go to many people who have helped in this anthology, and in particular to David Hay, Harry and Doreen Knipe, Loucilla Lavel, William Rollinson and Michael Davies-Shiel. My thanks, too, to the staff at Robert Hale where appreciation of Norman and his writings has extended over many years.

Index

The X, Y and Z Files
The 100-Year Experiment

First Printing: 2018
ISBN 978-1-9164785-0-3

Also available for Kindle from Amazon.

For all information contact Mr Slaine McRoth via email:
slainemcroth@yahoo.com

The X, Y and Z Files
The 100-Year Experiment

Sir James Gordon Josephson OBE

Edited by Slaine McRoth

Published by Slaine McRoth
2018